DIGITAL COPYRIGHT

DIGITAL
~~COPYRIGHT~~

Protecting intellectual property on the Internet • The Digital Millennium Copyright Act • Copyright lobbyists conquer the Internet • Pay per view...pay per listen...pay per use • The war against Napster • What the major players stand to gain • What the public stands to lose

JESSICA
~~LITMAN~~

Prometheus Books
59 John Glenn Drive
Amherst, New York 14228-2197

Published 2001 by Prometheus Books

Inquiries should be addressed to
Prometheus Books
59 John Glenn Drive
Amherst, New York 14228–2197
VOICE: 716–691–0133, ext. 207
FAX: 716–564–2711
WWW.PROMETHEUSBOOKS.COM

05 04 03 02 01   5 4 3 2 1

Library of Congress Cataloging-in-Publication Data

Litman, Jessica, 1953–
    Digital copyright / Jessica Litman.
        p. cm.
    Includes bibliographical references and index.
    ISBN 1–57392–889–5 (cloth : alk. paper)
    1. Copyright and electronic data processing—United States. I. Title.

KF3030.1 .L58 2000
346.7304'82—dc21   00–045917

Printed in the United States of America on acid-free paper

For Ari

CONTENTS

ACKNOWLEDGMENTS

I began the research reflected in this book fifteen years ago, and many people have helped me to formulate and clarify my thinking. Jon Weinberg has helped more than anyone; he asked me all the difficult questions (even before he married me). I cannot imagine writing anything without his help. Jon has read every word in this book at least a dozen times, and offered perceptive suggestions each time.

James Boyle suggested the idea for the book, and kept urging me to write it. Jane Ginsburg is a longtime friend and collaborator who has had to struggle to find any sentence she agrees with in my recent work. Jane's idea of the public good is very different from mine, for which I'm grateful. The opportunity to argue with someone who sincerely and without ulterior motive believes that we would all be better off if copyright protection were even stronger than it is now kept me honest. Pam Samuelson and I have worked together and in parallel on digital copyright issues for many years. Pam's work and thinking has greatly influenced mine. It was Pam's request for a paper that set me on the road leading to my proposal in chapter 12 for an alternative copyright system. Peter Jaszi's inspiration to recruit foot soldiers in the copyright wars to join the Digital Future Coalition gave me both something constructive to do with my outrage and the opportunity to learn how lobbyists work their backstage magic. American University gave me a home for a year that enabled me to see the story unfold from the front row. Diane Zimmerman and Rochelle Dreyfuss encouraged me to think more deeply about consumers' ideas of legal legitimacy. When I needed a particular succinct interpretive paradigm, Niva Elkin-Koren's work supplied it.

Of the many other people who helped me with the book or influenced my thinking, I owe special thanks to Hal Abelson, Jane Friedman, Seth Greenstein, Larry Lessig, and Dani Zweig for giving me crucial pieces in the puzzle.

INTRODUCTION

AMERICAN IDEAS OF FREEDOM ARE bound up with a vision of information policy that counts information as social wealth owned by all. We believe we are entitled to say what we think, to think what we want, and to learn whatever we're willing to explore. Part of the information ethos in the United States is that facts and ideas cannot be owned, suppressed, censored, or regulated; they are meant to be found, studied, passed along, and freely traded in the "marketplace of ideas."

In fact, information is regulated in this country as in others. We have an enormously complex collection of information law prescribing terms and conditions for a variety of different providers of information. Broadcasters are the most obvious example of regulated speakers, but we also have rules about what schools may teach and where protesters may demonstrate. The rules about how and when citizens can get information from the government are complex and arcane. Despite the web of regulation that surrounds some regions of free-speech law, however, the underlying concept holds true more often than not. In the United States, at least for the most part, we may say what we think, think what we want, and learn whatever we are willing to explore.

There are other corollaries, and we've gotten accustomed to them. We've been able to do our reading, viewing, and exploring privately and anonymously, and have come to view the ability to do so as a natural right. A world in which each word we read or image we view is monitored and recorded seems like the stuff of science fiction: unimaginable and, in any event, impossible in America.

The Internet has been hailed as the most revolutionary social development since the printing press. In many ways its astonishing growth has outstripped any historical analogy we can unearth. What has fueled much of that growth has been the explosion of new possibilities for connections—among people, among different formerly discrete packages of information, among ideas. It isn't that anyone would prefer to use a unix box (or even a Windows tcp/ip client) to find out what one can more easily read in the paper. Rather, one can interact with other people, and with the information one seeks, and do so directly at previously unthinkable speeds. Digital media and network connections, it is said, are the most democratic of media, promoting free expression and access to information wherever a computer can be hooked up to a telephone line.

In this celebration of new possibilities, we tend to emphasize the many things that become feasible when people have ready access to information sources and to other people not practically available before. The scope and the speed of interconnected digital networks make conversations easy that before were unimaginable. The almost utopian vision of a wired future seems to assume that the legal infrastructure of our information policy will continue to encourage us to speak, think, and learn as we will.

But the technological marvel that makes this interconnection possible has other potential as well. Digital technology makes it possible to monitor, record, and restrict what people look at, listen to, read, and hear.

Why, in the United States, would one want to do such a thing? To get paid. If someone, let's call him Fred, keeps track of what we see and hear, that enables Fred to ensure that we pay for our sights and sounds. Once information is valuable, an overwhelming temptation arises to appropriate that value, to turn it into cash. If the means of transforming information into a marketable and marketed commodity require a little invasion of privacy, a smidgen of information rationing, or a dollop of surveillance, well, that's the price of progress.

Perhaps it is; further, perhaps it's a price that many citizens would be more than willing to pay in order to preserve the current world dominance of American information and entertainment industries. Citizens are not, however, being asked, and their elected representatives turn out to be in no position to evaluate that bargain on their behalf. Meanwhile, the people who argue that the nation's prosperity requires a legal regime that enables information to be tightly controlled seem likely to prevail.

One of the most important devices being used to effect this transformation, ironically enough, is copyright law. No wonder so few people are paying attention. Copyright law has a well-earned reputation as a discipline both marginal and arcane. Copyright law questions can make delightful cocktail-party small talk, but copyright law answers tend to make eyes glaze over everywhere. Still, to the extent that the public considers copyright law at all, it appears to think that the law is designed to benefit authors for creating new works and thus to promote the progress of knowledge and art.

And, that's certainly the theory. The premise is that we want authors to have enough control over their works to enable them to extract some of the commercial value of those works—that's what lets them make a living creating works of authorship. At the same time, the purpose of the system is to benefit the public at large, and that works best when the rest of the value of the work can be enjoyed by the public at large. United States copyright law has until now divided up the value that inheres in works of authorship to permit authors (and their employers and publishers) to control and therefore profit from some uses of their works, while forbidding them from controlling others. Authors are given enough control to enable them to exploit their creations, while not so much that consumers and later authors are unable to benefit from the protected works. To take a simple example, copyright owners are entitled to prohibit others from making copies of their works, but copyright law gives them no rights to control whether or when people read them or use them.

Why the lines have been drawn where they are is a matter of some controversy. Some people insist that copyright owners are entitled to just enough control to provide an economic incentive for their creation, since the broad purpose of copyright is to promote knowledge by encouraging authors to create and disseminate their works. Others argue that the only uses of a work that are properly excluded from the copyright owner's control are the ones that have no significant economic value.

Technology now permits copyright owners of works in digital format to monitor and meter the consumption of their works. The ubiquity of digital technology in the information and entertainment industries and the rapid penetration of the Internet into Americans' lives have enabled the dissemination of an increasing amount of information on a pay-per-view basis. In the current milieu, the policy arguments over the rationale for copyright owners' imperfect control have taken on immense practical significance. If the reason that authors' and their publishers' control over uses of their works has been narrowly confined is to enable consumers and future authors to make the broadest possible use of protected creations that is consistent with the copyright system's encouragement of authorship, then digital technology changes very little. The fact that technology enables copyright owners to exercise more complete control is no reason to modify the copyright law to facilitate it. If, in contrast, the goal of copyright law is to place all feasible control over works of authorship firmly in the hands of copyright owners, new digital technology offers us the opportunity for the first time to come very close to perfecting the system.

The controversy over which view of the law is more nearly true is no longer academic. Over the past ten years, many have come around to the view that, in a networked digital world, limitations on copyright owners' control of their works are no longer desirable. Congress has added more than one hundred pages to the copyright statute, almost all of them billed as loophole-closers.[1] We've also seen the emergence of a new way of thinking about copyright: Copyright is now seen as a tool for copyright owners to use to extract all the potential commercial value from works of authorship, even if that means that uses that have long been deemed legal are now brought within the copyright owner's control.

In 1998, copyright owners persuaded Congress to enhance their rights with a sheaf of new legal and technological controls. Armed with those copyright improvements, copyright lawyers began a concerted campaign to remodel cyberspace into a digital multiplex and shopping mall for copyright-protected material. The outcome of that effort is still uncertain. If current trends continue unabated, however, we are likely to experience a violent collision between our expectations of freedom of expression and the enhanced copyright law. I wish I could be confident that copyright law would be the loser in such a fight.

NOTE

1. *See* Intellectual Property and Communications Omnibus Reform Act of 1999, Public L. 106-113 (1999); Digital Theft and Copyright Damages Improvement Act, Public L. 106-160 (1999); Digital Millennium Copyright Act, Public L. 105-204 (1998); No Electronic Theft (NET) Act, Public L. 105-147, 111 Stat. 2678 (1997); Anti-counterfeiting Consumer Protection Act , Public L. 104-153, 110 Stat. 1386, 1388 (1996); Digital Performance Right in Sound Recordings Act, Public L. 104-39, 109 Stat. 336 (1995); Audio Home Recording Act, Public L. 102-563, 106 Stat. 4237 (1992); Copyright Renewal Act, Public L. 102-307, 106 Stat. 264 (1992); Computer Software Rental Amendments, Public L. 101-650, 104 Stat. 5089, 5134 (1990); Copyright Remedy Clarification Act, Public L. 101-553, 104 Stat. 287 (1990).

ONE

COPYRIGHT BASICS

The Congress shall have the power . . .

To promote the Progress of Science and useful Arts, by securing for limited Times to Authors and Inventors the exclusive Right to their respective Writings and Discoveries.

—United States Constitution[1]

YOU DON'T NEED A DETAILED understanding of copyright law to read this book: a brief overview should give you enough to get by. The Statute of Anne, enacted by the British Parliament in 1710, is generally considered to be the world's first copyright law. The United States passed its first copyright statute in 1790. Early U.S. copyright laws required compliance with a variety of formalities (registration, copyright notice, renewal)[2] as a condition of copyright protection. Recent laws have dropped requirements for copyright notice, registration, or renewal, and have abandoned conditions limiting copyright to publicly distributed works. Today, copyright protection is automatic.

Copyright laws in the United States and elsewhere begin with the principle that neither the creator of a new work of authorship nor the general public ought to be able to appropriate all of the benefits that flow from the creation of a new, original work of authorship. If creators can't gain some benefit from their creations, they may not bother to make new works. If distributors can't earn money from the works, they may not bother to disseminate them. But all authors use raw material from elsewhere to build their works. Novelists, composers, sculptors, and programmers all incorporate into their works ideas, language, building blocks, and expressive details they first encountered elsewhere. If creators were given control over every element and use of the works they created, there would be little raw material left for later authors. Thus, both as a matter of fairness and as a matter of promoting learning by encouraging authors to create works and the public to consume them, copyright has always divided up the possible rights in and uses of a work, and given control over some of those rights to the creators and distributors and control over others to the general public.

When you buy a book today, you pay a flat fee to some bookseller rather than agreeing to be billed by the glance. You may read and reread the book, or any part of it. You may learn the stuff that's in it. You may talk about the book with your friends. You may loan your copy of the book to any friend who wants it. When you've finished with the book, you may resell it to a used bookstore or donate it to the local library, which may loan it out to anyone with a library card. You don't need the copyright owner's permission to do any of these things.

When you buy a musical recording on compact disc, you again pay some amount of money to own the thing. You have no further obligation to pay for each listen. The law permits you to make a tape of the recording for your car. You may resell the CD, or loan it out, even to friends who want to use it to make tapes for their cars. What you can't do without the copyright owners' permission is rent the CD out commercially, or broadcast it over the radio, or play it at a concert or in your restaurant, bar, or store.

When your child needs to consult an encyclopedia for a report on hive-building insects, you don't have to buy one; you can send her to the public library to look the stuff up. When she writes her report, she doesn't have to pay the encyclopedia company to use what she learned. When you see a building, you can snap a picture without paying the architect. When you go to a bookstore, you may skim the first chapter of a book before you buy it. When you turn on your car radio, you needn't pay the composers of the music you hear, or the artists who perform it. But you know at some level that in the process of writing music and delivering it to your ears, someone at some point has paid them something.

When you turn on your computer, you needn't pay a royalty to Microsoft or Apple® for the use of the operating-systems program that makes the computer work. We take this for granted, but it isn't natural law. It is the result of a complicated legal bargain that allocates the different benefits that flow from works of authorship to writers, to publishers, and to the public at large in a way intended to promote the progress of science and useful arts. There's no particular reason why we had to choose this system. We could have relied on the patronage system that gave us Shakespeare. We could have decreed that authors who create works of authorship have exclusive control over every use of their works for a year, or a decade, or a life, or forever.

Instead, we came up with a system designed to give some market-based financial compensation to people who create works, and to people who distribute them, without giving them extensive rights to prevent the use and reuse of those works by the public and by the authors of the future. The system is premised on the assumption that we can give authors and their publishers rights to control some ways of exploiting their works, and reserve the rest of the value of the works to the public at large.

Under the current copyright statute,[3] copyright vests automatically in original works of authorship as soon as they are "fixed in tangible form," i.e., embodied in a permanent, tangible object. No notice or registration is required.[4] The copyright in this book came into being as I typed the words that you are reading. The copyright in a song exists from the moment the song is first written down or recorded on tape, disc, or microchip. The copyright will belong either to the individual who created it (in which case it will last until seventy years after that person's death), or, if the work is created within the course of employment, to that individual's employer (in which case it will last for ninety-five years from its first public distribution).[5] It will give the copyright owner rights over the material the author added, but not over any preexisting material appropriated from elsewhere. The copyright will protect the expression in the work from being copied without permission, but will give no protection whatsoever to the underlying ideas, facts, systems, procedures, methods of operation, principles, or discoveries.[6] It may seem paradoxical that copyright fails to protect what for many works are their most valuable features, but that balance is a long-standing one; it derives, the U.S. Supreme Court tells us, from copyright's constitutional foundation.[7] The chief purpose of copyright is to promote learning, and learning would be frustrated if facts and ideas could not be freely used and reused.

United States copyright law gives authors a number of broad rights: the right to reproduce the work in fixed, tangible copies; the right to create adaptations; the right to distribute copies to the public; and the rights to perform publicly and display publicly. These rights are made subject in the statute to a variety of exceptions.[8]

Some of the exceptions are broad: under the "first sale doctrine," for example, the copyright owner has no right to control the distribution of a copy of a work after she has sold that copy.[9] The buyer can keep it, loan it, rent it, display it, or resell it to others. Another exception covers useful articles: If a protected photograph, painting, or sculpture embodies or depicts a useful article, anyone can reproduce the useful article, which is not itself subject to copyright protection. In other words, copyright protects a painting or photograph of an automobile, but gives no protection to the automobile itself.[10] Under the fair use privilege, a variety of otherwise infringing acts are excused for policy reasons.[11] (Common fair uses include quotations, parodies, photocopies for classroom use, and home video-taping of television programs.)

Most of the exceptions, though, are narrow and specific. Broadcasting organizations, for example, licensed to broadcast a musical recording, are allowed to make a copy of the work to facilitate the broadcast.[12] Libraries may make photocopies so long as they comply with a long list of conditions and limitations.[13] Cable television operators can retransmit broadcasts without the permission of the owners of the copyrights in the works being broadcast, so long as they pay a statutory license fee.[14] A small restaurant may play radio or television broadcasts for its customers, but may not play prerecorded music.[15] A church may play religious music during services.[16]

The presence of detailed exceptions shouldn't obscure the fact that some uses of copyrighted works are simply not subject to copyright owners' control at all. Copyright owners are given no control, for example, over *private* performance or display. Watching a videotape in your living room, showing the sculpture you just purchased to your cousin, or singing the latest Metallica hit to your friend over the telephone are simply not among the uses that the copyright owner has any right to prohibit or permit.[17] They have no power to prevent the owners of copies of their works from loaning them repeatedly. More fundamentally, copyright does not protect ideas, no matter how original, brilliant, or unique they may be.[18] $E=mc^2$ is in the public domain. Nor may copyright give owners legal rights over the functional or factual elements of their works. The design used for the onramps to the Triborough Bridge is not protected by copyright.[19] The facts reported in a biography of San Francisco Jewish families belong to no one.[20] Copyright owners do not own any of the ideas expressed in their works. They have no ownership of the functional or factual aspects of their works. They have no claim to any compensation when their readers learn and use their teachings.

All of this has worked more or less invisibly to the general public, because traditionally, copyright owners have had control over the sorts of uses typically made by commercial and institutional actors and little control over the consumptive uses made by individuals. That has permitted the copyright law to be drawn as a complex, internally inconsistent, wordy, and arcane code, since the only folks who really needed to know it were folks for whom copyright lawyers were an item of essential overhead. Most copyright infringement suits proceeded against businesses and institutions.

A law intended to be enforced against individual consumers would have needed to be structured differently; the current setup would strike many individuals as unfair. Under the current statute, anyone who invades the copyright owner's exclusive rights without a license or statutory privilege can be held liable for infringement.[21] The law has never required that an infringer be aware that she is violating another's copyright. It is copyright infringement to copy a protected work subconsciously and unknowingly;[22] it is also copyright infringement to perform or distribute copies of a work in the mistaken belief that one's use is licensed.[23] Successful plaintiffs in copyright-infringement suits can recover substantial damages without needing to prove any actual harm to the market for their works.[24] In addition, courts routinely order defendants to stop infringing activity, to surrender or destroy infringing copies, and to pay plaintiffs' lawyer bills.[25]

Digital technology changed the marketplace. It's a cliché that digital technology permits everyone to become a publisher. If you're a conventional publisher, though, that cliché doesn't sound so attractive. If you're a record company, the last thing you want is a world in which musicians and listeners can eliminate the middleman. But can you stop it, or at least delay it? Is the copyright law one tool that might help you do so?

NOTES

1. U.S. Const., art. I, § 8, cl. 8.

2. Until 1909, one secured copyright through registration. The copyright lasted for a fixed term, and could be renewed for an additional term if the copyright owner complied with renewal procedures. The 1909 act provided that one could secure copyright in some works by registering them, and in others by publishing them with the prescribed copyright notice. Registration was in any event necessary in order to apply for the renewal term. In either case, distributing copies to the public without the statutory notice forfeited the copyright. *See* Robert A. Gorman and Jane C. Ginsburg, *Copyright: Cases and Materials* 4–9, 339–43, 383–97(5th ed., Lexis Law Publishing, 1999).

3. The current statute was enacted in 1976 and has been amended periodi-

cally in the years since then. It is codified at 17 U.S.C. §§ 101-1332 (2000).

4. 17 U.S.C. § 102.

5. 17 U.S.C. §§ 201, 302.

6. 17 U.S.C. § 102(b).

7. *Feist Publications* v. *Rural Telephone Service*, 499 U.S. 340 (1991); *see also* *Baker* v. *Selden*, 101 U.S. 99 (1879).

8. 17 U.S.C. § 106.

9. 17 U.S.C. § 109. There are two narrow exceptions. Owners of copyrights in sound recordings and computer programs have the right to prohibit rental, but not loan, gift or resale, of copies of sound recordings or computer programs. Ibid.

10. 17 U.S.C. § 113.

11. 17 U.S.C. § 107.

12. 17 U.S.C. § 112(a).

13. 17 U.S.C. § 108.

14. 17 U.S.C. § 111. Federal Communications Commission regulations impose other restrictions that limit the ability to transmit particular works, and some of those regulations may constrain cable operators in ways that echo copyright limitations. See 47 U.S.C. § 325(b).

15. 17 U.S.C. § 110(5).

16. 17 U.S.C. § 110(3).

17. In *Columbia Pictures Industries, Inc.* v. *Professional Real Estate Investors*, 866 F.2d 278 (9th Cir. 1989), for example, motion picture studios sued a resort hotel that rented videodiscs for its guests to play on the large-screen TVs in their rooms. The court held that there was no *public* performance and therefore no infringement.

18. 17 U.S.C. § 102(b). *See Baker* v. *Selden*, 101 U.S. 99 (1879). Charles Selden devised a novel bookkeeping system that permitted accountants to condense six pages of accounts onto only two. Selden published several copyrighted manuals about his system, and hired an agent to travel through the country seeking to license the system and the ledger forms Selden had designed to go with it. An Ohio accountant, impressed with the Selden system but unable to pay Selden's price, adopted it anyway, and later peddled his version to other accountants. The United States Supreme court dismissed Selden's copyright infrigement suit:

> The very object of publishing a book on science or the useful arts is to communicate to the world the useful knowledge which it contains. But this object would be frustrated if the knowledge could not be used without incurring the guilt of piracy of the book.

101 U.S. at 103.

19. *See Muller* v. *Triborough Bridge Authority*, 43 F. Supp. 298 (S.D.N.Y. 1942).

20. *See Narell* v. *Freeman*, 872 F.2d 907 (9th Cir. 1989).

21. 17 U.S.C. § 501.

22. *See Bright Tunes Music Corp.* v. *Harrisongs Music, Ltd.*, 420 F. Supp. 177 (S.D.N.Y. 1976), *aff'd*, 722 F.2d 988 (2d Cir. 1983); *Fred Fisher* v. *Dillingham*, 298 F. 145 (S.D.N.Y. 1924).

23. *See, e.g., Lipton* v. *Nature Co.* 71 F.3d 464 (2d Cir. 1995).

24. 17 U.S.C. § 504(c).

25. *See Fogerty* v. *Fantasy, Inc.*, 510 U.S. 517 (1994); Gorman and Ginsburg, *Copyright*, at 729–30.

TWO
THE ART OF MAKING COPYRIGHT LAWS

C OPYRIGHT LAWYERS ARE A PECULIARLY myopic breed of human being. There is something fundamental about coming to understand that current law may make it technically illegal to watch a movie and then imagine what it would have looked like if the studio had cast some other actor in the leading role,[1] that renders one unfit for ordinary reflective thinking. Nonetheless, sometimes one can step back and perceive, in a dim sort of way, that one's tribe is doing something stupid. Realizing that doesn't get one very far. The institutional and legal structure of the copyright community makes it difficult to prevent foolish approaches to new technology.

Copyright laws become obsolete when technology renders the assumptions on which they were based outmoded. That has happened with increasing frequency since Congress enacted the first copyright law in 1790. Inevitably, new developments change the pitch of the playing field. Industries affected by copyright find that the application of old legal language to new contexts yields unanticipated results. They find themselves to be the beneficiaries of new advantages and the victims of new disadvantages, and respond about the way you would expect them to, with efforts to regain old benefits while retaining the new ones.

The first U.S. copyright statute, for example, gave authors exclusive rights to "print, reprint, publish or vend"—in other words, to control the reproduction and sale of copies.[2] A model based on compensating the author for the sale of every copy became unsatisfactory to authors when other means of exploiting works eclipsed the sale of copies. Consider, for instance, composers of popular music: So long as the chief source of revenue for popular songs was the sale of sheet music, composers fared well under the system. Although public performances of music might generate no royalties, musicians and singers performing the songs would need (purchased) sheet music in order to perform, so composers shared indirectly in

22

the performance revenues. Once it became possible to record a musical performance on a piano roll or phonograph record and to make and sell hundreds of those, or to broadcast performances over the radio, however, composers could be excluded from the additional proceeds generated by the recording or broadcast.[3] Establishments in the habit of performing music without seeking permission responded unenthusiastically to composers' proposals for a remedy. Thus, each technological advance inspired a dispute about whether it entitled copyright owners to expanded rights over their works. Each camp claimed the support of fundamental truth. Even King Solomon would have had trouble deciding between them every time the problem arose: there are only so many times you can threaten to slice up a baby before its putative mothers get wise.

About one hundred years ago, Congress got into the habit of revising copyright law by encouraging representatives of the industries affected by copyright to hash out among themselves what changes needed to be made and then present Congress with the text of appropriate legislation. By the 1920s, the process was sufficiently entrenched that whenever a member of Congress came up with a legislative proposal without going through the cumbersome prelegislative process of multiparty negotiation, the affected industries united to block the bill. Copyright bills passed only after private stakeholders agreed with one another on their substantive provisions. The pattern has continued to this day.

A process like this generates legislation with some predictable features. First of all, no affected party is going to agree to support a bill that leaves it worse off than it is under current law. This means that negotiating industries need to identify some potential surplus they can divide up among themselves to get enough support for new proposals, and that surplus most often comes at the expense of outsiders. Here's a simple example: copyright terms have been getting longer and longer. Between 1978 and 1998, most copyrights expired at the end of their seventy-fifth year. As Mickey Mouse, who first appeared in 1927, came face to face with the imminent expiration of his copyright, Disney's eyes turned toward Europe, where a number of countries had recently lengthened their copyright terms to match Germany's term of life of the author plus seventy years.[4] Proprietors of aging but still profitable works asked Congress to tack twenty additional years onto the term of every extant copyright. A copyright term that is twenty years longer makes both licensors (or owners) and licensees (commercial users) better off, because licensors get an extra twenty years on their revenue stream, and licensees get an extra twenty years of exclusivity. The proposal, therefore, enjoyed widespread support. It posed problems for publishers of public domain books, who would be prevented from bringing out particular works for two additional decades. Many of them had plans to bring out editions of works due to enter the public domain within the next few years.[5] Most publishers, however, were enthusiastic and the publishers' lobbies pushed it. It was also a problem for libraries, which can make more extensive use of public domain works than they can of copyright-protected works, so the proposal's supporters agreed to a library exception to the twenty-year term extension. That still isn't great for members of the public, who are (the Constitution tells us) supposed to get unfettered access to all protected works after a limited period of copyright, but the general public doesn't sit at the negotiating table.

Second, there's a premium on characterizing the state of current law to favor one's position, since current law is the baseline against which proposals are negotiated. So, if university libraries, say, are liable under current law if they make lots of photocopies of law-review articles at the request of professors who want file copies, library associations are likely to be more willing to support legislation that gives them a partial, limited, contingent exemption from this sort of photocopying in return for tacking twenty more years onto the copyright term. If, however, current library photocopying practices are perfectly legal, people who want to get libraries to sign off on term extension need to come up with something else to offer as a bribe.

Third, the way these things tend to get settled in the real world is by specifying. Libraries say, "We need a privilege to make copies for patrons who request them." Book publishers say, "Well, okay, you can make the copies but other folks can't" (so we need a definition of libraries who qualify for the privilege), "and you can only make one copy for each patron, and you can make them only in these circumstances." Television broadcasters say, "We need to make copies so that we can edit a program to include commercials and station ID." So movie studios and music publishers say, "Well, okay, *you* can make one copy but other folks can't" (and now we have a new specific privilege and a definition of broadcasters who get to use it), "but you can only make one copy, and you can make it only in these circumstances, and after six months you have to destroy it." Record companies say, "*We* need a license to make copies so we can make all those records and tapes and CDs that bring royalties into composers' pockets without having to call up the copyright owner and ask permission for every song." So composers and music publishers say, "Well, you can have a statutory license, but you have to pay for it, and you have to send us monthly royalty statements, and you can only make records for the home user, not for jukeboxes or Muzak®."[6]

You see the pattern. As the entertainment and information markets have gotten more complicated, the copyright law has gotten longer, more specific, and harder to understand. Neither book publishers nor libraries have any interest in making the library privilege broad enough so that it would be useful to users that aren't libraries, and neither movie studios nor broadcast stations have any interest in making the broadcaster's privilege broad enough to be of some use to say, cable television or satellite TV, so that doesn't happen. Negotiated privileges tend to be very specific, and tend to pose substantial entry barriers to outsiders who can't be at the negotiating table because their industries haven't been invented yet. So negotiated copyright statutes have tended, throughout the century, to be kind to the entrenched status quo and hostile to upstart new industries.

The Internet has generated a lot of hype in the past decade, and that has encouraged the people who run the current information and entertainment industries to look at it as at least as much of a threat as an opportunity. The Internet sometimes gets characterized as a giant copying machine that facilitates widespread and undetectable copyright infringement. That's about 50 percent hype—the Internet facilitates widespread copying, but it also facilitates detection of copying. Still, you can see how it would be a scary idea. The Internet also gets painted as the next new thing that will replace conventional newspapers and television and phonograph records in our lives. That's also probably hype, but you can see how that notion might bother newspaper publishers and television networks and record companies. The Internet gets promoted as a new market we'll use to sell everything from computer software to vacation homes, and while that may be an attractive idea, it's far from clear that the current market leaders in the sales of computer software and vacation homes are going to be the new market leaders in the new medium.

So, this new Internet thing hits the radar screen, and it's big, and it's scary, and everybody wants a piece of it. The commercial lawyers scurry off to redraft the Uniform Commercial Code to cover electronic contracts,[7] and the civil-liberties lawyers worry about strong encryption and sexually explicit content. And in the early 1990s, the dominant players in the entertainment and information industries got cracking on reforming the copyright law to make the Internet safe for the then-leading copyright owners.

Copyright owners argued that the United States currently dominated the world in film, music, television, computer software, and databases, and if the Internet weren't made safe for copyright owners, either all the people in all the other countries would get together and steal all our stuff, or U.S. copyright owners would decline to put their stuff on the Internet (because it wasn't safe) and the United States might lose the advantage of world leadership on this new medium. (Neither claim turned out to be true in practice, to the extent we can gather empirical evidence one way or the other, but they are the sort of claims that have always sold well to Congress.)

When we get to the down-and-dirty of formulating actual proposals for legislation, the first tactic of interested parties is to claim that extant copyright law already gives them whatever it is they want. (When it came to the Internet, it was a little hard to square this argument with the alternative argument that U.S. industries would stay out of the online market until Congress strengthened copyright protection, but that claim was already proving to be demonstrably false.) The dynamics of copyright negotiation make it important for interests seeking legislation to claim that they already have all, or at least most, of whatever it is they are asking for. If you want Internet service providers to be held liable for their subscribers' infringing activities, for example, it will be easier to accomplish this if you claim that current law imposes such liability (but that you would be willing to bargain toward a suitably narrow limitation) than to demand that Congress impose that liability in the first instance. But, Congress had enacted the current copyright law more than twenty years earlier, so it would have been hard to argue that Congress had the Internet in mind. To make the case that copyright law already provided the enhanced protection they wanted, copyright owners needed some statutory language to hang their new improved interpretation on. That limited their options.

Thus constrained, the claim that some people made was this: the copyright statute gives the copyright owner the exclusive right to reproduce protected works in "copies," subject only to the exceptions enumerated in the statute. (I mentioned some of these earlier: privileges for libraries and broadcasters and record companies and the like to make limited numbers of copies in particular situations.) A computer works by reproducing things in its volatile Random Access Memory, and anything that exists in volatile memory could, at least in theory, be saved to disk (the argument continued), so each appearance of any portion of a work in any computer's random access memory is a reproduction in a copy within the meaning of the statute.[8] That would mean—since there are no enumerated exceptions for Internet-related uses—that the copyright owner has the legal right to control, enjoin, or collect money for every single appearance of a work in the memory of any computer anywhere. Moreover, since the reproduction right is the "fundamental" copyright right (after all, that's why we call it *copy*right), any diminution in this important fundamental right would impede the progress of science and the useful arts.

If you think about the argument for a moment, you can see that, if it sells, it gives copyright owners control not only over every time America Online uses pictures of Captain Kirk and Mr. Spock to advertise its *Star Trek* chat group, but also over every time an AOL subscriber uses her computer to view the ad, and also over every computer-to-computer transmission the packets of data make to get from AOL's webserver to the user's computer. That means that, in theory, AOL, and its subscriber, and the proprietors of the University of Illinois computer and the MCI computer that the data happen to travel through on that particular day are all copyright infringers, even though they may have no way of knowing that these anonymous electrons infringe Paramount's proprietary rights.

They couldn't mean that, right? But they did. And, as a practical and political matter, it turned out to be a brilliant legal argument. Copyright owners who want to ensure that they control—and can charge money for— any appearance of their works in any computer anywhere, argued that Congress gave them that right twenty years ago, and that all they were asking for now was some support for their efforts to enforce it. The argument succeeded—copyright owners were able to persuade Congress to pass the Digital Millennium Copyright Act, which encourages the use of technological protections to facilitate a pay-per-view, pay-per-use system using some sort of automatic debit payment before anyone can have access to anything.[9] The ingeniousness of the argument depended in part on its corollary: if a copyright owner's rights were infringed every time parts of a work passed through a computer, then the current users of the Internet (and of computers, fax machines, compact disc players, and quite possibly ordinary telephone service), and the folks who operated all the equipment they used, were lawbreakers and could be held liable for hundreds of thousands of dollars in damages *each*. That bogeyman convinced many of the stakeholders to go along with a basic scheme predicated on copyright owners' right to continuing control of each attempt to see, read, hear, or use their works, in return for a specific exemption insulating each of them from liability.

Politically, then, the argument was understandable, even inspired. As a matter of policy, though, it carried horrific implications. Setting the basic compensable unit of copyright (which is also the basic infringing unit) at the ephemeral RAM copy in volatile memory sets it at a place that implicates the fundamental operation of computers on what is essentially an atomic level. It means that all appearance of works in computers—at home, on networks, at work, in the library—needs to be effected in conformance with, and with attention to, copyright rules. That's new. Until now, copyright has regulated multiplication and distribution of works, but it hasn't regulated consumption. If you buy a book, or even borrow a book, you're free to read it as many times as you like. You can loan it to somebody else. You can sell it or give it away or even rent it out. You can't make copies of it, but you can use it and use it and use it again. But, if every time a work appears in the Random Access Memory of your computer, you are making an actionable copy, then we have for the first time given copyright owners extensive control over the consumption of their works. Each time you opened Microsoft Word to edit a document, you would need Microsoft's permission. Each time you used your computer's CD-ROM drive to listen to a CD you had purchased, you would need a license from the record company. Each time you viewed a Web page with a picture of Mickey Mouse, you would first need to secure permission from Disney.

By using so basic an atomic unit, we're proposing to put copyright rules in place as the most basic "rules of the game" in cyberspace. If we adopt that model, it is unavoidable that the answers to a lot of questions that we're used to thinking about as questions central to our information policy, are going to be answers that derive, first, from the copyright view of the universe. I'm not talking only about questions like whether a person who writes something is entitled to get paid when another person reads it. The current digital copyright agenda seeks to supply copyright answers to a whole range of basic policy questions ranging from who is entitled to access, to what, and on whose terms, to whether citizens have any privacy interest whatsoever in personal data. These are the sorts of questions with which the American legal system has struggled for some years under the umbrella of information policy, but the digital copyright agenda supplies copyright answers to all of them. And because copyright lawyers talk to each other too much, we can't even see how crazy that idea looks from the outside world.

Copyright law rules reflect a variety of characteristics that make them unsuitable for the basic infrastructure of our information policy. Let me start with a basic one: copyright rules are complicated and hard to understand. There are a lot of reasons for that, but the most obvious one is that our copyright rules were hammered out by copyright lawyers to adjust the commercial relations among their clients. Sometimes the best solution to any particular dispute involves drawing some peculiarly counterintuitive lines. So long as the rules are being drawn by copyright lawyers for their clients (all of whom, by definition, have copyright lawyers), it doesn't much matter that the only way to know what the rules say is to commit a two-hundred-some page statute to memory. That's what copyright lawyers are paid for. But once we try to make these rules apply to the everyday activities of every person on the planet, a set of rules that only lawyers—and, indeed, only specialists—could be expected to be able to work with won't do. And, in fact, it's even worse than that, because a number of the rules that copyright lawyers take for granted are so very counterintuitive that people commonly refuse to believe that they could possibly be the rules.

A simple example here are the rules governing when bars, restaurants, and stores need a copyright license to play the radio or television or recorded music where their patrons can hear it. The basic rules were settled years ago. Copyright owners have the exclusive right to authorize public performance of their works. Most small businesses playing recorded music and many businesses playing television or radio, therefore, needed to buy a performing license to do so. ASCAP,* BMI,† and SESAC—all music performing rights societies who represent composers—were delighted to sell performance licenses to any establishment that wished to play music. Licenses were cheap, a matter of a few hundred dollars per year. Nonetheless, because proprietors of small businesses found the well-settled rules incredible, dozens of them went to court to protect their supposed right to play music—every year—at a cost of hundreds of thousands of dollars, because they couldn't believe that these rules were really the rules. And they always lost. Even so, the next year there were another dozen small business owners who were determined to litigate, and they lost too.[10] Members of the general public commonly find copyright rules implausible, and simply disbelieve them.

Now, the copyright answer to this difficulty, by which I mean the answer that copyright interests are suggesting that the world adopt, is to

---

*American Society of Composers, Authors and Publishers (ASCAP)
†Broadcast Music, Inc. (BMI)

encourage the use of technological devices that make unauthorized copying or use impossible, and the enactment of stiff laws to penalize anyone for hacking around or disabling these devices. That way, people won't have to know what the rules are because it will be impossible for most of them to break them. (This is like installing a device in every automobile that disables it from going any faster than fifty-five miles per hour. This used to be the speed limit, but nobody believed in it, nobody obeyed it, and now it's history.) Which illustrates another basic problem: the information policy solutions devised by copyright lawyers negotiating among themselves are inevitably copyright-centric. Copyright law has a narrow focus. It has never paid attention to a whole host of important interests that have traditionally informed our information policy, and copyright analysis turns out to have very little room in it to do so.

In addition to free speech concerns, information policy takes account of issues related to equity, competition, ensuring a diversity of viewpoints, securing ready and affordable access to important sources of information, privacy—all issues that are at best tangential to copyright law and in some cases wholly alien.

Until recently, that problem was of more theoretical than real concern. So long as copyright governed the transactions among commercial and institutional entities, but left most individuals alone, it was usually possible to strike a deal to do whatever it was you needed to do. In addition, one or more of the designated copyright-affected industries might have interests that coincided, at least roughly, with those of individual members of the public. Consumers, for example, have a limited home-recording-for-personal-use privilege that was secured for them by the litigation and legislative negotiation of the manufacturers of home recording equipment.[11]

But the threat and promise of the Internet has induced those of us who are copyright lawyers to an act of breathtaking hubris. We define a set of rules that we say ought to be the basic copyright rules of the road, and then we construe those rules to govern every single way that information coded in electrons can move from one computer to another. We didn't ask whether these rules will be sufficiently sensitive to the core policies that have animated our information law for years and years; we just said, "Oh, it's never been a problem before. . . ." But with a change that radical, there may not be any business or institutional interests that are likely to act as representatives of the public interest. Instead, what you see are Internet service providers, or telephone companies who say: "Well, gee, it's okay with me if all my subscribers have a lot of exposure for reading legal content you don't want them to read, so long as you write a provision into the law that ensures that *I'm* exempt."[12]

If Congress were in the habit of looking hard at copyright proposals to see whether their substantive provisions were good policy, or would interact in good ways with other policies, one might have expected this exercise to come to an early end. People who aren't copyright lawyers, after all, would look at copyright lawyers' claims to control all digital uses of any copyrighted work and say, "There's something wrong with this picture." But, because the tradition in copyright legislation involves getting a bunch of copyright lawyers to sit at a bargaining table and talk with one another, a lot of important questions were never asked.

In 1998, copyright lobbyists persuaded Congress to enact a twenty-six-thousand-word, fifty-page coda to the copyright statute setting forth a new and convoluted series of rights and exceptions for digital copyright. Among other innovations, the new law for the first time purports to make it illegal for individual consumers to gain unauthorized access to copies of techno-logically protected works, even copies they own. There are a great many exceptions: for computer-security experts engaged in testing the security of a particular computer system, for example, or for law-enforcement officers investigating crimes, but they are cast in prose so crabbed and so encum-bered with conditions as to be of little use to anyone who doesn't have a copyright lawyer around to explain which hoops to jump through.

U.S. copyright law is based on a model devised for print media, and expanded with some difficulty to embrace a world that includes live, filmed, and taped performances; broadcast media; and, most recently, dig-ital media. The suitability of that model for new media is controversial. As one might expect, to the extent that current legal rules make some parties "haves" and others "have-nots," the haves are fans of the current model, while today's have-nots suggest that some other model might be more appropriate for the future. Meanwhile, copyright lawyers, who, after all, make their living interpreting and applying this long and complex body of counterintuitive, bewildering rules, insist that the current model is very close to the platonic ideal, and should under no circumstances be jetti-soned in favor of some untried and untrue replacement. They naturally prefer to make the copyright rules they know the rules that all of us need to operate under whenever we encounter copyrighted works. Congress, for its part, is content to let them make the rules they want to.

That puts us in very real danger of adopting a set of rules for our information society that few of us can live with. Deferring to the copyright bar to write those rules will serve us badly, but persuading Congress to use another approach is, at best, unlikely to succeed. Since members of Congress are disinclined to ask the right questions without prodding from their constituents, it has become crucially important for the general public to appreciate the huge stake it has in what questions are asked and how these questions are answered.

NOTES

1. 17 U.S.C. § 106(2) gives the owner of a copyright the exclusive right to prepare derivative works, which the statute defines broadly to include any adaptation in any form, regardless of whether that adaptation is ever embodied in a permanent copy or communicated to another human being. There is no requirement that the adaptation be commercial. The unauthorized creation of an adaptation is itself an invasion of the copyright owner's rights.

2. The first U.S. copyright statute, Act of May 31, 1790, ch. 15, § 1, 1 Stat. 124, gave copyright owners the "sole right and liberty of printing, reprinting, publishing and vending."

3. Until the enactment of the copyright act of 1909, copyright owners realized no revenues from the sales of piano rolls and phonograph records, because they were not deemed to be "copies" of the music. See *White-Smith Music Publishing Co. v. Apollo Co.*, 209 U.S. 1 (1908). Until Congress established a public performance right for musical works in 1897, composers had no right to receive royalties from public performances.

4. Supporters characterized this as a proposal for international copyright term harmonization. In fact, both Europe and the United States have a dual copyright term. Copyrights that vest initially in the individual who creates a work endure for the life of the author plus seventy years, while copyrights that vest initially in employers or corporations last for a fixed term. Before the recent U.S. term extension, authors' life-based copyrights were longer in Europe than in the United States, while copyrights in works made for hire lasted longer in the United States than in Europe. After term extension, both the United States and Europe follow a life-plus-seventy term, but the U.S. term for works made for hire is nearly twice as long as the comparable term in Europe. Mickey Mouse, and other Disney copyrights, are works made for hire.

5. *See Eldred* v. *Reno*, 74 F.Supp.2d 1 (D.D.C. 1999).

6. *See* 17 U.S.C. § 108 (library reproduction); 17 U.S.C. § 112 (broadcaster reproduction); 17 U.S.C. § 115 (record company reproduction).

7. *See* Jane Kaufman Winn and Michael Rhoades Pullen, *Dispatches from the Front: Recent Skirmishes Along the Frontiers of Electronic Contracting Law*, 55 Business Lawyer 455 (1999).

8. Copyright law has long distinguished between "fixed" hard reproductions, like books and photographic slides or prints, which the statute defines as "copies," and unfixed ephemeral reproductions, like television broadcasts, slide projections, and screen displays. Under the current law, copyright protection does not vest until a work is fixed in a tangible copy, and section 106(1) prohibits reproduction in fixed copies but not ephemeral unfixed reproduction. The reasons for the distinction are largely historical, *see* New York University Law Review, *Study #3: The Meaning of "Writings" in the Copyright Clause of the Constitution* (1956), reprinted in 1 Studies on Copyright 43 (Arthur Fisher Memorial Edition, 1963), but the statutory scheme of rights and exceptions is organized around the principle.

9. *See* Digital Millenium Copyright Act, Public L. 105-304(1998) (codified at 17 U.S.C. §§ 101, 104, 114, 512, 1201–1204).

10. After more than eighty years, bar and restaurant owners' refusal to credit the public performance rules finally paid off. Periodically, small-business owners went to Congress and asked Congress to fix the law to make it right, and music-copyright owners pulled out all the stops to prevent Congress from doing so. *See, e.g., Oversight Hearing on Music Licensing in Restaurants and Retail and Other Establishments Before the Subcommittee on Intellectual Property and Judicial Administration of the House Committee on the Judiciary,* 106th Cong. 1st sess. (July 17, 1997); *Music Licensing Practices of Performing Rights Societies: Oversight Hearing Before the Subcommittee on Intellectual Property and Judicial Administration of the House Committee on the Judiciary,* 103d Cong., 2d sess. (February 23–24, 1994). When copyright owners approached Congress with a request that it extend the term of all copyrights for an additional twenty years, bar and restaurant owners used it as a hostage. Small-business owners threatened to block term extension unless composers agreed to an expanded privilege to play radio and television programming. The term extension bill passed Congress with an expanded bar and restaurant music performance exemption attached to it. *See* Sonny Bono Copyright Term Extension Act of 1998, Pub. L. No. 105-298, 112 Stat. 2827 (codified at 17 U.S.C. §§ 110(5), 301–304).

11. *See* Audio Home Recording Act of 1992 (codified at 17 U.S.C. § 1008); *Sony v. Universal City Studios*, 464 U.S. 417 (1984). More on that privilege in chapter 10, where we will meet Napster.

12. *See, e.g., NII Copyright Protection Act of 1995: Hearing on H.R. 2441 Before the Subcommittee on Courts and Intellectual Property of the House Committee on the Judiciary*, 104th Cong., 2d sess. (February 8, 1996) (testimony of Scott Purcell, Commercial Internet Exchange); ibid. (testimony of Stephen M. Heaton, Compuserve, Inc.); *Copyright Infringement Liability of Online and Internet Service Providers, Hearing Before the Senate Judiciary Committee*, 105th Cong., 1st sess. (September 4, 1997)

(testimony of George Vradenburg III, America Online, Inc., on behalf of the Ad Hoc Copyright Coalition).

A person familiar with the negotiations being conducted during the 105th Congress over the issue of Internet Service Provider liability for copyright infringement described a proposal made by a Senate staffer to give individual subscribers a limited privilege to browse the Internet at home. The proposal, he said, received an unenthusiastic reception from both content owners and the Internet service providers. The providers insisted that a privilege for their subscribers was unnecessary, so long as liability could not be imposed on the service providers for subscribers' infringement. The compromise that emerged from the negotiations gave service providers an exemption from liability for their subscribers' posts so long as they cooperated with aggrieved content owners by promptly removing or blocking access to material subject to a copyright owner's complaint, and by identifying offending subscribers when served with appropriate papers. That compromise was embodied in the Digital Millennium Copyright Act, enacted in 1998. Digital Millennium Copyright Act, Public L. 105-304, 112 Stat. 2860 (1998) (codified at 17 U.S.C. § 512).

THREE
COPYRIGHT AND COMPROMISE

I f history bores you, you should skip this chapter. My purpose here is to present a very abbreviated history of United States copyright lawmaking in the twentieth century.[1] The story shows the evolution of our copyright legislative process, and demonstrates why it tends to produce perverse statutes. It also makes clear how daunting a task it would be to attempt to reform it.

This is a story about private parties, vested interests, and the inexorable pace of technological change. Throughout this century, members of Congress have introduced innumerable copyright bills, held hearings on many, reported some, and enacted few. Congress last enacted a general overhaul of the copyright law a quarter-century ago, in 1976. Since then, Congress has been inundated with proposals to revise copyright law in light of new technology.

The pressures put by new technology on the current copyright statute have sparked disputes over whether the current copyright statute can adjust to the climate of rapid technological change. When such disputes arise, interested parties on all sides tend to raise familiar arguments. One camp, typically, claims that current technology differs profoundly from prior developments and calls into question the assumptions on which our copyright laws are based. Another camp insists that copyright law has always faced the problem of technological change and accommodated it with remarkable success. The current challenge, the argument continues, is not qualitatively different from previous challenges. The copyright statute is equal to the task, and needs no major change. (The argument is more a rhetorical device than an article of faith, so it is not unusual to see the proponents of one side taking the opposite view depending on what proposal is on the table.[2])

Although the dispute is commonly framed in terms of the historical elasticity of the copyright law, the law's ability to stretch itself around new technology has been less than inspiring. Any given copyright law will be more hospitable to some sorts of technological change than to others. Interests who find themselves, usually more by reason of accident than design, in a favorable legal position will naturally resist proposals to tinker with it. Revising the law to make room for new developments, then, has often been a difficult feat to pull off. The legislative process that Congress has come to rely on for copyright revision has exacerbated the problem.

A century ago, Congress confronted the dilemma of updating and simplifying a body of law that seemed too complicated and arcane for legislative revision. To solve that problem, Congress and the Copyright Office settled on a scheme for statutory drafting that featured meetings and negotiations among representatives of industries with interests in copyright. That scheme dominated copyright revision during the legislative process that led to the enactment of the 1909 Copyright Act.[3] Congress and the Copyright Office continued to rely on meetings and negotiations among interested parties for subsequent efforts at copyright revision. The efforts during the 1920s and 1930s to amend the copyright law to permit adherence to the Berne Convention for the Protection of Literary and Artistic Works, an international treaty mandating automatic copyright protection without any requirements for copyright notice or registration, rested upon interindustry negotiations and collapsed when those negotiations collapsed. The twenty-one-year effort that culminated in the enactment of the 1976 Copyright Act again depended upon officially sponsored meetings among those with vested interests in copyright. The copyright amendments that finally enabled the United States to join the Berne Convention in 1989 involved a similar process. The 1992 Audio Home Recording Act resulted from a protracted, multiparty negotiation among composers; music publishers; record companies; performers; and the manufacturers of tapes, tape recorders, and other home electronic equipment.[4] The efforts to write copyright amendments that make specific provision for digital media relied heavily on interindustry negotiations and stalled whenever those negotiations stalled. Indeed, the informal understanding among copyright scholars and practitioners is that copyright revision is, as a practical matter, impossible except through such a process.

The process Congress has relied on for copyright revision, however, has shaped the law in disturbing ways. The interindustry negotiations that resulted in the 1909 Copyright Act sought to revise a body of law based on an old model in order to enable it to embrace a variety of new media.

Industries for whom the old law worked well sought to retain their advantages; industries that found the old law inadequate sought profound changes in the way the copyright statute treated them. Affected interests compromised their disputes by treating different industries in disparate ways. The draft bill that emerged from the conferences among industry representatives defined particular copyright rights with reference to the type of work in which copyright was claimed, and the statute enacted in 1909 retained the draft bill's essential strategy. Authors of particular classes of works were granted specific, enumerated rights; rights differed among the classes of copyrightable works. Thus, the 1909 act gave the proprietor of the copyright in a dramatic work the exclusive right to present the work publicly, the proprietor of the copyright in a lecture the exclusive right to deliver the work in public for profit, the proprietor of the copyright in a musical composition the exclusive right to perform the work publicly for profit except on coin-operated machines, and the proprietor of the copyright in a book no performance or delivery right whatsoever.

The drafters of the 1976 statute, still in effect today, pursued similar goals to different conclusions. Congress and the Copyright Office again depended on negotiations among representatives of an assortment of interests affected by copyright to draft a copyright bill. During twenty-one years of inter-industry squabbling, the private parties to the ongoing negotiations settled on a strategy for the future that all of them could support. Copyright owners were to be granted broad, expansive rights, including future as well as currently feasible uses of copyrighted works. Each of the copyright users represented in the negotiations, meanwhile, received the benefit of a privilege or exemption specifically tailored to its requirements, but very narrowly defined. The 1976 act solved the problem of accommodating future technology by reserving to the copyright owner control over uses of copyrighted works made possible by that technology. Broad, expansive rights were balanced by narrow, stingy exceptions.

The process leading to the 1998 enactment of the Digital Millennium Copyright Act extended the familiar multilateral, interindustry negotiation to the point of self-parody. Copyright owners secured new rights defined in language designed to prevent the discovery of loopholes, and granted a diverse roster of powerful players narrow, detailed, and incomprehensibly drawn exceptions.

A comparison of the immediate futures of these laws reveals that they failed the future in similar ways. Narrow provisions became inapplicable or irrelevant as technology developed, while those interests absent from the meetings of industry representatives encountered significant legal barriers to their activities. The inflexibility of specific provisions distorted the balance that the statute's drafters envisioned when it was enacted, and interested groups came running to Congress to plead for quick fixes. Broad rights and broad exceptions consistently swallowed up their specific counterparts.

An exploration of how the process of drafting copyright statutes through negotiations among industry representatives became entrenched, and what that process has cost us in our efforts to deal rationally with technology, demonstrates how little has changed in the past century. The new technologies have grown more complex, and the number of affected interests has multiplied, but the essence of the disputes and the rhetoric in which they are cast are much the same.

1900–1909: THE FIRST CONFERENCES

Until the copyright revision that culminated in the 1909 act, the legislative process accompanying copyright enactments differed little from the process yielding most statutes: interested parties sent petitions to Congress. The majority of bills were drafted by representatives of affected interests, who then requested members of Congress to introduce the bills, wrote petitions to Congress in their support, and testified in their favor during hearings of the House and Senate Patent Committees, which had jurisdiction over patent, trademark, and copyright bills. By 1900, the body of copyright law was a pastiche of inconsistent amendments grafted on a basic structure that conflated (and sometimes confused) copyrights, patents, and trademarks. Efforts toward general statutory revision foundered as a "result of difficulties in obtaining a quorum of the Patents Committee to give attention to this subject."[5]

Beginning in 1901, Thorvald Solberg, the recently appointed first Register of Copyrights,[6] pleaded repeatedly with Congress to appoint a special commission to revise the copyright law. Members of the Senate Patent Committee, however, were hostile to the idea of a commission. The Librarian of Congress, Herbert Putnam, suggested that Congress instead pass a resolution authorizing the Library of Congress to convene a conference of experts and interested parties to consider a codification of the copyright laws. The members of the Senate Patent Committee concluded that it would be improper for Congress to authorize such a conference, but suggested that they would be delighted if the Librarian were to call an unauthorized conference on his own motion.

The Librarian of Congress followed the Patent Committee's suggestion and, in 1905, invited representatives of authors, dramatists, painters, sculptors, architects, composers, photographers, publishers of various sorts of works, libraries, and printers' unions to a series of meetings in New York City. The invitees represented the beneficiaries of the rights granted by existing copyright statutes. The Librarian did not invite representatives from the newer interests that had not yet received statutory recognition; the motion picture industry, the piano roll industry, and the "talking machine" (phonograph) industry received no invitations. No invitee commented on their absence.

A year later, a bill emerged from the conferences. Congress held joint House-Senate committee hearings. It quickly became clear that the doubts of Senate Committee members about the propriety of a conference of private interests had been well-founded. Witnesses who had not been invited to the conferences found the whole procedure scandalous. Indeed, some went so far as to suggest that Congress was being hoodwinked by a monopolistic conspiracy. The Librarian of Congress became increasingly defensive.

The copyright bill produced by the conferences conferred significant advantages upon composers and music publishers, who had participated, at the expense of the piano roll and talking machine industries, which had not. Case law of the period held that the manufacture of piano rolls did not infringe the copyright in the underlying musical composition. The bill, however, gave copyright owners the exclusive right to make or sell any mechanical device that reproduced the work in sounds, thus making the unlicensed manufacture of piano rolls and phonograph records illegal. The opposition from piano roll and talking machine companies to the bill derived significant weight from their complaints about the process, and dominated the 1906 hearings. At the request of the House and Senate committees, the bill's original authors drafted a substitute bill limiting the mechanical reproduction provisions that the piano roll and talking machine interests opposed. Nonetheless, a majority of the House Committee voted to delete the mechanical reproduction subsection completely. A minority of the House Committee filed a dissenting report supporting a third version of the disputed subsection. The majority of the Senate Committee reported favorably on a bill incorporating yet a fourth version, while the Senate minority report supported the House Committee majority's position.

None of the bills reached a vote, and, in the following year (1908), a proponent of each of the four camps introduced a bill reflecting its position. At the joint hearings held on the four bills, testimony was as divisive as it had been two years earlier. At the end of the hearings, a representative of popular songwriters suggested that the songwriters might sit down with the piano roll and talking machine manufacturers and the music publishers' association in order to agree on a compromise solution. Representative Frank Currier (R-N.H.), the chairman of the House Committee, urged the parties to adopt such a plan, and a spokesman for the piano roll industry disclosed that he had, in fact, begun to explore negotiations with his opponents earlier in the day. Representative Currier assured the witnesses that, if they could reach agreement, the bill would pass. The Senate Committee chairman echoed his enthusiasm for the plan and adjourned the hearings.

The copyright bill introduced in February of 1909 included a solution that embodied the agreement of the affected parties. The relevant provision differed from prior proposals; it established a compulsory license for mechanical reproductions of music and entirely exempted the performance of musical compositions on coin-operated devices. The bill also incorporated a side agreement or two that the private parties had reached along the way.[7] It was enacted within the month.

1910–1912: THE CONFERENCES REPRISED

At the same time the committees were struggling with the revision bill, the Kalem Company hired a writer to read General Lew Wallace's *Ben Hur*, and write a scenario for a motion picture, which it then produced (complete with chariot race). Kalem advertised the picture as "Positively the Most Superb Moving Picture Spectacle ever Produced in America in Sixteen Magnificent Scenes." Kalem had not, of course, bothered to secure a license from Wallace or his publisher. The motion picture industry had been operating without concern for the copyright laws. A few motion pictures had been registered for copyright as "photographs," but the industry was paying no more attention to the copyrights in works it used for its raw material than had the piano roll and talking machine industries before it. The copyright in *Ben Hur* belonged to Harper Brothers Publishers, and Harper Brothers slapped the Kalem Company with a copyright infringement suit.

In 1911, the United States Supreme Court held that the exhibition of the movie infringed the copyright in the novel.[8] The Kalem Company settled the suit for $25,000. The motion picture industry woke up and got in touch with its congressmen.

Motion pictures had barely been mentioned in the hearings on the 1909 act; the motion picture industry had not been invited to the original conferences, and had not bothered to attend the congressional hearings. After *Kalem Co.* v. *Harper Brothers*, however, the motion picture industry faced the prospect of liability under a statute that had been drafted without its interests in mind. It prepared a bill to amend the copyright statute to limit the motion picture industry's exposure in copyright infringement actions and asked Rep. Edward Townsend (D-N.J.)[9] to introduce the bill in Congress.[10]

Townsend introduced the movie industry bill in January of 1912; the House Patent Committee scheduled it for hearings that same month. The committee made no initial effort to notify interested parties of the pending bill. A representative of the live-theater industry, however, learned of the hearings and showed up at them without invitation. The hearings that followed threatened to become a replay of the talking machine dispute. Most of the witnesses who testified before the committee were the same people who testified in 1906 and 1908. Although some of them represented different interests this time around, their arguments and counterarguments had a familiar ring. As was the case in the earlier hearings, opponents of the legislation testified that its supporters were conspirators in thrall to a dastardly trust.

To head off a full-scale reenactment, Rep. Joshua Alexander (D-Mo.) suggested that the parties negotiate privately to reach a compromise solution, and twice asked the committee to adjourn its hearings to permit the private negotiations to continue. The parties reached an agreement in March of 1912 and turned their draft of a bill over to Representative Townsend for introduction. The agreement resolved the theater industry's objections to the bill, but disadvantaged authors of nondramatic works, who had not been involved in the controversy. The Copyright Office questioned the wisdom of aspects of the compromise, but the committee reported the bill with only minor changes. Enactment followed swiftly.

1914–1940: NEW PLAYERS JOIN THE GAME

The lesson an industry observer might have expected to learn from the preceding saga of copyright legislation was that interested parties were well advised to work out their differences before involving Congress. And, indeed, that was precisely what affected industries attempted to do with all subsequent efforts at copyright revision. Seeking interindustry consensus, however, became significantly more complicated in the years that followed.

Shortly after the enactment of the Townsend amendment in 1912, the structure of industries affected by copyright changed dramatically. In 1914, representatives of music publishers and composers formed the American Society of Composers, Authors, and Publishers (ASCAP) to enforce its members' nominal rights to perform their musical compositions publicly for profit. ASCAP began a campaign to pool its members' copyrights and then use collective action to force businesses to purchase performance licenses. On November 2, 1920, the first commercial radio broadcasting station opened with a broadcast of the Warren G. Harding election returns. Radio receiving set manufacturers pioneered radio broadcasting as a promotional device; other concerns soon recognized the potential of radio advertising. Within a few years, there were radio stations throughout the nation. During the 1920s, the motion picture industry grew more powerful. U.S. companies produced "talkies" and began exporting their movies to Europe.

Despite the enactment of the Townsend amendment, motion picture producers grew increasingly uncomfortable with the formalities of a copyright statute written without attention to their needs. Representatives of the motion picture industry met with writers' representatives in New York and agreed to convene private copyright conferences, along the model of those that produced the 1909 act, to work out a consensus on copyright revision. Representatives of writers, book and periodical publishers, printers, labor unions, librarians, and motion picture producers met in conferences over a number of years and hammered out the details of a copyright revision bill. Motion picture counsel completed a draft of the bill, and Rep. Frederick William Dallinger (R-Mass.) introduced it in 1924. Participants in the conferences, however, had not sought the advice of broadcasters or the talking machine industry and had sought, but not received, the advice of composers and music publishers. Nor had the representatives of motion picture producers consulted the theater owners who exhibited their films. When the supporters of the Dallinger bill arrived in front of the House Patent

Committee, they discovered that the industries they failed to invite to their conferences were pursuing their own agenda.

Both motion picture theaters and radio stations used popular music in their programs. Apparently, theater and station owners gave copyright infringement little thought until ASCAP showed up on their doorsteps demanding royalties. When ASCAP went to court and got injunctions, radio stations and motion picture theater owners went to Congress to seek ASCAP's abolition. Members of Congress introduced various bills to restrict ASCAP's activities, to exempt radio stations and theater owners from liability for infringement, or to narrow the right to perform musical compositions publicly for profit. The Patent Committee scheduled hearings on pending legislation, and the two legislative agendas collided in the House Committee hearing room.[11]

In hearings before the House Patent Committee, numerous witnesses testified that the copyright law was inadequate and needed revision. They disagreed sharply, however, on the form that revision should take. Most of the witnesses endorsed one of a half-dozen bills pending before the committee and testified solemnly that adoption of any of the other bills would bring the progress of science and the useful arts to a screeching halt. Reps. Sol Bloom (D-N.Y.) and Fritz Lanham (D-Tex.) expressed their frustration with the testimony, and Bloom inquired whether any solution to the various disputes would be feasible. An author of the Dallinger bill suggested that the lawyers for the interests affected by copyright have another try at the conference approach over the summer. House Committee members endorsed the suggestion, with the proviso that the list of invitees be broader than before. Rep. Randolph Perkins (R-N.J.) pointedly suggested the importance of including broadcasters, while Representative Bloom proposed that members of the House Committee also attend. After some bickering among witnesses about starting points for discussion, Perkins persuaded them to give the idea of further conferences serious consideration. Bloom successfully moved the appointment of a subcommittee to oversee the effort.

The committee appointed Sol Bloom to head a five-person subcommittee. The meetings began the following April (1925) and continued for nearly a year. The list of invitees was initially expansive. In an early meeting, however, representatives of ASCAP had a rancorous exchange with representatives of the National Association of Broadcasters, and the broadcasters withdrew in a huff.[12]

After numerous meetings, representatives of almost all of the participating industries agreed on the text of a bill. The centerpiece of the bill would have enabled the United States to adhere to the Berne Convention. The language and structure of the bill reflected its compromise nature. Individual clauses had been created through several series of bilateral negotiations and fit together awkwardly. It also lacked any accommodation for the absent broadcasters' concerns. Nonetheless, the bill, introduced by Rep. Albert Vestal (R-Ind.) as the Vestal bill in the 69th Congress, had a long list of endorsements. The broadcasting industry, of course, opposed the bill bitterly and allied with the talking machine industry and the theater owners to block it. Simultaneously, they pursued legislation to permit businesses to perform or broadcast music without a license.

The Vestal bill languished in Congress for several years, accumulating opposition from libraries, periodical publishers, academics, and a splinter group of theatrical producers, as well as broadcasters, motion picture producers, and the talking machine industry. In 1930, supporters of the Vestal bill intensified their efforts toward enactment. During the 71st Congress, the House Patent Committee held further hearings on the Vestal bill. Authors' representatives met with representatives of organizations opposed to the bill throughout the night during the hearings and reached further compromises on disputed provisions. Witnesses thus explained to the House Committee that they had opposed the bill during the previous day's testimony, but were now willing to endorse it. Members of the committee urged that further negotiations proceed with dispatch. Representative Lanham suggested that one dispute be settled on the spot, in the hearing room and during the testimony.[13] As a result of the hasty negotiations, the House Committee reported the Vestal bill favorably, observing that "practically all of the industries and all the authors have united in support of this revision."

"Practically all the industries," of course, was not quite the same as all of the industries. Industries that had gotten little satisfaction from the conferences persuaded members of Congress to press their proposals on the floor of the House. The House of Representatives voted in favor of the Vestal bill only after adopting floor amendments restricting ASCAP's activities and permitting anyone to play phonograph records or radio broadcasts in public so long as the performances were nonprofit. The amendments, however, failed to mollify the bill's opponents. When the House referred the bill to the Senate, representatives of broadcasters, radio and phonograph manufacturers, and motion picture theater owners demanded that the Senate hold hearings to receive testimony in opposition to the bill. After listening to the testimony, the committee settled on a series of amendments and reported a by now complex, and internally inconsistent, Vestal bill to the Senate floor, where it got caught in a filibuster on another matter.

In the following Congress, the House Committee started over. The new committee chairman, Democrat William Sirovich of New York City, had been both a physician and a playwright before becoming a politician, and believed he could cut through the obstacles preventing copyright revision. Sirovich scheduled extended hearings and met privately with industry representatives. He then introduced a bill that embodied his notion of a fair compromise. In the face of opposition from the motion picture theater owners, map publishers, and broadcasters, he revised the bill to incorporate their suggestions. Motion picture producers and distributors and ASCAP denounced the changes. Chairman Sirovich rushed the bill to the House floor under a special rule, but the opposition of other members of the House Patent Committee killed the bill before it could be put to a vote.

Meanwhile, private negotiations began to collapse in the face of the Depression economy. Organizations that made concessions in the spirit of compromise in 1926, 1928, or 1930 were no longer satisfied with their bargains. At the suggestion of a representative of organized labor, the Senate Committee on Foreign Relations asked the State Department to organize an informal committee of State Department, Copyright Office, and Commerce Department representatives to oversee further private negotiations. The interdepartmental committee held a series of conferences with representatives of affected interests. They drafted a bill that proved to be acceptable to broadcasters and to the other interests that had opposed the Vestal bill. Writers, composers, publishers, motion picture producers, and organized labor, however, found the bill completely unacceptable and promptly got off the bandwagon. Strong support from the administration enabled the bill to pass the Senate, but strong opposition from interested parties caused it to perish in the House.

With copyright revision stalled in Congress, a private foundation attempted to restart it. In 1939, the National Committee on International Intellectual Cooperation called its own copyright conferences. After sixteen months of meetings, it was unable to arrive at a bill that everyone would support. The committee drafted a bill nonetheless. The bill went nowhere. After twenty years of private negotiations, the Second World War intervened, and efforts to revise the copyright statute died.

SHORTCHANGING THE FUTURE

Throughout the various conferences held between 1905 and 1940, interests that were absent from the bargaining table were shortchanged in the compromises that emerged. The Librarian of Congress's conferences in 1905 and 1906 excluded the piano roll and talking machine interests; the bill that emerged disadvantaged them. The motion picture industry attended none of the negotiations that resulted in the 1909 act and found the statute a significant hindrance. The 1912 negotiations between motion picture and theater industries to frame the Townsend amendment yielded a compromise that handicapped authors and publishers of nondramatic works, who did not participate. The conferences in the 1920s that led to the Dallinger bill included no representatives of the broadcasting industry; the Dallinger bill gave publishers and composers rights at the broadcasters' expense. The broadcasters walked out of the conferences that produced the Vestal bill; the Vestal bill addressed none of the broadcasters' concerns.

At first glance, this observation seems intuitively obvious. Parties who are negotiating would seem to have no incentive to safeguard the interests of their absent competitors. On further consideration, however, the persistent shortchanging of absent interests seems more startling. The battles that preceded the enactment of the 1909 act should have demonstrated to the participants that interests excluded from negotiations could effectively block legislation. Many of the participants in the later conferences had been privy to the 1906 and 1908 hearings. Even had the threat been dismissed or forgotten, the controversy that surrounded the Dallinger bill should surely have persuaded conference participants to make some accommodation for absent parties in connection with the Vestal bill. Yet, the compromises that were made emerged only after face-to-face bargaining, either within the conferences or at the last minute in response to congressional pressure.

The parties had an interest in drafting legislation that Congress would enact. That interest should have persuaded them to incorporate language that absent groups would find acceptable. The pressures of the negotiation process, however, made it difficult to accommodate groups who were not participating in the bargaining. The division of rights among competing interests became increasingly complex and interdependent. The compromises that emerged from the conference approach were rarely merely bilateral. Authors conditioned concessions to motion picture producers on their receipt of concessions from organized labor who in turn demanded something from publishers. In the ensuing complex web of interrelated concessions, the hypothetical demands of absent parties got lost.

The understandable tendency of stakeholders to view representatives of the upstart future as poachers on previously settled territory also influenced the course of negotiations. Composers, sheet music publishers, and musicians divided up the world in a satisfactory manner before the producers of piano rolls and talking machines entered their markets. Novelists, dramatists, photographers, book publishers, and theatrical producers had comfortable niches before motion picture theaters came on the scene. Excluding newcomers from the benefits conferred by copyright legislation may have seemed like a necessary corollary to protecting one's turf.

Indeed, the interests that had not yet come into being when the negotiations took place were the quintessential excluded parties. They posed a potential competitive threat to all current stakeholders yet they couldn't lobby against legislation. As one might expect, then, they were the parties most likely to find that the negotiated compromises operated to their disadvantage. The industries that chafed most under the provisions of the 1909 act, for example, were the motion picture and broadcast industries: the former barely begun and the latter not yet imagined at the time the Librarian of Congress called his conference in 1905.

The motion picture and broadcast industries found the 1909 act particularly inhospitable because it required emergent industries to adapt themselves to ill-fitting molds. The drafters of the 1909 act had crafted the language to settle particular, specific interindustry disputes.[14] The extent to which the 1909 act's category-specific language encompassed new technology was difficult to predict. Although the specificity of terms initially provided security to the affected industries, the growth of new forms and methods made the language seem increasingly ambiguous. The development of the mimeograph machine, which allowed the production of many copies of text using a wax stencil rather that metal type, for example, created doubts about the reach of a provision requiring all books to "be printed from type set within the limits of the United States, either by hand or by the aid of any kind of type-setting machine, or from plates made within the limits of the United States from type set therein."[15] When the word roll, a piano roll with lyrics printed alongside the perforations that produced the music, superseded the simple piano roll, it was unclear whether the compulsory license for mechanical reproductions of music permitted the addition of printed lyrics.

The statutory language posed more radical problems for the new media. The infant industries found the 1909 act ambiguous and its application to their activities uncertain until the courts issued an authoritative ruling. Courts, in turn, struggled to apply the 1909 act's language to facts that its drafters never envisioned. As case law developed, the application of copyright law to new technology depended more on linguistic fortuity than anything else.

Determining the scope of copyright protection for motion pictures, for example, required courts to decide such questions as whether the exhibition of a motion picture constituted "publication" within the meaning of the 1909 act. Was a motion picture, specifically enumerated in subsections (l) and (m) of section 5, also a "dramatic or dramatico-musical composition" as specified in subsection 5(d), or, if not, could it still be deemed a "drama" for the purposes of subsection 1(d)? If so, was exhibiting the film a "performance"? Should projecting the frames of a motion picture be characterized as making a "copy" of the motion picture or as "dramatizing" it? Radio broadcasting posed similar problems. Was the broadcast of music to receiving sets in individuals' homes a public performance? Was broadcasting at no charge to listeners a performance for profit? Was it a public performance for profit to install a radio receiving set and loudspeakers in hotel guest rooms?[16]

1950–1961: RETURNING TO CONFERENCE

By the end of the Second World War, industries had been operating within the confines of the 1909 act for a third of a century. Everybody criticized the law as outmoded; it had, after all, been drawn to accommodate the requirements of particular media before the advent of radio, jukeboxes, sound motion pictures, Muzak®, and television. The affected industries accommodated the arcane law through combinations of trade practice, collectively bargained form contracts, and practical contortions. Where the copyright statute failed to accommodate the realities faced by affected industries, the industries devised expedients, exploited loopholes, and negotiated agreements that superseded statutory provisions. The broadcast industry formed its own performing rights society to compete with ASCAP. The recording industry developed a form license that incorporated the basic concept of a compulsory license for mechanical reproduction, but at more favorable terms, and used it instead of the license conferred by the statute. The motion picture industry established an ASCAP-like operation to deal with unauthorized exhibition of films. An enterprising group of talking machine manufacturers used the copyright exemption for the performance of musical compositions on coin-operated devices to launch the jukebox industry, and marketed jukeboxes to establishments that wished to play music but not to pay royalties. Each accommodation, however, was soon perceived as an entitlement and became one more obstacle to agreement.[17]

The subject matter of copyright remained frozen in the form it had taken in 1912. More recently developed works were copyrightable only to the extent they could be analogized to the statutory list of works subject to copyright, and received rights whose scope was limited by the category in which they best fit. Decorative lamp bases and children's toys, for example, could be registered as "works of art" or "reproductions of a work of art." Motion pictures and television programs recorded on film could be copyrighted as unpublished motion picture photoplays. Live or videotaped television programs, radio programs, and phonograph records were deemed uncopyrightable. The copyright businesses had developed a practice of dividing up copyright rights and administering them separately. Composers of musical works, for example, controlled their rights to perform music publicly for profit, and licensed those rights through ASCAP. The rights to reproduce the music in sheet music, phonograph records, or motion pictures, however, was controlled by music publishing companies, who were the copyright owners of record. The copyright law allowed for none of this: it treated copyright as a single, unitary right that could be owned by only one person at any given time.[18] New technological uses waited in the wings. Cable television, xerographic photocopying, and digital computers were all invented in the 1940s.[19] It was difficult to figure out what provisions of the copyright law would apply to the new technologies and what effects the technologies would have on the copyright law.

To revive the process of comprehensive copyright revision, Congress returned to a suggestion that it had rejected summarily fifty years before. In 1956, it appropriated funds for the appointment of a special committee of copyright experts.[20] The Register of Copyrights, Arthur Fisher, initially conceived a three-year revision process that would depart significantly from the familiar conferences. Fisher envisioned a committee of copyright experts acting in a purely advisory capacity, while the Copyright Office's research division performed comprehensive studies of prior revision efforts, copyright laws of other nations, and each of the major substantive issues involved in copyright revision. The committee's job would be to offer comments and suggestions, but not to make policy. Fisher hoped to keep the policy-making process insulated within the Copyright Office to avoid the partisan wrangling that infected prior legislation.

The Librarian of Congress appointed a panel of twenty-nine copyright experts, the majority of whom were lawyers active in the American Bar Association. The panelists' ideas about their appropriate role differed from the Register's, and they soon began requesting that they convene in a forum that would permit the thrashing out of policy. The Copyright Office acceded to requests to convene meetings of the panelists for substantive discussions but insisted upon its prerogative to formulate recommendations for legislation without further consultation.

The American Bar Association established a shadow committee, including many of the panelists in its membership. The committee embarked on an effort to formulate substantive proposals at the same time as it monitored the Copyright Office's revision efforts. While the Copyright Office struggled to digest the studies and the panelists' suggestions and to write a report in relative seclusion, the panelists themselves were meeting with interested parties in ad hoc groups and symposia to articulate substantive consensus.

In 1960, shortly before the Copyright Office completed the Register's Report to Congress, outlining recommendations for a revision bill, Register Fisher died. His successor, Register Abraham Kaminstein, abruptly shifted gears. While Fisher appeared to have viewed the history of interindustry compromise as a weakness of prior revision efforts, Kaminstein seemed to read the record differently. He argued that such compromise was the keystone of achieving copyright revision and that the goal of enacting a modern copyright statute was worth herculean efforts to encourage compromise among interested parties.

Register Kaminstein began working toward conciliation and narrowly averted a crisis that threatened to derail the revision program. The substance of the Register's Report had been poorly received by the Bar, a number of whose members insisted that they would prefer the current outmoded statute to one following the Register's recommendations. Kaminstein announced that the Copyright Office was willing to abandon unpopular proposals. He expanded the membership of the panel of experts and arranged meetings with interested parties to encourage them to compromise with one another. The result was, in essence, a return to the conference process. Six years of study had produced the Register's Report. Another five years of conferences produced a bill that reflected the consensus of the conference participants and bore little resemblance to the Register's recommendations. It took an additional eleven years in Congress for the interested parties to compromise on extraneous issues and late-breaking problems. When the parties finally compromised on nearly every provision in the bill, Congress would enact the 1976 Copyright Act.[21]

PRIVATE PARTIES AND VESTED INTERESTS

The stormy history of past revision efforts led the Copyright Office to conclude that the only copyright bill that would pass was one built on a network of negotiated compromises. The Copyright Office concentrated much of its energy on identifying affected interests and including their representatives in the negotiations. But, of course, it wasn't possible to invite every affected interest. Some interests lacked organization and had no identifiable representatives. In the 1905 conferences, the Library of Congress had tried unsuccessfully to recruit representatives of composers to participate. Music publishers purported to speak for composers and were the only representatives available. In the conferences convened in the 1960s, painters and sculptors did not attend and the Copyright Office's efforts to seek them out proved unsuccessful. Choreographers, theatrical directors, and computer programmers sent no representatives because they had no representatives to send. Other interests that would have profound effect on copyright did not yet exist at the time of the conferences. Just as there had been no commercial broadcasters to invite to the conferences in 1905, there were no videocassette manufacturers, direct satellite broadcasters, digital audio technicians, personal computer users, motion picture colorizers, online database subscribers, or Internet service providers to invite in 1960.

Nor could the rest of us be there. The amorphous "public" comprises members whose relation to copyright and copyrighted works varies with the circumstances. Many of us are consumers of copyrighted songs and also consumers of parodies of copyrighted songs, watchers of broadcast television and subscribers to cable television, patrons of motion picture theaters and owners of videotape recorders, purchasers and borrowers and tapers of copyrighted sound recordings. Although a few organizations showed up at the conferences purporting to represent the "public" with respect to narrow issues, the citizenry's interest in copyright and copyrighted works was too varied and complex to be amenable to interest-group championship. Moreover, the public's interests were not somehow approximated by the push and shove among opposing industry representatives. To say that the affected industries represented diverse and opposing interests is not to say that all relevant interests were represented.

The conference participants began as the members of the Library of Congress's panel of experts and were all established members of the copyright bar. Other representatives joined the conferences as particular conflicts arose. Register Kaminstein invited representatives of current beneficiaries of the statute to participate in discussions of cutbacks in their statutory benefits. Lawyers on the panel solicited participation from their other clients. As with the conferences on earlier legislation, however, participants were almost exclusively those who already had a sizable economic investment in copyright matters under current law. Although these participants undoubtedly interacted with copyrighted works outside of their professional capacity, they failed to bring that perspective to bear on the conference negotiations.

Perhaps the most patent example of the partisan perspective that dominated the negotiations is illustrated in the treatment of the issue of private use, an issue that became increasingly vexing in the years after the 1976 act took effect. Presumably, all industry representatives made private use of copyrighted works in their individual capacities. Yet, the issue of the appropriate scope of permissible private use of copyrighted works received little explicit attention during the revision process. Representatives were too busy wrangling over commercial and institutional uses to talk about the behavior of individuals in their homes. The aggregate agendas developed in the conferences of private parties reflected systematic, if unintentional, bias against absent interests. The fact that private use had no defenders and received no explicit treatment in the revision conferences, therefore, had substantive results on the legality of private use under the revision bill.

The public, of course, does have a designated representative; acting as that representative is Congress's job description. A few congressional committee staff members did attend some of the copyright conferences as observers, but stayed above the fray. The unspoken premise of the conference process was that Congress would enact any bill that everyone else could agree on. Ultimately, that is what Congress did.

The nature of this process introduces particular difficulties into the enterprise of statutory interpretation. This type of drafting process makes it exceedingly difficult to speak of legislative intent if by legislative intent one means the substantive intent of members of Congress. Even if one avoids that dilemma by ascribing to Congress an intent to enact the substance of the deals forged in conferences, one nonetheless may encounter difficulty in identifying any overall purpose pervading the text of the statute. The compromises that evolve through the conference process can be multilateral and interrelated, but may not incorporate any common vision or strategy. Courts must apply this legislation to parties, works, and situations that never arose during the conference process, and to industries that could not be present.[22]

Moreover, the complexity and specificity of multiparty compromises exacerbates the problem. If a compromise is negotiated between monolithic interests, between, for example, all artists and all art users, we can find roughly defined representatives in the negotiating process for the interests that develop in the future. Applying a compromise negotiated among encyclopedia publishers, popular music composers, motion picture producers, novelists, and dramatists, however, to a situation involving the importers of unicorn figurines[23] can be substantially more troublesome. This reveals the difficulty of jettisoning any effort to find coherence in such a statute and attempting to interpret it as if it were a contract. If the industry to which a court is trying to apply the statute was neither represented in negotiations nor in privity with someone who was there, it is difficult to assess how the metaphorical contract allocates the risks of ambiguity.

As it happens, however, the conferences that led to the 1976 act did finally settle on a common strategy and did allocate the risks of ambiguity. Indeed, industry representatives explained the strategy to Congress in unusually explicit terms. The bills that became the 1976 act possessed a coherence that previous revision legislation lacked, although that coherence emerged as a by-product of the efforts to achieve interindustry consensus. Register Kaminstein suggested early on that the key to general revision would be to draft a copyright bill that benefited each of the competing interests. In that, the conferences succeeded. The bill that emerged from the conferences enlarged the copyright pie and divided its pieces among conference participants so that no leftovers remained.

1961–1976: BROAD RIGHTS AND NARROW EXCEPTIONS

In 1961, two months after Register Kaminstein filed the controversial Register's Report, he convened a meeting of an augmented panel to discuss copyright revision.[24] Kaminstein invited the original twenty-nine panelists, chairmen of bar association committees, delegations from a dozen federal agencies and departments, and representatives of several interests that had until then been excluded. Kaminstein announced that the purpose of the meeting was for the assembled government and industry representatives to use the recommendations made in the Register's Report as the foundation for the development of interindustry consensus. The meeting was the first of a series of meetings and with each meeting the number of interests represented on the panel increased. Between panel meetings, the panelists met with one another in search of compromises, and the Copyright Office urged additional meetings and negotiations among affected interests. During these discussions, the Copyright Office and industry representatives hammered out the substance of a revision bill.

In the 1961 Register's Report, the Copyright Office suggested only modest changes in the law: the codification of courts' solutions to assorted copyright problems, the clarification and simplification of language, and the removal of some anomalies created by technological change or historical accident. Meetings with representatives of affected interests, however, produced proposals to broaden rights and narrow exemptions and privileges. Suggestions for broad or general privileges evolved through negotiations to very specific ones.

For example, the performance right developed through the conferences into something much broader than the Register had initially proposed, with much narrower exceptions. The 1909 act gave the owner of the copyright in a musical work the exclusive right to perform the work publicly for profit, subject to the jukebox exemption. A 1952 amendment extended the right of public performance for profit to lectures, sermons, and other nondramatic literary works. Unlike copyright owners in musical works, owners of copyrights in dramatic works had had exclusive rights all over public performances, whether for profit or not, since 1856, while motion picture copyright owners had no explicit public performance right at all. The Register's 1961 Report recommended that musical and nondramatic literary works continue to have a public performance for profit right and that motion pictures be given a public performance right with no for-profit qualification. Representatives of authors and composers, however, demanded control over nonprofit as well as for-profit performances. Joined by motion picture producers, they simultaneously pressed the Register to define the public performance right more broadly. The Copyright Office drafted a provision granting copyright owners a general exclusive right to perform the work publicly, subject to express exceptions allowing educational and religious performances, charitable benefits, and retransmissions of television and radio broadcasts without permission.

The response from the panelists was guardedly positive; they shifted their emphasis to requesting that the exceptions be radically narrowed. Representatives of industries that performed copyrighted works were willing to go along so long as the exemptions and privileges set forth in the bill continued to shield their activities. Industry representatives got together in meetings sponsored by the Copyright Office or subcommittees of the bar associations and tried to come to terms on the scope of exceptions to the performance right.

In 1964, the Copyright Office circulated a draft bill with a more expansive definition of public performance and further restrictions and conditions on specifically worded exemptions and privileges. Panelists insisted that the exemptions and privileges were still too broad, general, and ambiguous. Claimants of privileges and exemptions complained that the language of the bill was still unclear. Another round of meetings produced an even more conditional and restrictively worded series of exemptions and privileges. By the time the 1965 bill was ready for congressional hearings, the broadly defined public performance right had become encumbered with specifically worded exceptions permitting limited public performances for classroom teaching, educational television transmissions within educational institutions, religious services, charitable benefits, cable retransmissions at no charge, transmission to private hotel rooms, and reception of broadcasts in public places. By the time Congress enacted a revision bill in 1976, these exceptions and privileges had grown still more numerous, more narrowly worded, and more detailed. For example, the 1965 revision bill declared that noncommercial cable transmissions of broadcast programming required no permission.[25] By 1976, the noncommercial cable television exemption had been replaced by a detailed system of statutory licenses spelled out in nine pages of impenetrable prose.[26]

That pattern of evolution pervaded the revision bill. Copyright owners wanted the broadest possible rights with the narrowest possible exceptions.

Many representatives of interests that used copyrighted works were agreeable to such a strategy on the condition that such exceptions explicitly
cover their activities. In addition, some insisted that the product of their
use of preexisting copyrighted works itself be copyrightable and entitled to
the expansive rights. Thus, the field of copyrightable subject matter grew
progressively more inclusive. The Copyright Office had committed itself to
seeking a consensus solution, and consensus jelled around a strategy of
granting broad rights in an expansive field of copyrightable works and subjecting the rights to specific, narrowly tailored exceptions.

The bill introduced in Congress in 1965 followed this scheme. In the
first of a long series of congressional hearings on copyright revision,
Deputy Register George Cary explained the bill's approach:

> The problem of balancing existing interests is delicate enough, but the bill
> must do something even more difficult. It must try and foresee and take
> account of changes in the forms of use and the relative importance of the
> competing interests in the years to come, and it must attempt to balance
> them fairly in a way that carries out the basic constitutional purpose of the
> copyright law.
>
> Obviously, no one can foresee accurately and in detail the evolving
> patterns in the ways authors' work will reach the public 10, 20, or 50 years
> from now. Lacking that kind of foresight, the bill adopts a general
> approach of providing compensation to the author for future as well as
> present uses of his work that materially affect the value of his copyright. As
> shown by the jukebox exemption in the present law, a particular use which
> may seem to have little or no economic impact on the author's rights today
> can assume tremendous importance in times to come. A real danger to be
> guarded against is that of confining the scope of an author's rights on the
> basis of the present technology, so that as the years go by his copyright
> loses much of its value because of unforeseen technical advances.
>
> For these reasons the bill reflects our belief that authors' rights should
> be stated in the statute in broad terms and that the specific limitations on
> them should not go any further than is shown to be necessary in the
> public interest.[27]

Thus, a strategy born by accident of accretion had acquired its rationale.
The revision bill spelled out five expansively defined exclusive rights: the
right to reproduce or copy the work, the right to make derivative works or
adapt the work, the right to distribute the work, the right to perform the

work publicly, and the right to display the work publicly. It then subjected the exclusive rights to a variety of narrowly drawn exceptions.

Not all of the disputes were resolved through the prelegislative process. When Congress held its first hearings on the revision bill in the tenth year of the revision program, several controversies remained, and more disputes arose as the rapid pace of technological change created new players and new problems. Significantly, however, none of the unresolved controversies concerned the overall structure and approach of the bill. Almost all of the disputes involved specific details of particular privileges and exemptions. Members of Congress declined, for the most part, to respond to the controversies by attempting to arrive at policy solutions of their own devising. Instead, Congress involved itself in the mediation process, urging opposing interests to meet, cajoling them to reach agreement, and sometimes sitting down with them and demanding that they compromise. During the eleven additional years that it took to produce a bill that every industry representative would be willing to support, the solutions to inter-industry disputes became progressively more complicated and detailed. From the inclusive group conferences, negotiations evolved into interlocking bilateral and trilateral deals. The deals themselves worked to the advantage of the interests party to them and to the comparative disadvantage of others. The longer the negotiations on a particular dispute continued, the narrower and more specific was the resulting solution.

NEGOTIATED STATUTES AND TECHNOLOGICAL POLICY

In 1976 Congress finally enacted the modern copyright statute it had labored over so long, and the Senate Judiciary Committee optimistically dissolved its Subcommittee on Patents, Trademarks and Copyrights. For those familiar with the struggles to apply the 1909 act to developing technology, however, the 1976 act should have seemed designed to fail the future in predictable ways. Broadly phrased general provisions have inherent flexibility. Narrow, specific provisions do not. Most of the 1976 act's limitations on copyright owners' expansive rights were cast in narrow, specific language. Yet, in order to answer the questions that the future will present, a statute needs flexible language embodying general principles.

New players that technological change will introduce into the game have a particularly compelling need for flexible statutory provisions. The representatives of yet-to-develop technology cannot be present in a bargaining room filled with current stakeholders. They must, therefore, rely on such general and flexible provisions as the statutory scheme includes. The narrower and more specific the prose is, the less likely it is that a statutory provision will be sufficiently flexible to be responsive to technological change, and the more quickly the provision will be outdated.

A process that relies upon negotiated bargains among industry representatives, however, is ill-suited to arrive at general, flexible limitations. The dynamics of interindustry negotiations tend to encourage fact-specific solutions to interindustry disputes. The participants' frustration with the rapid aging of narrowly defined rights inspired them to collaborate in drafting rights more broadly, but no comparable tendency emerged to inject breadth or flexibility into the provisions limiting those rights. The only general limitations reflected in the current copyright statute were devised by courts in the nineteenth century, before Congress turned to a revision strategy resting upon meetings among affected interests. Although these provisions have survived the press of technological change better than the narrow and specific limitations that pervade the 1976 act, they have not been equal to the task of providing the flexibility necessary to respond to the developments that have arrived with the future.[28]

In the years since the 1976 act took effect, the legislative process engendered a variety of amendments designed to respond to particular challenges. Arriving at enactable language required protracted bargaining among diverse industries. Disputes were resolved by crafting ever more specific wording, to ensure that the statutory language could not be read to privilege unanticipated uses. The laws that have emerged have had an extraordinarily short shelf life. Many of them were obsolete before their effective date.

The limited statutory license permitting cable television broadcasts in return for the payment of statutory royalties into a fund to be divided among copyright owners, for instance, was phrased too narrowly to cover home satellite dish television. After being sued for copyright infringement, satellite carriers demanded a license of their own. The major affected copyright-owner interests—movie studios and music publishers—had little to lose from agreeing to extend the cable license to satellites. Although they opposed statutory licenses in principle, there were no feasible alternative models in operation for funneling royalties to the myriad copyright owners whose rights were implicated in each broadcast signal. A satellite license offered them revenue that was otherwise uncollectable as a practical matter.

Network broadcasters and cable companies, however, were resistant. While they had fought bitterly over the details of the cable license, they were united in this instance in their opposition to extending concessions to a new industry likely to compete with both of them. Neither broadcasters nor cable system operators owned copyrights in the underlying programming, but they were able to use their seats at the bargaining table to block the expansion of the cable license to satellite TV. In 1988, Congress enacted the Satellite Home Viewer Act,[29] granting satellite carriers a new and more restrictive license to transmit television signals to home satellite dishes for private home viewing. The statutory license fee was calculated differently for satellites than the comparable cable license, and resulted in sharply higher fees. Network and cable representatives insisted upon a further, crucial limitation: satellite transmission of network and network affiliate signals would be permitted *only* for subscribers who could not receive such signals via either conventional broadcast or cable subscription.[30] In the 1990s, satellite carriers sought to lure disaffected customers from cable by offering them both their local broadcast stations and premium satellite signals. What stopped them wasn't technological barriers but legal ones, inserted into the copyright act at the behest of satellite's competition. Seeking to press their advantage, network broadcasters filed copyright infringement suits against satellite carriers, claiming that the satellite companies were supplying network signals to subscribers not entitled to receive them. Bills to reform the satellite license to provide parity with cable attracted substantial congressional support, but foundered on the opposition of cable and broadcast interests.[31] Finally, in 1999, Congress enacted a narrow set of provisions modestly reducing satellite license fees and enabling satellite carriers eventually to provide local signals to subscribers on the same terms available to cable so long as the satellite carriers comply with technical and legal restrictions designed to require them to behave as if they were cable operators running cable infrastructure.[32] The amendments did not disturb the other disparities.

In 1992, Congress enacted the Audio Home Recording Act (AHRA),[33] a law seeking to address the potential problem posed by digital reproduction of sound recordings. Digital reproduction posed a potent threat, record companies argued, because it permitted the recording of countless perfect copies. Everyone in possession of a digital copy could create many more. Digital tape recorders had become common equipment in professional recording studios, and consumer models had recently been introduced to the Japanese market. Composers and record companies sought to prevent the manufacture or importation of digital recorders for the consumer market, complaining that they could facilitate widespread piracy. Protracted negotiations among record companies, composers, music publishers, performers, and consumer electronics manufacturers yielded a complex agreement ultimately enacted as the AHRA. In return for technical and monetary concessions, copyright owners agreed that they would abandon both their attempts to prevent the sale of digital recording devices and their controversial and unenforceable claims against consumers for private copying of recorded music. The law contains an explicit provision prohibiting suit against consumers for creating noncommercial digital or analog copies of musical recordings.[34] In return, device manufacturers agreed to pay a royalty on every digital recording device or digital tape sold. The royalties were to be distributed among composers, music publishers, record companies, and performers, according to a formula that was both complex and maddeningly vague.[35] Manufacturers also agreed to a provision requiring every digital audio recording device to be equipped with technological copy controls. The controls were to permit an unlimited number of first-generation copies from an original or commercial digital recording, but were to prevent any copying of copies. The rationale for the provisions was that the device and tape tax would compensate rights holders for unauthorized first-generation copies, but not for serial copies. The required technological fix, in essence, disabled consumer digital recording devices from implementing their superiority to analog devices. Perhaps that is part of the reason that digital tape recorders and digital tape failed to sell very well.

Another part of the reason, though, was that computers soon developed sound cards capable of playing high-fidelity sound over computer speakers. Computer hardware manufacturers had demanded an exemption from the AHRA's provisions. The definition of devices subject to the AHRA had been carefully and narrowly drafted to ensure that computers need not incorporate serial copy management systems. Computer disks were not subject to the tape tax. The statute required the Commerce Department to keep a careful eye on the situation and to set up a procedure to verify compliance with the statute's technical provisions. The department has never done so. The royalty provisions of the AHRA have generated insignificant funds. The serial copyright management technology may have doomed the market for the devices, which in any event are hardly on the consumer electronic product radar screen. The most common methods of consumer digital recording, those involving computers, are exempt from the act's royalty and serial copy management system requirements. The only part of the law that still casts a large shadow is the one permitting consumers to make non-commercial digital or analog copies of musical recordings without fear of copyright infringement liability. At the time, that concession seemed cheap. The U.S. Supreme Court's opinion in the famous Betamax case, *Sony* v. *Universal Studios*,[36] indicated that private consumer copying of recorded or broadcast content was in many cases privileged under the statute's fair use provisions. To the extent that consumer copying was actionable, moreover, enforcement would have seemed at least unpopular and overreaching, and very possibly impossible, since it would have required copyright owners to monitor consumers' private behavior and sue them for acts committed in the privacy of their homes. Not so many years afterwards, however, the growth of the Internet has made that provision the most important thing that copyright owners would take back if they could. Perhaps they can.

If negotiated copyright statutes turn out to be so unworkable, why is it that Congress continues to rely on private interests to work out the text of bills? One reason may be that, until recently, copyright issues seemed to be the province of a very narrow slice of the citizenry, hardly worth the cost of bringing oneself up to speed. The negotiation process delegates everything to people who are, after all, the real copyright experts, and allows Congress to exploit their accumulated expertise. The participants are the people who will have to order their day-to-day business relations with one another around the provisions of the legislation. They can bring their perspective on the real world in which they interact to bear on the law with which they will have to live.

The process permits a give-and-take among a wide field of players whose competing interests are exceedingly complex. The universe of current stakeholders does not divide easily into monolithic camps. There may be no simple, overarching principles that can easily define how all of these actors should order their interactions with one another. Putting all of them into a room and asking them not to come out until they have agreed to be bound by the same rules may be the most efficient approach to formulating law that will work well enough for each of them, although not necessarily for the rest of us.

The process also makes copyright revision politically feasible. If one could overcome the difficulties in educating members of Congress in a technical legal field with little publicity value, and find ways to impart enough knowledge about the complex inner workings of the myriad affected industries, one would still face daunting obstacles to coming up with enactable legislation. Every adjustment to the copyright statute will disadvantage some current stakeholder, who will be someone's constituent. Perhaps a statute might be enacted over that stakeholder's pitched opposition; but efforts to accomplish that in the past have not succeeded. If the stakeholder will instead agree to accept the disadvantage in return for an advantage conceded by another stakeholder, there will be no pitched opposition and the bill will be much more likely to go through.

The need to balance concessions in order to achieve such agreement, of course, imposes constraints on the sort of legislation that is likely to emerge from the process. Unless the participants become convinced that the new legislation gives them no fewer benefits than they currently enjoy, they are likely to press for additional concessions. It must, therefore, be expected that any successful copyright legislation will confer advantages on many of the interests involved in hammering it out, and that those advantages will probably come at some absent party's expense. But nobody need take the responsibility for making difficult political choices associated with selecting the interests that the legislation will disadvantage. Indeed, the process is almost tailormade to select those interests thoughtlessly and automatically, as a by-product of ongoing negotiations.

It is the seeming inevitability of bias against absent interests, and of narrow compromises with no durability, that makes such a process so costly. Each time we rely on current stakeholders to agree on a statutory scheme, they produce a scheme designed to protect themselves against the rest of us. Its rigidity leads to its breakdown; the statute's drafters have incorporated too few general principles to guide courts in effecting repairs.

It would seem naive to suggest that Congress simply reclaim its legislative responsibilities and write a revised copyright statute embodying general principles instead of negotiated deals. Current stakeholders have controlled the playing board for nearly a century, and would doubtless prefer to keep it that way. Although they squabble with one another over specifics, they have managed to unite in fierce opposition to copyright revision bills drafted without their participation. The 1990s saw an astonishing increase in copyright-related campaign contributions—making it increasingly unlikely that Congress would support a movement to divest copyright stakeholders of responsibility for drafting copyright legislation.

Members of Congress have continued to encourage negotiated solutions. Interested parties meet with each other but cling to provincial negotiating postures. Current stakeholders are unwilling to part with short-term statutory benefits in the service of long-term legal stability. Those disfranchised by current law lack the bargaining chips to trade for concessions. Thus, the process is unlikely to produce any balanced legislative proposals.

Furthermore, the process is securely entrenched. The inquiry relevant to copyright legislation long ago ceased to be "is this a good bill?" Rather, the inquiry has been, and continues to be "is this a bill that current stakeholders agree on?" The two questions are not the same.

Negotiations among current stakeholders tend to produce laws that resolve existing interindustry disputes with detailed and specific statutory language, which rapidly grows obsolete. Such laws consign the disputes of the future to resolution under models biased in favor of the status quo. A copyright law cannot make sensible provision for the growth of technology unless it incorporates both the flexibility to make adjustments and the general principles to guide courts in the directions those adjustments should take. The negotiation process that has dominated copyright revision throughout this century, however, is ill adapted to generate that flexibility. It cannot, therefore, be expected to produce statutes that improve with age.

NOTES

1. This chapter is adapted from a much longer article, *Copyright Legislation and Technological Change*, published in 1989 in the Oregon Law Review at 68 Oregon Law Review 275. Readers in search of detailed citations can find them in the footnotes to that article.

2. On September 4, 1997, for example, the Recording Industry Association of America testified before the Senate Judiciary Committee that extant copyright law was "flexible enough to handle the ever changing technology of the Internet." The Senate should therefore resist calls to limit the infringement liability of Internet service providers for infringing acts committed by their subscribers. *See Copyright Infringement Liability of Online and Internet Service Providers, Hearing Before the Senate Judiciary Committee*, 105th Cong., 1st sess. (September 4, 1997) (testimony of Cary Sherman, Recording Industry Association of America). Two weeks later, the Recording Industry Association of America explained to the House Subcommittee on Courts and Intellectual Property that Internet piracy of American recordings made it imperative to adopt amendments designed to prevent any circumvention

of copyright protection systems, and to do so quickly. *See Hearing on H.R. 2281 and H.R. 2180 Before the Subcommittee on Courts and Civil Liberties of the House Judiciary Committee,* 105th Cong., 1st sess. (September 17, 1997) (testimony of Johnny Cash and Hilary Rosen, Recording Industry Association of America).

3. Copyright Act of March 4, 1909, 35 Stat. 1075, *repealed by* 1976 General Revision of Copyright Law, Pub. L. No. 94-553, 90 Stat. 2541 (1976) [Hereinafter 1909 Act].

4. Audio Home Recording Act of 1992, Public L. 102-563, 106 Stat. 4237 (codified at 17 U.S.C. §§ 1001–1010). The act required, for the first time, that digital recording devices be equipped with technology to prevent the recording of second-generation copies, imposed a royalty tax on the sale of blank digital tapes and recording devices, and permitted (first-generation) consumer audiotaping without infringement liability. The audio recording device prohibition was sufficiently controversial that, after the introduction of legislation in 1987, four years of negotiations among record companies, hardware manufacturers, songwriters, music publishers, and performing rights societies were required to reach agreement on the form and specifications of a limited prohibition. *See* H.R. Rep. 873 pt. 1, 102d Cong., 2d sess. 14-18 (1992); Gary S. Lutzker, *Note, DAT's All Folks: Cahn v. Sony and the Audio Home Recording Act of 1991—Merrie Melodies or Looney Tunes,* 11 Cardozo Arts & Entertainment Law Review 145 (1992). During the legislative process, the prohibition was narrowed and narrowed again to ensure that it would not be construed to apply to devices other than home audio recording devices. As enacted, it was balanced by a provision preventing the imposition of copyright liability for noncommercial copying of audio recordings, or for manufacturing, importing, or selling audio recorders. See 17 U.S.C. § 1008.

5. The material in this section is drawn from *Library of Congress, Copyright in Congress, 1789–1904* (1976 reprint of 1905 ed.), as well as annual fiscal year reports filed by the Register of Copyrights, the congressional hearings and bill texts reprinted in the multivolume E. F. Brylawski and A. Goldman, *Legislative History of the 1909 Copyright Act* (Fred B. Rothman, 1976), and the Congressional Record.

6. The office of Register of Copyrights was established in order to centralize the responsibility for registering copyrights (hence the name). The Copyright Office, headed by the Register, is a department of the Library of Congress, and is thus part of the legislative branch. The first Register, Thorvald Solberg, was paid an annual salary of $3,000, and supervised twenty-nine clerks. The current Register, Mary Beth Peters, presides over a far larger operation. The office still registers copyrights (although registration is no longer required), and maintains a publicly searchable catalogue of registered works. It also provides expert advice to Congress about pending copyright legislation and the current operation of the copyright law, advises the executive branch in connection with international copyright treaties, and administers the complex statutory licenses for cable systems, record producers, noncom-

mercial broadcasters, satellite carriers, manufacturers or importers of digital audio recorders and tape, and the cablecast and webcast of digital audio transmissions.

7. Authors' representatives and representatives of the printers' union, for example, reached an agreement over which works would lose their copyrights if they were printed using type set outside of the United States. Books written in foreign languages could be typeset abroad, but works written in English were required to be printed from type set in the United States. That agreement was incorporated into section 15 of the 1909 act.

8. *Kalem Co. v. Harper Bros.*, 222 U.S. 55 (1911).

9. During the early 1910s, the motion picture industry was concentrated in New Jersey, Philadelphia, and New York City. Congressmen representing districts in which motion picture producers were located spearheaded the industry's efforts to amend the copyright statute in the House of Representatives.

10. Most of the information in this section appears in the congressional hearings held on the Townsend amendment. *See Townsend Copyright Amendment: Complete File of Arguments on H.R. 15,263 and H.R. 20,596 Before the House Committee on Patents*, 62d Cong., 2d sess. (1912); *Townsend Copyright Amendment: Hearing on H.R. 22,350 Before the House Committee on Patents*, 62d Cong., 2d sess. (1912). *See also* H.R.Rep. No. 756, 62d Cong., 2d sess. (1912).

11. Again, I have drawn most of my information from the House and Senate Hearings. *See Copyrights: Hearings on H.R. 6250 and H.R. 9137 Before the House Committee on Patents*, 68th Cong., 1st sess. (1924); *Copyrights: Hearings on H.R. 11,258 Before the House Committee on Patents*, 68th Cong., 2d sess. 475-79 (1925); *To Amend the Copyright Act: Hearings on S. 2328 and H.R. 10,353 Before the Joint Committee on Patents*, 69th Cong., 1st sess. 236-39 (1926); *Copyright: Hearings on H.R. 10,434 Before the House Committee on Patents*, 69th Cong., 1st sess. 15-17 (1926); *General Revision of the Copyright Law: Hearings on H.R. 6990 Before the House Committee on Patents*, 71st Cong., 2d sess. (1930); *General Revision of the Copyright Law: Hearings on H.R. 12,549 Before the Senate Committee on Patents*, 71st Cong., 3d sess. (1931); General Revision of the Cong., 1st sess. (1932); *International Copyright Union: Hearings on S. 1928 Before the Senate Committee on Foreign Relations*, 73d Cong., 2d sess. (1934); *Revision of the Copyright Laws: Hearings before the House Committee on Patents*, 74th Cong., 2d sess. 221-60 (1936). *See also* A. Goldman, *The History of U.S.A. Copyright Law Revision From 1901 to 1954*, reprinted in *Subcommittee on Patents, Copyrights and Trademarks of the Senate Committee on the Judiciary*, 86th Cong., 1st sess., Copyright Law Revision (Committee Print 1960).

12. Nathan Burkan, representing ASCAP, declared that composers would never give in to the demands of broadcasters. Paul Klugh, executive chairman of the National Association of Broadcasters, insisted that Burkan's remarks were inappropriate and demanded that he retract them. Burkan refused. The broadcasters responded by boycotting all subsequent meetings. *See Copyright Hearings on H.R. 10434 Before the House Subcommittee on Patents*, 69th Cong., 1st sess. 193-94 (1926).

13. When William Warner, of the National Publishers' Association, alluded to a disagreement between authors and periodical publishers over the ownership and scope of serialization rights, Representative Lanham suggested that Warner interrupt his testimony in order to permit authors to express their views and then negotiate an immediate resolution. *See General Revision of the Copyright Law: Hearings on H.R. 6990 Before the House Committee on Patents,* 71st Cong., 2d sess. 155 (1930).

14. The 1909 act's strategy for reconciling competing demands among industry representatives was to specify rights and remedies within subject matter categories. The conferences began in 1905 with each organization's articulation of its wish list. Each of the affected interests sought to retain the advantages it enjoyed under current law, while eliminating features that worked to its detriment. Where wishes appeared irreconcilable, the parties suggested differentiation of provisions along subject matter lines. The solutions to many disputes were provisions detailing the particular rights attaching to particular categories of works, the particular actions that constituted infringement of those rights, and the particular remedies available for those infringements. The bill introduced in 1906 followed this strategy. For example, the original bill varied the term of copyright among different classes of works, from twenty-eight years for prints and labels to life of the author plus fifty years after death for musical compositions. In addition, it placed a ten-year limit on the exercise of the exclusive dramatization right in a book. In tinkering with the bill, the House and Senate committees removed some of the distinctions but added others. Thus, Congress replaced the variable copyright terms with a uniform renewable term of twenty-eight years. On the other hand, the 1906 bill treated the performance rights in musical compositions and dramatic compositions similarly. The bill that Congress enacted gave the rights different scope and established different remedies for their infringement.

15. 1909 Act § 15. Congress amended the section in 1926 to prevent the forfeiture of copyrights in mimeographed books. *See* Act of July 3, 1926, 44 Stat. 818.

16. *See, e.g., Patterson* v. *Century Prod.,* 93 F.2d 489 (2d Cir.1937); *Tiffany Prods.* v. *Dewing,* 50 F.2d 911 (D.Md.1931); *Metro Goldwyn Mayer Distrib.* v. *Bijou Theatre,* 3 F.Supp. 66 (D.Ma.1933); *Jerome H. Remick & Co.* v. *American Auto. Accessories,* 5 F.2d 411 (6th Cir.1925); *Jerome H. Remick & Co.* v. *General Elec.,* 4 F.2d 160 (S.D.N.Y.1924); *M. Witmark & Sons* v. *L. Bamberger & Co.,* 291 F.2d 776 (D.N.J.1923); *Buck* v. *Jewell-LaSalle Realty,* 283 U.S. 191 (1931).

17. The broadcasters' performing rights association, Broadcast Music, Inc., was established in 1939 as a performing rights society owned entirely by broadcasters. Like ASCAP, it licensed its entire repertory of compositions for a flat fee. The music publishers' solution to the compulsory license was the Harry Fox Agency. The Fox Agency operates as an arm of the National Music Publishers Association, and offers a form license to record companies in lieu of the statutory compulsory license. The Fox license is less onerous for record companies because it allows one-stop shopping and permits them to remit royalties less frequently. The popularity of juke-

boxes frustrated composers' attempts to repeal what came to be called the "jukebox exemption" until 1976, when Congress replaced it with a statutory compulsory license carrying a nominal annual royalty. In 1989, the jukebox license was superseded by a provision encouraging representatives of jukebox operators to negotiate with representatives of composers and music publishers on a collective license and making copyright office arbitration available to resolve disputes. *See* 17 U.S.C. § 116. By that time, however, jukeboxes were no longer ubiquitous.

18. *See* Abraham L. Kamenstein, Divisibility of Copyrights, reprinted in *Subcommittee on Patents, Trademarks and Copyrights of the Senate Committee on the Judiciary*, 86th Cong., 1st sess., Copyright Law Revision Study Number 11 (1960). The law was even more complicated because it required that every published work bear a copyright notice naming the copyright owner. The practice in periodical publishing involved a complicated series of conveyances of the copyrights in individual articles in a periodical from author to publisher and back again, with detours for licensees of subsidiary rights, in order to enable the periodical publisher to own the copyright for purposes of initial publication while permitting the author of the article to retain all other rights. *See* ibid.

19. Rural appliance merchants deployed early cable television systems to enlarge the local market for television by improving reception. The first documented cable television transmission took place in 1948. By 1952, fourteen thousand households were cable subscribers.

John Mauchley and J. Presper Eckert used vacuum tubes to build the ENIAC computer in 1946. They went on to build UNIVAC, the first commercial mainframe computer, in 1951.

The precursor to the Xerox photocopier was introduced in 1948, but didn't take off until Xerox marketed an easier to use machine in 1959.

20. In addition to transcripts of the conferences and Congressional hearings, and the texts of documents prepared by the Copyright Office for Congress, I have relied on news reports and ABA section reports during the period. Most of the legislative history of the 1976 Copyright Revision Act is collected in George S. Grossman, *Omnibus Copyright Revision Legislative History* (1976) (microfiche), and indexed in *Kaminstein Legislative History Project, Copyright Act of 1976* (1983).

21. General Revision of Copyright Law, Pub.L. No. 94-553, 90 Stat. 2541 (1976) (codified as amended at 17 U.S.C. §§ 101–810). *See generally Jessica Litman, Copyright Compromise and Legislative History*, 72 Cornell Law Review 857 (1987).

22. Courts have struggled to apply the 1976 act to cases involving videocassette recorders, communications satellites, computer software, electronic databases, and the Internet. *See, e.g., Matthew Bender & Co. v. West Publishing Co.*, 158 F.3d 674 (2d Cir. 1998) (electronic database); *Lotus Development Co. v. Borland International*, 49 F.3d 807 (1st Cir. 1995), *aff'd by an equally divided Court*, 516 U.S. 233 (1996) (computer software); *West Publishing v. Mead Data Cent.*, 799 F.2d 1219 (8th Cir.1986), *cert. denied*, 479 U.S. 1070 (1987) (electronic database); *Hubbard Broadcasting v. Southern*

Satellite Systems, 777 F.2d 393 (8th Cir.1985), *cert. denied,* 479 U.S. 1005 (1986)(satellite TV); *Eastern Microwave* v. *Doubleday Sports,* 691 F.2d 125 (2d Cir.1982), *cert. denied,* 459 U.S. 1226 (1983)(satellite TV); *Religious Technology Center* v. *Netcom On-Line Communications Services, Inc.,* 907 F. Supp. 1361 (N.D. Cal. 1995) (Internet); *Universal City Studios* v. *Sony Corp. of Am.,* 480 F.Supp. 429 (C.D. Cal.1979), *aff'd in part, rev'd in part,* 659 F.2d 963 (9th Cir.1981), *rev'd,* 464 U.S. 417 (1984) (VCRs). The courts' efforts to apply the statute in these cases have been criticized widely. The statutory language, however, gave courts little guidance. The fact-specific provisions of the statute do not contemplate such exotic creatures; the paucity of provisions articulating more general principles has relegated courts to ad hoc decision making.

23. The meaning of the statute's two-part definition of "work made for hire," see 17 U.S.C. § 101, generated a four-way Circuit split until it was resolved by the U.S. Supreme Court in *Community for Creative Non-Violence* v. *Reid,* 490 U.S. 730 (1989). The controversial Second Circuit opinion that sparked the conflict among the circuits was *Aldon Accessories* v. *Spiegel, Inc.,* 738 F.2d 548 (2d Cir.), *cert. denied,* 469 U.S. 982 (1984). *Aldon Accessories* construed the definition as applied to novelty unicorn figurines.

24. The material in this section is drawn from the sources cited above in note 15.

25. *See* H.R. 4347, 89th Cong., 1st sess. § 109 (1965).

26. *See* Public Law 94-553 § 111, 90 Stat. 2541, 2550-2558 (1976).

27. *Copyright Law Revision: Hearings on H.R. 4347 Before the Subcommittee on Courts, Civil Liberties and the Administration of Justice of the House Committee on the Judiciary,* 89th Cong., 1st sess. 32-33 (1965) (testimony of George Cary, Deputy Register of Copyrights).

28. The best known of these general limitations is the controversial doctrine of fair use. Fair use originated as a judicially created, implied limitation on copyright owners' rights. One of its earliest American expressions came in the 1841 case of *Folsom* v. *Marsh,* 9 F. Cas. 342 (No. 4901) (C.C.D. Mass. 1841). Fair use evolved in the case law into a privilege to use a reasonable portion of a copyrighted work for a reasonable purpose, but the privilege eluded precise definition. Defendants commonly invoked the privilege in cases involving parody, biography, or scholarly research.

The 1961 Register's Report suggested that the revision bill give explicit recognition to the fair use doctrine. *See U.S. Library of Congress Copyright Office, Report of the Register of Copyrights on the General Revision of the U.S. Copyright Law 25* (1961). The proposal proved controversial; conference participants disagreed on the scope of fair use under extant law and also disagreed on the wisdom of reducing their understanding to statutory text. The Copyright Office's efforts to negotiate a compromise before presenting a bill to Congress failed when the issue of fair use became tangled with the issue of educational use.

Representatives of educational institutions requested a statutory exemption for educational use. Authors and publishers refused; they insisted that educators were already abusing the copyright law and should receive no further privileges beyond those the fair use doctrine already permitted. Educators responded that fair use was too unpredictable a doctrine for them to rely on; moreover, because most fair use cases arose in commercial contexts, they gave little guidance to the doctrine's application in a nonprofit educational setting. The Register and the House Subcommittee's general counsel convened several series of meetings; members of Congress urged further negotiations. Ultimately a compromise emerged, encompassing both the language of a statutory fair use section and the language of the House and Senate Reports to accompany it. The resulting statutory provision combined language from the Register's initial proposal with examples of educational use. The accompanying passages in the House and Senate Reports grew by accretion to include the authors' and publishers' early demand that the goal of the statutory provision was "to restate the present judicial doctrine of fair use, not to change, narrow or enlarge it in any way"; the educators' demand for an extensive discussion of photocopying for classroom use; and the text of letters from representatives of affected interests together with exceedingly detailed guidelines on classroom reproduction that the representatives had negotiated among themselves. See Jessica Litman, Copyright Legislation and Technological Change, see note 1 above, at 340–41; Jessica Litman, Copyright, Compromise and Legislative History, 72 Cornell Law Review 857, 875–77 (1987).

29. Public L. No. 100-667, 102 Stat. 3489 (1988) (codified as amended at 17 U.S.C. § 119).

30. 17 U.S.C. § 119(2)(B). There's a great deal of dispute about whether the tests to ascertain whether a subscriber could, with an appropriate antenna, receive local network affiliate broadcasts over- or underestimate eligible subscribers. Subscribers who cannot receive broadcast signals but do subscribe to cable can become eligible for satellite television by canceling their cable subscription and sitting in a dark room for ninety days. See Satellite Home Viewer Improvements Act, Hearing on S. 247 Before the Senate Committee on the Judiciary, 106th Cong., 1st sess. (1999).

31. See S. 247 Hearing, above in note 30.

32. Intellectual Property and Communications Omnibus Reform Act of 1999 §§ 1001–1012, Public L. 106-113 (1999) (codified at 17 U.S.C. §§ 119, 122). The law restored access to distant network signals for most customers who had received them before October 31, 1999, but only temporarily.

33. Public. L. 102-563, 106 Stat. 4237 (1992) (codified at 17 U.S.C. §§ 1001–1010).

34. 17 U.S.C. § 1008.

35. Sections 1004–1008 require that the funds be split into different pots of money for the benefit of record companies, performers, composers, and music publishers, and specify the percentage of the total that each group should receive. The statute contains no instructions on the difficult task of apportioning money among different claimants within a class, beyond an exhortation to encourage all claimants to agree among themselves.

36. 464 U.S. 417 (1984).

FOUR
A THOUGHT EXPERIMENT[1]

I MAGINE THAT YOU HAVE BEEN retained as the public's copyright lawyer. One morning, your client, the public, walks into your office to consult you about a deal that it has been offered. It seems that all of the industries with substantial economic stakes in copyright have gotten together and written up a proposal. Here it is: the 1976 copyright statute. It's well over one hundred pages long, and, frankly, it's a little hard to decipher.[2] Your client stayed up all night to read it, and can't seem to make head or tail of it. In any event, your client drops this heavy tome on your desk.

Client: "So, whaddya think? Should I sign it? Is it a good deal?"

You (temporizing): "It depends. What sort of a bargain do you want?"

Client: "Look; I'm not out to get something for nothing. I understand that authors won't write stuff if they can't get paid. I want them to make new works and I'm willing to pay them to do so. I want to encourage authors to write as many new works as they can. As for me, I want to be able to read, see, hear, or download any work in captivity, and pay appropriate royalties for doing so.[3] Will this proposal let me do that?"

Would you recommend that your client sign on the dotted line?

I would not. The text we're considering wasn't really written with your client's interests in mind. Most of it was drafted by the representatives of copyright-intensive businesses and institutions, who were chiefly concerned about their interaction with other copyright-intensive businesses and institutions. For that reason, there is much in the statute that speaks to the behavior of a public television station or a cable system operator with respect to the programming it might transmit,[4] and very few words addressing the behavior of a consumer with respect to the programming she might watch or record. You can find a fair amount of language relevant to the actions of a publisher bringing out an author's new novel, and the film producer who seeks to adapt the story for the screen,[5] but not much about the actions of the police officer who buys and reads the book, rents and sees the film, and wishes the producer had not cast Tom Cruise in the leading role.[6] The law has a specific provision for retail stores who play the radio for their customers, but no language that seems to contemplate fraternities who play loud music for their neighbors.[7] Thus, the statute fails to discuss your client's ability or obligation to pay appropriate royalties in return for access, and there is no provision securing your client's opportunity to read, see, hear, or download copyrighted works.

One can draw different conclusions from the paucity of language speaking to the behavior of individuals who are consuming rather than exploiting copyrighted material. One conclusion commonly voiced is that the statute really doesn't address the legal obligations of individuals acting in their private capacities. An equally plausible interpretation, favored by copyright owners and copyright lawyers, is that the statute forbids private individuals, acting without permission, to invade the copyright owner's broad rights unless their behavior falls within an express statutory exception. Not many of these specific exceptions address individuals' private actions, which means that individuals are routinely prohibited from doing the sorts of things that businesses have statutory exemptions for unless they first secure the copyright owner's permission. For example, the statute permits record companies to create musical arrangements for songs in the course of recording them. Consumers, though, have no such privilege, and creating an unauthorized arrangement violates composers' rights to create "derivative works," regardless of whether the arrangement is publicly performed or commercially exploited.[8] It follows that, if consumers are liable whenever they engage in behavior within the terms of the copyright owner's exclusive rights without an express exemption, you break the law when you play music by ear on the piano in your living room. Similarly, since the derivative work right contains no express exemption for six-year-olds, your children ought not to act out *Star Wars*. Either way, it doesn't seem as if the agreement on your desk is something you should advise your client to sign.

Content owners and copyright lawyers insist that ordinary people should look at unlicensed music, and unlicensed software, and unlicensed digital reading material the same way they see stolen personal property, and should treat them accordingly. Just as consumers believe that it is wrong to pocket a diamond ring without paying for it, they should understand that it is equally wrong to play a song without paying for it.[9] Yet as fiercely as some copyright owners embrace this principle, they seem oblivious of some of its important implications.

If ordinary people are to see copyrights as equivalent to tangible property, and accord copyright rules the respect they give to other property rules, then we would need, at a minimum, to teach them the rules that govern intellectual property when we teach them the rules that govern other personal property, which is to say in elementary school. The problem, though, is that our current copyright statute could not be taught in elementary school, because elementary school students couldn't understand it. Indeed, their teachers couldn't understand it. Copyright lawyers don't understand it.[10] If we are going to teach the copyright law to schoolchildren, then we need the law to be sensible, intuitive, and short enough that schoolchildren can hold its essential provisions in their heads. What we have now is not even close.

It is unrealistic to imagine that we could make members of the public conduct their daily affairs under rules thought up by and for major players in copyright-affected industries simply by announcing that they must. If the public is to play by copyright rules, then those rules must be designed with the public's interests in mind.

Let's return to my thought experiment. The public has hired you to act as its copyright lawyer. Acting in your new role, you review the current statute, and you chat with your client about where to go from here:

You: Look. I think the copyright concept is a good one, but I'm not happy with the details. There are a bunch of places where I think the language is unfortunate, and not in your long-term best interest. Let me take it home and see if I can draft up a counter-proposal that'll meet your needs, here.

Client: Gee. That's great; that's what I hoped you'd say. But, this time, when you're writing it up, could you make it real short? I don't read so fast, and this is important to me. I want to understand what it says.

So, you have yourself a drafting project. Your job is to construct a copyright law that affords members of the public the opportunity to read, see, hear, and otherwise experience, download, buy, borrow, and keep copies of all, or at least most, of the works that are out there, while according ample compensation to the authors and publishers of copyrighted works, and encouraging them to produce and disseminate as many copyrighted works as they are able to. The law should be about three pages long, should strike more folks than not as more fair than not, and should be sufficiently intuitive to appeal to schoolchildren.

Imagine now that, after a couple of hours of concentrated work, you come up with some language that meets these specifications. For the purposes of the thought experiment it isn't important what the language actually says. Let's simply imagine that you manage to come up with something short, clear, and fair. Your client reads it, understands it, and approves it. You take it over to Congress. Or maybe you send it to the newspapers. Perhaps you sign on to the Internet and post it for all to read. You have only one final problem: Congress isn't going to enact it.

As the previoius chapter made clear, the only way that copyright laws get passed in this country is for all of the lawyers who represent the current stakeholders to get together and hash out all of the details among themselves. In the past, this process has produced laws that are unworkable from the vantage point of people who were not among the negotiating parties, and it won't generate any better results this time. Whatever the strengths of the negotiated legislation approach to an area as complex as copyright, the statutes that result from the process are long, complex, and counterintuitive. The dynamics inherent in the negotiation process discourage brevity and intuitive appeal. Lawyers representing affected interests respond to the issues raised by new technology by ratifying all of the "accidents" that favor their clients and repudiating the "accidents" that work to their disadvantage. The time-honored approach is to claim that the first sort of accident is no accident at all but part of Congress's grand design, while the second sort of accident is a completely unintended, unexpected "loophole." If interested parties disagree on which accidents are which, there is a predictable negotiated solution. Negotiating stakeholders have always resolved differences through specificity and detail. By the time we're done, the new statute is even worse than the old one. And while it is easy to claim that the interplay among all of the interests affected by copyright provides a proxy for the public interest, the statutes that this interplay produces demonstrate that it isn't so.

Our current copyright law is a descendent of the copyright laws in force a century ago, which were designed to bring order to the interaction among affected industries. Because affected industries, and their lawyers, were invited to draft those rules themselves, the law became so technical, detailed, and counterintuitive that those industries now need to bring their copyright lawyers along to tell them how to play. If the law is intended to govern only the behavior of players with substantial economic stakes in copyright-affected matters, there is not much wrong with that degree of complexity. As soon, however, as the law is claimed to control the ordinary behavior of ordinary members of the public going about their ordinary daily business, then that species of law will no longer serve. No solution will seriously address the public's interests unless the public sits at the negotiating table and insists that it do so.

That is supposed to be Congress's job, of course. Congress is the public's copyright lawyer. Yet, as I've discussed, Congress lacks the interest, expertise, and institutional memory to represent the public on this particular project, and has found significant political benefits in deferring to the interests the legislation affects. Thus, what Congress has done more often than not is delegate the job of coming up with legislation to interested private parties, which is how the statute got so long and convoluted in the first place.

Congress, of course, has its *own* copyright lawyer, who is in some sense charged with the responsibilities Congress has abdicated. That is the Copyright Office's job. The Copyright Office has both expertise and institutional memory; it has functioned as Congress's copyright lawyer and copyright expert for almost a century. Unfortunately, the Copyright Office has tended to view copyright owners as its real constituency, and has spent the past ten years moving firmly into the content industry's pocket. The reasons are unexceptional: The office has a limited budget, and relies on the goodwill of its regular clients. Copyright Office policy staff often come from and return to law firms that regularly represent copyright owners. Perhaps most importantly, the Copyright Office relies on the copyright bar to protect it from budget cuts and incursions on its turf. When Sen. Orrin Hatch introduced a bill that would have transferred the Register's copyright policy-making authority to a new administrative agency,[11] for example, the copyright bar rallied in opposition to the change.[12] Thus, it is unsurprising that the Register has routinely given positions advanced by the content industry her enthusiastic endorsement.

That leaves the public's interest essentially unrepresented in the copyright legislative process. But this is only a thought experiment. The public has no copyright lawyer, and none of the lawyers involved in making copyright laws can afford to view the public's interests as sufficiently compelling to override the immediate pressing needs of their various clients. The resulting legislation shows it.

NOTES

1. Portions of this chapter are adapted from an article published as *The Exclusive Right to Read*, at 13 Cardozo Arts & Entertainment Law Journal 29 (1994).

2. The 1909 Copyright Act occupied twelve pages of the United States Code. As originally enacted, the 1976 Copyright Act was sixty-one pages long. By 1995, a variety of amendments had expanded its length to 142 pages. Today it is 205 pages long.

3. I've appropriated the turns of phrase from Dani Zweig, who, in another life, posted reviews of science-fiction books to Usenet news. Dr. Zweig spent some years as a software-design professor before taking a software quality-control position in the private sector.

4. *See* 17 U.S.C. §§ 111, 118.

5. *See, e.g.,* 17 U.S.C. §§ 106, 201, 203.

6. *See Anne Rice Jabs Stake into Cruise,* USA Today, May 23, 1994, at 2D. In theory, the police officer who succumbs to temptation and imagines the film as it might have looked if Daniel Day Lewis had been cast in Tom Cruise's role may be violating the copyright owners' exclusive rights under 17 U.S.C. § 106 (2) to prepare derivative works, since the right to prepare derivative works is violated by any adaptation involving originality on the adapter's part, even if it is never embodied in tangible form. See H.R. Rep. 1476, 94th Cong., 2d sess. 62 (1976); see also chapter 2, note 1, in this book.

7. Playing loud music for your neighbors is performing it publicly. Public performances of copyrighted works are copyright infringement unless privileged by sections 107–19. Section 110(5) contains a limited privilege to play radio or television programs. Section 110(5)(A) permits use in public of a single radio or television, so long as the program is not further transmitted. Section 110(5)(B) expressly privileges the use of televisions or radios (but not records, tapes, or discs) to play music (but not other works) in bars, restaurants, and small commercial establishments. No comparable provision exists for use of a boom box in public, or the playing of automotive stereo equipment in a car with its windows rolled down.

8. The privilege to make a new musical arrangement appears in the compulsory license provision for making records. See 17 U.S.C. § 115(a)(2). It is a limited privilege that comes into play only for songs that have already been released in recorded form, and that applies only where the purpose of the new arrangement is to make records, CDs, or tapes to be distributed to the public for private use. (There is no provision that gives musicians or composers such a privilege in connection with their work, although they routinely create arrangements before seeking the copyright owner's permission.) The right to create derivative works, in 17 U.S.C. § 106, purports to give copyright owners control over creative adaptations of their works, regardless of whether those adaptations are later commercially exploited. The deriv-

ative work has been described by federal judge Alex Kosinski as "hopelessly over-broad." *See Micro Star, Inc.* v. *Formgen, Inc.,* 154 F.3d 1107, 1110 (9th Cir. 1998).

9. This completely ignores a crucial distinction between diamond rings and songs. Only one person may keep a particular diamond ring in his pocket at any given time, while an unlimited number of people can play a particular song at any given time.

10. I make this statement with no intention of being hyperbolic. Anyone with access to the Internet can join a number of online virtual communities in which copyright law is discussed by groups including experts and interested laypeople. One story I like to tell involves a debate that went on for a couple of months on a wonderful copyright mailing list that had more than one thousand subscribers, many of whom were prominent experts in the field. The debate was over whether one could dedicate one's electronic postings to the public domain, and, if so, how might that be accomplished, and could one, having done that, attach any conditions to the further distribution of the contents of those posts? Participants were not sure that it was possible to dedicate works to the public domain anymore, after the Berne Implementation Act (Pub. L. No. 100-568, 102 Stat. 2853 (1988)); they were not sure how, if it were possible, one could accomplish it; they could not agree on what words to use. None of these folks were copyright naïfs; both the original inquirer and most of the posters offering views on this particular issue had substantial copyright backgrounds. But, if one thousand sophisticated people with enormous copyright expertise among them cannot over a two-month period resolve this simple a question, then the law has gotten way too complicated for any purpose; it surely cannot be taught to schoolchildren.

11. S.1961, 104th Cong., 2d sess. (1996). The new agency would have combined the Copyright Office with the Patent and Trademark Office under the leadership of then-Commissioner of Patents Bruce Lehman. We will see a great deal of Commissioner Lehman in chapter 6.

12. *See The Omnibus Patent Act of 1996: Hearing on S. 1961 Before the Senate Judiciary Committee,* 104th Cong., 2d sess (1996).

FIVE

CHOOSING METAPHORS

A public domain work is an orphan. No one is responsible for its life. But everyone exploits its use, until that time certain when it becomes soiled and haggard, barren of its previous virtues. Who, then, will invest the funds to renovate and nourish its future life when no one owns it? How does the consumer benefit from that scenario? The answer is, there is no benefit.

— Jack Valenti[1]

THE COPYRIGHT LAW ON THE books is a large aggregation of specific statutory provisions; it goes on and on for pages and pages. When most people talk about copyright, though, they don't mean the long complicated statute codified in title 17 of the U.S. Code. Most people's idea of copyright law takes the form of a collection of principles and norms. They understand that those principles are expressed, if sometimes imperfectly, in the statutory language and the case law interpreting it, but they tend to believe that the underlying principles are what count. It is, thus, unsurprising that the rhetoric used in copyright litigation and copyright lobbying is more often drawn from the principles than the provisions.

One can greatly overstate the influence that underlying principles can exercise over the enactment and interpretation of the nitty-gritty provisions of substantive law. In the ongoing negotiations among industry representatives, normative arguments about the nature of copyright show up as rhetorical flourishes, but, typically, change nobody's mind. Still, normative understandings of copyright exercise some constraints on the actual legal provisions that the lobbyists can come up with, agree on, convince Congress to pass, and persuade outsiders to comply with. The ways we have of thinking about copyright law can at least make some changes more difficult to achieve than others.

Lawyers, lobbyists, and scholars in a host of disciplines have reexamined and reformulated copyright principles over the past generation, in ways that have expanded copyright's scope and blinded many of us to the dangers that arise from protecting too much, too expansively for too long. That transformation has facilitated the expansion of copyright protection and the narrowing of copyright limitations and exceptions.

At the turn of the century, when Congress first embraced the copyright conference model that was to trouble us for the rest of the century, the predominant metaphor for copyright was the notion of a quid pro quo.[2] The public granted authors limited exclusive rights (and only if the authors fulfilled a variety of formal conditions) in return for the immediate public dissemination of the work and the eventual dedication of the work in its entirety to the public domain.[3]

As the United States got less hung up on formal prerequisites, that model evolved to a view of copyright as a bargain in which the public granted limited exclusive rights to authors as a means to advance the public interest. This model was about compensation:[4] it focused on copyright as a way to permit authors to make enough money from the works they created in order to encourage them to create the works and make them available to the public. That view of the law persisted until fairly recently.

If you read books, articles, legal briefs, and congressional testimony about copyright written by scholars and lawyers and judges fifty years ago, you find widespread agreement that copyright protection afforded only shallow and exception-ridden control over protected works. Forty, thirty, even twenty years ago, it was an article of faith that the nature of copyright required that it offer only circumscribed, porous protection to works of authorship. The balance between protection and the material that copyright left unprotected was thought to be the central animating principle of the law. Copyright was a bargain between the public and the author, whereby the public bribed the author to create new works in return for limited commercial control over the new expression the author brought to her works. The public's payoff was that, beyond the borders of the authors' defined exclusive rights, it was entitled to enjoy, consume, learn from, and reuse the works. Even the bounded copyright rights would expire after a limited term, then set at fifty-six years.

A corollary of the limited protection model was that copyright gave owners control only over particular uses of their works.[5] The copyright owner had exclusive rights to duplicate the work. Publishing and public performance were within the copyright owner's control. But copyright never gave owners any control over reading, or private performance, or resale of a copy legitimately owned, or learning from and talking about and writing about a work, because those were all part of what the public gained from its bargain. Thus, the fact that copyright protection lasted for a very long time (far longer than the protection offered by patents); the fact that copyright protection has never required a government examination for originality, creativity, or merit; and the fact that copyright protects works that have very little of any of them was defended as harmless: because copyright *never* took from the public any of the raw material it might need to use to create new works of authorship, the dangers arising from overprotection ranged from modest to trivial.

There was nearly universal agreement on these points through the mid-1970s. Copyright was seen as designed to be full of holes. The balance underlying that view of the copyright system treated the interests of owners of particular works (and often those owners were not the actual authors) as potentially in tension with the interests of the general public, including the authors of the future; the theory of the system was to adjust that balance so that each of the two sides got at least as much as it needed.[6] In economic terms, neither the author nor the public was entitled to appropriate the entire surplus generated by a new work of authorship.[7] Rather, they shared the proceeds, each entitled to claim that portion of them that would best encourage the promiscuous creation of still newer works of authorship.

If you're dissatisfied with the way the spoils are getting divided, one approach is to change the rhetoric. When you conceptualize the law as a balance between copyright owners and the public, you set up a particular dichotomy—some would argue, a false dichotomy[8]—that constrains the choices you are likely to make. If copyright law is a bargain between authors and the public, then we might ask what the public is getting from the bargain. If copyright law is about a balance between owners' control of the exploitation of their works and the robust health of the public domain, one might ask whether the system strikes the appropriate balance.[9] You can see how, at least in some quarters, this talk about bargains and balance might make trouble. Beginning in the late 1970s and early 1980s, advocates of copyright owners began to come up with different descriptions of the nature of copyright, with an eye to enabling copyright owners to capture a greater share of the value embodied in copyright-protected works.[10]

In the last thirty years, the idea of a bargain has gradually been replaced by a model drawn from the economic analysis of law, which characterizes copyright as a system of incentives.[11] Today, this is the standard economic model of copyright law, whereby copyright provides an economic incentive for the creation and distribution of original works of authorship.[12] The model derives a lot of its power from its simplicity: it posits a direct relationship between the extent of copyright protection and the amount of authorship produced and distributed—any increase in the scope or subject matter or duration of copyright will cause an increase in authorship; any reduction will cause a reduction.

The economic analysis model focuses on the effect greater or lesser copyright rights might have on incentives to create and exploit new works. It doesn't bother about stuff like balance or bargains except as they might affect the incentive structure for creating and exploiting new works. To justify copyright limitations, like fair use, under this model, you need to argue that authors and publishers need them in order to create new works of authorship,[13] rather than, say, because that's part of the public's share of the copyright bargain. The model is not rooted in compensation, and so it doesn't ask how broad a copyright would be appropriate or fair; instead it inquires whether broader, longer, or stronger copyright protection would be likely to lead to the production of more works of authorship.

The weakness in this model is that more and stronger and longer copyright protection will always, at the margin, cause more authors to create more works—that's how this sort of linear model operates. If we forget that the model is just a useful thought tool, and persuade ourselves that it straightforwardly describes the real world, then we're trapped in a construct in which there's no good reason why copyrights shouldn't cover everything and last forever.

Lately, that's what seems to have happened. Copyright legislation has recently been a one-way ratchet, and it's hard to argue that that's bad within the confines of the conventional way of thinking about copyright. In the past several years we've seen a further evolution. Copyright today is less about incentives or compensation than it is about control.[14] What ended up persuading lawmakers to adopt that model was the conversion of copyright into a trade issue: The content industries, copyright owners argued, were among the few in which the United States had a favorable balance of trade. Instead of focusing on American citizens who engaged in unlicensed uses of copyrighted works (many of them legal under U.S. law), they drew Congress's attention to people and businesses in other countries who engaged in similar uses. The United States should make it a top priority, they argued, to beef up domestic copyright law at home, and thus ensure that people in other countries paid for any use of copyrighted works abroad. United States copyright law does not apply beyond U.S. borders, but supporters of expanded copyright protection argued that by enacting stronger copyright laws, Congress would set a good example for our trading partners, who could then be persuaded to do the same. Proponents of enhanced protection changed the story of copyright from a story about authors and the public collaborating on a bargain to promote the progress of learning, into a story about Americans trying to protect their property from foreigners trying to steal it.

That story sold. It offered an illusion that, simply by increasing the scope and strength and duration of U.S. copyright protection, Congress could generate new wealth for America without detriment or even inconvenience to any Americans. That recasting of the copyright story persuaded Congress to "improve" copyright protection and cut back on limitations and exceptions.[15]

The upshot of the change in the way we think about copyright is that the dominant metaphor is no longer that of a bargain between authors and the public. We talk now of copyright as property that the owner is entitled to control—to sell to the public (or refuse to sell) on whatever terms the owner chooses. Copyright has been transformed into the right of a property owner to protect what is rightfully hers. (That allows us to skip right past the question of what it is, exactly, that ought to be rightfully hers.) And the current metaphor is reflected both in recent copyright amendments now on the books and in the debate over what those laws mean and whether they go too far.

One example of this trend is the piecemeal repeal of the so-called first sale doctrine, which historically permitted the purchaser of a copy of a copyrighted work to sell, loan, lease, or display the copy without the copyright owner's permission, and is the reason why public libraries, video rental stores, and art galleries are not illegal.[16] The first sale doctrine enhanced public access to copyrighted works that some were unable to purchase. Because the first sale doctrine applies only to copies of a copyrighted work, it became increasingly irrelevant in a world in which vast numbers of works were disseminated to the public through media such as television and radio, which involved no transfer of copies. Copyright owners who did distribute copies of their works, however, lobbied for the first sale doctrine's repeal. Congress yielded to the entreaties of the recording industry to limit the first sale doctrine as it applied to records, cassette tapes and compact discs in 1984, and enacted an amendment that made commercial record rental (but not loan or resale) illegal.[17] After the computer software industry's attempts to evade the operation of the first sale doctrine—by claiming that their distribution of software products involved licenses rather than sales[18]—received an unenthusiastic reception in court,[19] Congress partially repealed the first sale doctrine as it applied to computer programs.[20] Bills to repeal the first sale doctrine for audio/visual works were introduced in Congress,[21] but never accumulated enough support to be enacted. The actual bites these laws took out of the first sale doctrine were small ones, but in the process, the principle that the doctrine represents has been diminished.

If we no longer insist that people who own legitimate copies of works be permitted to do what they please with them, that presents an opportunity to attack a huge realm of unauthorized but not illegal use. If copyright owners can impose conditions on the act of gaining access, and back those conditions up with either technological devices, or legal prohibitions, or both, then copyright owners can license access to and use of their works on a continuing basis. Technological fences, such as passwords or encryption, offer some measure of control, and enhanced opportunities to extract value from the use of a work. The owner of the copyright in money management software, for example, could design the software to require purchasers of copies to authorize a small credit card charge each time they sought to run the program. The owner of the copyright in recorded music could release the recording in a scrambled format, and rent access to descramblers by the day. Technological controls, though, are vulnerable to technological evasion, which is where the part about legal controls comes in.

When copyright owners demanded the legal tools to restrict owners of legitimate copies of works from gaining access to them, Congress was receptive. Copyright owner interests argued that, in a digital age, anyone with access to their works could commit massive violations of their copyrights with a single keystroke by transmitting unauthorized copies all over the Internet. In order for their rights to mean anything, copyright owners insisted, they were entitled to have control over access to their works—not merely initial access, but continuing control over every subsequent act of gaining access to the content of a work.[22] Thus, to protect their property rights, the law needed to be amended to prohibit individuals from gaining unauthorized access to copyrighted works.[23]

Augmenting copyright law with legally enforceable access control could completely annul the first sale doctrine. More fundamentally, enforceable access control has the potential to redesign the copyright landscape completely. The hallmark of legal rights is that they can be carefully calibrated. Copyright law can give authors control over the initial distribution of a copy of a work, without permitting the author to exercise downstream control over who gets to see it. Copyright law can give authors control over the use of the words and pictures in their books without giving them rights to restrict the ideas and facts those words and pictures express. It can give them the ability to collect money for the preface and notes they add to a collection of Shakespeare's plays without allowing them to assert any rights in the text of those plays. It can permit them to control reproductions of their works without giving them the power to restrict consumption of their works. Leaving eye-tracks on a page has never been deemed to be copyright infringement.

Copyrighted works contain protected and unprotected elements, and access to those works may advance restricted or unrestricted uses. Access controls are not so discriminating. Once we permit copyright owners to exert continuing control over consumers' access to the contents of their works, there is no way to ensure that access controls will not prevent consumers from seeing the unprotected facts and ideas in a work. Nor can we make certain that the access controls prevent uses that the law secures to the copyright owner, while permitting access when its purpose is to facilitate a use the law permits. If the law requires that we obtain a license whenever we wish to read protected text, it encourages copyright owners to restrict the availability of licenses whenever it makes economic sense for them to do so. That, in turn, makes access to the ideas, facts, and other unprotected elements contingent on copyright holders' marketing plans, and puts the ability of consumers to engage in legal uses of the material in those texts within the copyright holders' unconstrained discretion. In essence, that's an exclusive right to use. In other words, in order to effectively protect authors' "exclusive rights" to their writings, which is to say, control, we need to give them power to permit or prevent any use that might undermine their control. What that means is that a person who buys a copy of a work may no longer have the right to read and reread it, loan it, resell it, or give it away. But the law has been moving away from that principle for years.

A second example of this trend is the campaign to contract the fair use privilege. Fair use was once understood as the flip side of the limited scope of copyright.[24] The copyright law gave the copyright holder exclusive control over reproductions of the work, but not over all reproductions.[25] The justifications for fair use were various; a common formulation explained that reasonable appropriations of protected works were permissible when they advanced the public interest without inflicting unacceptably grave damage on the copyright owner. Fair use was appropriate in situations when the copyright owner would be likely to authorize the use but it would be a great deal of trouble to ask for permission, such as the quotation of excerpts of a novel in a favorable review or the use of selections from a scholarly article in a subsequent scholarly article building on the first author's research. Fair use was also appropriate in situations when the copyright owner would be unlikely to authorize, such as parodies and critiques, under a justification Prof. Alan Latman described as "enforced consent." The social interest in allowing uses that criticized the copyright owner's work, for example, outweighed the copyright owner's reluctance to permit them. Fair use was appropriate whenever such uses were customary, either under the implied-consent rubric or as a matter of enforced consent. Fair use was finally asserted to be the reason that a variety of uses that come within the technical boundaries of the exclusive rights in the copyright bundle, but were difficult to prevent, like private copying, would not be actionable.[26]

Recent reformulations of the fair use privilege, however, have sought to confine it to the implied assent justification. Where copyright owners would not be likely to authorize the use free of charge, the use should no longer be fair. The uses that were permitted because they were difficult to police are claimed to be a subset of the impliedly permitted uses; should copyright owners devise a mechanism for licensing those uses, there would, similarly, no longer be any need to excuse the uses as fair.[27] In its most extreme form, this argument suggests that fair use itself is an archaic privilege with little application to the digital world: where technology permits automatic licensing, legal fictions based on "implied assent" become unnecessary.[28] Limiting fair use to an implied assent rationale, moreover, makes access controls seem more appealing. Thus, the fact that access controls would make no exception for individuals to gain access in order to make fair use of a work is said to be unproblematic. Why should fair use be a defense to the act of gaining unauthorized access?

By recasting traditional limitations on the scope of copyright as loopholes, proponents of stronger protection have managed to put the champions of limited protection on the defensive. Why, after all, should unde-sirable loopholes not now be plugged? Instead of being viewed as altruists seeking to assert the public's side of the copyright bargain, library organi-zations, for example, are said to be giving aid and comfort to pirates. Instead of being able to claim that broad prohibitions on technological devices are bad technological policy, opponents of the copyright-as-control model are painted as folks who believe that it ought to be okay to steal books rather than to buy them. And when educators have argued that everyone is losing sight of the rights that the law gives the public, they have met the response that the copyright law has never asked authors to subsi-dize education by donating their literary property.

Then there's the remarkable expansion of what we call piracy. Piracy used to be about folks who made and sold large numbers of counterfeit copies. Today, the term "piracy" seems to describe *any* unlicensed activity—especially if the person engaging in it is a teenager. The content industry calls some behavior piracy despite the fact that it is unquestionably legal. When a consumer makes a noncommercial recording of music by, for example, taping a CD she has purchased or borrowed from a friend, her copying comes squarely within the privilege established by the Audio Home Recording Act. The record companies persist in calling that copying piracy even though the statute deems it lawful.[29]

People on the content owners' side of this divide explain that it is tech-nology that has changed penny-ante unauthorized users into pirates, but that's not really it at all. These "pirates" are doing the same sort of things unlicensed users have always done—making copies of things for their own personal use, sharing their copies with their friends, or reverse-engineering the works embodied on the copies to figure out how they work. What's changed is the epithet we apply to them.

If we untangle the claim that technology has turned Johnny Teenager into a pirate, what turns out to be fueling it is the idea that *if* Johnny Teenager were to decide to share his unauthorized copy with two million of his closest friends, the *effect* on a record company would be pretty sim-ilar to the effect of some counterfeit CD factory's creating two million CDs and selling them cheap. Copyright owners are worried, and with good reason. But, in response to their worry, they've succeeded in persuading a lot of people that any behavior that has the same effect as piracy must *be* piracy, and must therefore reflect the same moral turpitude we attach to piracy, even if it is the same behavior that we all called legitimate before.

Worse, any behavior that *could potentially cause the same effect* as piracy, even if it doesn't, must also be piracy. Because an unauthorized digital copy of something *could* be uploaded to the Internet, where it *could* be downloaded by two million people, even making the digital copy is piracy. Because an unauthorized digital copy of something could be used in a way that could cause all that damage, making a tool that makes it *possible* to make an unauthorized digital copy, even if nobody ever actually makes one, is itself piracy, regardless of the reasons one might have for making this tool. And what could possibly be wrong with a law designed to prevent piracy?

My argument, here, is that this evolution in metaphors conceals immense sleight of hand. We as a society never actually sat down and discussed in policy terms whether, now that we had grown from a copyright-importing nation to a copyright-exporting nation, we wanted to recreate copyright as a more expansive sort of control. Instead, by changing metaphors, we somehow got snookered into believing that copyright had always been intended to offer content owners extensive control, only, before now, we didn't have the means to enforce it.

NOTES

1. *Copyright Term Extension Act: Hearing on H.R. 989 Before the Subcommittee On Courts and Intellectual Property of the House Committee on the Judicary,* 104th Cong., 1st sess. (June 1, 1995) (testimony of Jack Valenti, Motion Picture Association of America).

2. *See* Jessica Litman, *The Public Domain,* 39 Emory Law Journal 965, 977-92 (1990).

3. *See, e.g., London* v. *Biograph,* 231 F. 696 (1916); *Stone & McCarrick* v. *Dugan Piano,* 210 F. 399 (ED La 1914).

4. I'm indebted to Professor Niva Elkin-Koren for this insight. See Niva Elkin-Koren, *It's All About Control: Copyright and Market Power in the Information Society* (7/00 draft).

5. *See, e.g., U.S. Library of Congress Copyright Office, Report of the Register of Copyrights on the General Revision of the U.S. Copyright Law* 6, 21–36 (1961).

6. *See, e.g., Chaffee, Reflections on the Law of Copyright,* 45 Columbia Law Revview 503 (1945); Report of the Register of Copyrights, note 5 above, at 6.

7. Economists would say that the authorship of a new work creates a benefit that exceeds the costs of authoring it. That is the reason why the public benefits when authors create new works. The excess benefit is a surplus. It falls to the law to determine how that surplus should be allocated. Classically, copyright law accorded

the author a portion of the surplus thought to be necessary to provide an incentive to create the work, and reserved the remaining benefit to the public.

8. *See, e.g.*, Jane C. Ginsburg, *Authors and Users in Copyright*, 45 Journal of the Copyright Society of the USA 1 (1997).

9. *See* Benjamin Kaplan, *An Unhurried View of Copyright* 120–22 (Columbia University Press, 1967); Stephen Breyer, *The Uneasy Case for Copyright: A Study of Copyright in Books, Photocopies and Computer Programs*, 84 Harvard Law Review 281 (1970).

10. One series of writings explored the possibility of characterizing copyright as a natural right, on the theory that works of authorship emanated from and embodied author's individual personalities. *See, e.g.*, Edward J. Damich, *The Right of Personality: A Common Law Basis for the Protection of the Moral Rights of Authors*, 23 Georgia Law Review 1 (1988); Justin Hughes, *The Philosophy of Intellectual Property*, 77 Georgetown Law Journal 287 (1988); John M. Kernochan, *Imperatives for Enforcing Authors' Rights*, 11 Columbia-VLA Journal of Law & the Arts 587 (1987). Ignoring for the moment that, at least in the United States, the overwhelming majority of registered copyrights were corporately owned, these thinkers posited the model of author who creates all works from nothing. The parent/progeny metaphor was popular here—authors were compared with mothers or fathers; their works were their children. Therefore, the argument went, they were morally entitled to plenary control over their works as they would be over their children.

11. *See, e.g.*, Paul Goldstein, *Derivative Rights and Derivative Works in Copyright*, 30 Journal of the Copyright Society 209 (1982); Wendy J. Gordon, *Fair Use as Market Failure: A Structural and Economic Analysis of the Betamax Case and Its Predecessors*, 82 Columbia Law Review 1600 (1982); William M. Landes and Richard Posner, *An Economic Analysis of Copyright*, 18 Journal of Legal Studies 325 (1989).

12. *See, e.g.*, Dennis Karjala, *Copyright in Electronic Maps*, 35 Jurimetrics Journal 395 (1995); Alfred C. Yen, *When Authors Won't Sell: Parody, Fair Use and Efficiency in Copyright Law*, 62 University of Colorado Law Review 1173 (1991).

13. *See* Wendy J. Gordon, *Toward a Jurisprudence of Benefits: The Norms of Copyright and the Problems of Private Censorship*, 57 University of Chicago Law Review 1009, 1032-49 (1990); Litman, note 2 above, at 1007–12.

14. Again, I'm indebted to Professor Elkin-Koren for the taxonomy. *See* Elkin-Koren, note 4 above.

15. I have told that story in some detail in Jessica Litman, *Copyright and Information Policy*, 55 Law & Contemporary Problems (Spring 1992), at 185.

16. *See* 17 USCA § 109; see generally John M. Kernochan, *The Distribution Right in the United States of America: Review and Reflections*, 42 Vanderbilt Law Review 1407 (1989).

17. Record Rental Amendment of 1984, Pub. L No 98-450, 98 Stat 1727 (1984) (codified as amended at 17 USCA §§ 109, 115).

18. *See* Pamela Samuelson, *Modifying Copyrighted Software: Adjusting Copyright Doctrine to Accommodate a Technology,* 28 Jurimetrics Journal 179, 188–89 (1988).

19. In *Vault Corp.* v. *Quaid Software, Ltd.*, 847 F2d 255 (5th Cir 1988), the court rejected such a license and the state law purporting to enforce it because the court found it to be inconsistent with federal copyright law, which gives purchasers of copies of computer programs the rights that the shrink-wrap license attempted to withhold.

20. Computer Software Rental Amendments Act of 1990, Pub. L. No. 101-650, 104 Stat 5089, 5134 §§ 801–804 (codified at 17 USC § 109). Like the Record Rental Act, the CSRA prohibits commercial software rental, but not resale, gift, or loan.

21. *See* S. 33, 98th Cong, 1st sess. (January 25, 1983), in 129 Cong. Rec. 590 (January 26, 1983); H.R. 1029, 98th Cong., 1st sess. (January 26, 1983), in 129 Cong. Rec. H201 (January 27, 1983); Home Video Recording, Hearing Before the Senate Committee on the Judiciary, 99th Cong, 2d sess. (1987).

22. *See* Jane C. Ginsburg, *Essay: From Having Copies to Experiencing Works: the Development of an Access Right in U.S. Copyright Law,* in Hugh Hansen, ed., *U.S. Intellectual Property: Law and Policy* (Sweet & Maxwell, 2000).

23. I discuss the access-control amendments extensively in chapter 9. As enacted, they prohibit individuals from circumventing any technological devices designed to restrict access to a work, and make it illegal to make or distribute any tool or service designed to facilitate circumvention. *See* 17 U.S.C. § 1201. The law imposes substantial civil and criminal penalties for violations. *See* 17 U.S.C. §§ 1203, 1204.

24. *See, e.g.*, Alan Latman, *Study # 14: Fair Use 6-7* (1958), reprinted in 2 Studies on Copyright, Studies on Copyright 778, 784–85 (Arthur Fisher Memorial Edition 1963).

25. *See Folsom* v. *Marsh*, 9 Fed Cas. 342 (1841); H. Ball, The Law of Copyright and Literary Property 260 (Bender, 1944); L. Ray Patterson, *Understanding Fair Use*, 55 Law and Contemporary Problems (Spring 1992), at 249.

26. *See generally* Latman, note 24 above at 7–14, 2 Studies on Copyright at 785–92; Lloyd Weinreb, *Commentary: Fair's Fair: A Comment on the Fair Use Doctrine*, 105 Harvard Law Review 1137 (1990).

27. *See, e.g.*, Jane C. Ginsburg, note 8 above, at 11–20 (1997); *American Geophysical Union* v. *Texaco*, 60 F.3d 913 (2d Cir. 1995).

28. *See, e.g.*, Tom W. Bell, *Fared Use v. Fair Use: The Impact of Automated Rights Management on Copyright's Fair Use Doctrine*, 76 N. Carolina Law Review 101 (1998).

29. *See, e.g.*, *Music on the Internet: Is There an Upside to Downloading? Hearing Before the Senate Judiciary Committee*, 106th Cong., 2d sess. (July 11, 2000) (remarks of Hilary Rosen, RIAA).

COPYRIGHT LAWYERS
SET OUT TO COLONIZE
CYBERSPACE

I N 1992, THE "INFORMATION SUPERHIGHWAY" suddenly sprang into the news and became a media darling. Introduced as part of the election campaign, the Superhighway, it was promised, would usher in a new era of American competitiveness and economic power by enabling us all to harness digital technology to access a new, twenty-first-century technological marvel that would supersede conventional media.

If one were currently a dominant player in what has suddenly been dubbed a "conventional" medium, one might find this possibility threatening. Some entrepreneurs saw the Information Superhighway as a new expanse of undiscovered geography to be annexed and colonized. Other stakeholders, though, viewed the uncharted contours of this new information space as a frightening and lawless frontier to be tamed and subdued. Policy makers, lobbyists, and journalists of both persuasions began to sit down with one another to figure out what this new beast would look like and how it could best be turned to American and industry advantage.

What happened next was a failure of imagination. Most of the high-level policy makers and lobbyists, and most of the reporters they spoke with, were completely innocent of the Internet and only slightly more conversant with computers. For some, computers were infuriating boxes that sat on their secretaries' desks, and could be operated only by people young enough to know how to program a VCR. For others, computers were wonderful automatic typewriters and calculators that ran word processing and spreadsheet software, and perhaps a virtual solitaire game as well. In 1992, after all, only about five million people were connected to the Internet.

In any event, the dominant early model of the Information Super-highway-to-be was some fantasy digital network that would provide Americans everywhere with access to five hundred television channels, 480 or so of which would allow them to view endless variations of pretty much the same programs they were already watching. The other channels might be "interactive": these were commonly envisioned as next-generation home shopping channels that would permit one to engage in one-stop impulse purchasing merely by pressing a few buttons on the remote control.

With their imaginations thus constrained, well-meaning policy makers fell into an understandable fallacy. If America were to retain (or regain) economic world dominance through the deployment of this Information Superhighway, the infrastructure would need to be built and funded by American private industry, who were unlikely to invest in it unless it looked likely to be profitable. Profitability would require a large potential customer base seeking to buy the things the Information Superhighway could offer them and the equipment and service required to use it. But consumers weren't likely to spend their dollars on five hundred television channels, and a newfangled sort of computer-television-box to watch them with, unless there were shows playing on the channels. So a first, and absolutely necessary, step to promoting the new technological and economic miracle was to find a way to induce the private sector to develop content for the new medium in sufficient quantity to make it attractive to potential subscribers, equipment manufacturers, and Information Superhighway subscription services.

Shortly after President Clinton's inauguration, the White House rechristened the clichéd Information Superhighway as the more bureaucratic "National Information Infrastructure" and appointed an "Information Infrastructure Task Force" to formulate government policy related to the whatever-it-was. The task force split itself into committees and working groups, and appointed advisory bodies and councils from the private sector.[1] Content issues were delegated to the Information Policy Committee, which appointed a Working Group on Intellectual Property chaired by Patent Commissioner Bruce Lehman. Lehman had represented the computer software industry on copyright issues before his appointment to the Patent Office; his senior staff included former copyright lobbyists for the computer and music recording industries. They maintained extensive informal communication with private-sector copyright lobbyists as they geared up to formulate administration copyright policy. The actual membership of the working group was drawn from government agencies and departments across the executive branch. Members complained privately, however, that they were figureheads: all decisions were made and all documents were drafted by the commissioner and his senior staff without any consultation.

In November of 1993, the Lehman Working Group held a public

hearing for the purpose of getting on the record what it was that current market leaders in the information and entertainment industries wanted— and didn't want—if they were to invest in the National Information Infra- structure.[2] What most of them said they wanted, indeed needed, was exten- sive control of all uses of their works and minimal government interfer- ence.[3] To all appearances, the Working Group staff then set out to secure it for them.

In July 1994, the Lehman Working Group issued a draft "Green Paper" report, containing its preliminary analysis of copyright issues affecting and affected by the Information Infrastructure, and its suggestions for copyright revision.[4] Many of its suggestions echoed those made by industry repre- sentatives in the public hearing. The draft report recommended what it characterized as minor clarifications of well-settled principles, and modest alterations to better secure copyright owners' control over works they pro- duce. The minor changes it recommended, however, appeared to many interested observers to attempt a radical recalibration of the intellectual property balance.

The Green Paper predicated its legal analysis on the assertion that one reproduces a work every time one reads it into a computer's random-access memory. Although the report cited no authority for its position, in fact a handful of cases in the early 1990s had considered loading software into random-access memory to create an actionable copy.[5] What may have been the watershed moment in the transition from an incentive model of copy- right to a control model came when a customer service manager for a com- puter company named MAI Systems quit his job and went to work for a business that maintained and repaired computer systems designed by other companies, including his original employer. MAI sued him and his new employer on a slew of different grounds. The judge apparently decided that this guy was scum, and he handed down one of those unfortunate opin- ions where the plaintiff prevails on every single claim and the defendant's every argument is wrong.[6] To get to the conclusion that the plaintiff was entitled to an injunction for willful copyright infringement, though, the court had to get past the fact that turning on someone's computer to ser- vice it would not normally be seen as infringing the copyright in the soft- ware. So, the court held that every time the employee or his new business turned on a customer's computer, the operating system software was loaded into random-access memory, which created an unauthorized copy.

As the Lehman Working Group put the finishing touches on its Green

Paper, a couple of other courts adopted the MAI court's holding in cases involving competing computer service businesses.[7] If every time something is loaded into random-access memory without the copyright owner's express permission, an actionable copy is made, that analysis could apply to text files, or digital music files, or any other file in digital form. So, we have this crazy but brilliant theory under which every unlicensed use of any work in digital form is potentially an infringement. For all works encoded in digital form, any act of reading or viewing the work would require the use of a computer (or a digital processor in a CD, digital audio or digital video player), and would, under this interpretation, involve an actionable reproduction. The Lehman Working Group urged the view that that copyright does, and should, assure the right to control each of those reproductions to the copyright owner.[8]

The next issue that the Green Paper addressed related to *transmissions* of copies of protected works. There, the Green Paper found the state of the law regarding copyright owners' control to be less than clear. The statute assimilated transmissions to performances, and gave copyright owners the exclusive right to authorize transmissions that resulted in public performances or displays, but no rights over transmissions that resulted in only private performances or displays. (Singing Metallica's hits to your friends or playing your Metallica CD over the telephone is a private performance and poses no copyright problems.) Most transmissions, the Working Group insisted, should be deemed public performances or displays. If one-to-one transmissions of works were considered to be private performances, extant copyright law would exclude them from the copyright owner's control, even though such transmissions might substitute for the purchase of copies. The Green Paper therefore recommended amending the law to enhance copyright holders' legal rights to control transmissions of their works. The Lehman Working Group suggested that instead of, or in addition to, considering transmissions to be performances, the law should treat them as distributions of copies, thus plugging the potential loophole.[9]

In addition, the Working Group complained, "if a transaction by which a user obtains a 'copy' of a work is characterized as a 'distribution,' then, under the current law, the user may be entitled to make a like distribution without the copyright owner's permission (and without liability for infringment)."[10] That was because the first sale doctrine allowed the owner of a lawfully made copy to sell, loan, rent, or otherwise pass that copy along. The Working Group therefore suggested that the statute be amended to provide that the first sale doctrine not apply to any transmission. Noting the difficulty of enforcing copyright rights against individual consumers, the Lehman Working Group endorsed copyright owners' use of copy-protection technology to prevent individuals from committing infringement. Because technology can be hacked, however, the Working Group concluded that the law should be amended to prohibit any circumvention of anticopying systems, and forbid the creation or sale of any device or service intended to defeat such systems. Instead of merely making unauthorized reproduction illegal, the proposal sought to make it as close to impossible as the law could bring it.

The release of the Green Paper inspired great enthusiasm among the motion picture, recording, and computer software industries, and dismay among libraries, composers, writers, online service providers like America Online® and Compuserve®, and the makers of consumer electronic devices and computer hardware. The Lehman Working Group held public hearings on the Green Paper, and made the hearing transcripts available for a brief period over the Internet. They solicited public comment via email. They put together a not-so-informal multilateral negotiation among representatives of copyright owners and representatives of schools and libraries to try to reach an agreement on the scope of fair use in the digital environment. Commissioner Lehman would later tell Congress that there had never been a more open process than the Working Group's consideration of the issues before it.[11]

At the same time, Commissioner Lehman demonstrated a firm idea of what it was the Working Group would eventually conclude, and a willingness to manipulate the process to cause the record to better support the recommendations he expected to reach. The official members of the Lehman Working Group were kept in the dark about the conclusions they would be reported to have reached until the last minute. When a large number of comments on the Green Paper turned out to be negative, Commissioner Lehman insisted that the naysayers didn't understand what they were talking about.

The Lehman Working Group predicated its arguments about the need for enhanced copyright protection in the context of the National Information Infrastructure (NII) on the assertion that, unless copyright owners were given expansive rights over the material they made available, no material would be made available. The NII was depicted as a collection of empty pipes, waiting to be filled with content. By 1994, the only explanation for that depiction was the one that turned out to be true: most of the people involved in formulating the substance of the Lehman Working Group Green Paper were unacquainted with the Internet, and had no opportunity to compare their imaginary NII of the future with the flourishing Internet that was already out there. The Lehman Working Group continued to view its charge as defining rules that would supply sufficient incentives to inspire the private sector to build a new global information infrastructure so that they could fill it with proprietary content. They failed to see the digital network already in use that grew larger every day.

The Working Group's final report, first promised for the early spring of 1995, was delayed until May, until June, and finally until September. The Working Group staffers had received written and e-mailed comments from 150 different people and organizations, listened to five days of public testimony, and had innumerable meetings with private groups. The Working Group's response to all of the public comments turned out to be largely stylistic. The rhetoric of the final report was more balanced than the language of the Green Paper. The substantive recommendations, though, were essentially unchanged.

The final report was not the florid endorsement of enhanced copyright protection that its predecessor draft report was. The Green Paper's approach had been twofold: the draft contained revisionary interpretations of current law that enhanced copyright owners' control over their works, and suggestions for further fortifying that control. The Working Group's White Paper spent most of its ink on the revisionary interpretation leg of the strategy: it asserted that most of the enhanced protection copyright owners might want was *already available* under current law, at least so long as that law was properly interpreted, and it contained a long exegesis of what the properly interpreted copyright law should be read to provide.[12] The difference was largely one of style rather than substance, as the White Paper ended up adopting most of the recommendations tentatively included in the Green Paper, but instead of characterizing them as desirable amendments, it depicted them as well-settled and uncontroversial interpretations of the current law.

Thus, the White Paper concluded that so long as the meaning of the current copyright law, and the way that law should be read to apply to new technology, were clarified, then the current law was "fundamentally adequate and effective."[13] The White Paper, therefore, took on the task of interpreting current law to resolve any ambiguities that might arise in the context of new technology. Using the tools that good lawyers use when engaged in such tasks,[14] the White Paper carefully explained that just about every ambiguity one could imagine, properly understood, should under the best view of current law be resolved in favor of the copyright holder.

That approach enabled the authors of the White Paper to come to conclusions that would strike anybody but a copyright lawyer as extravagant. Most notably, since any use of a computer to view, read, reread, hear, or otherwise experience a work in digital form would require reproducing that work in a computer's memory, and since the copyright statute gives the copyright holder exclusive control over reproductions,[15] everybody would need to have either a statutory privilege or the copyright holder's permission to view, read, reread, hear, or otherwise experience a digital work, each time she did so.[16] The purchaser of an e-book would need permission each time she read any part of that e-book; the owner of a compact disc would need a license every time she listened to the music on the disc. Someone catching sight of an image posted on the World Wide Web would need the permission of the owner of the copyright in that image (who might not be the person who posted the image) each time it appeared on her computer screen. Not only individuals, but their Internet service providers and the proprietors of any computers that assisted in the transfer of files were, and should be, liable for copyright infringement in these cases, regardless of whether they knew someone's intellectual property rights were being invaded, or even what content was moving through their equipment. Once it was understood that current copyright law in fact so provided, the White Paper argued, there was little need to amend it to make express provision for new technology; only minor adjustments would be required. Thus, the White Paper neatly avoided addressing the policy question of whether copyright *should* be defined in terms that convert individual users' reading of files into potentially infringing acts, by insisting that Congress chose to set it up this way when it enacted the current law in 1976.

The Lehman Working Group's White Paper suggested that only modest improvements would be necessary to secure to copyright owners the expansive rights Congress had granted them twenty years earlier. Of a number of purportedly minor amendments, two were key. First, the Working Group repeated its earlier recommendation in the Green Paper that Congress amend the statute to recognize that unauthorized transmissions violate the copyright owner's distribution right as well as the reproduction, performance, and display rights. (There was no need, the White Paper assured its readers, to amend the first sale doctrine since it was clear that it had no application to transmissions.) Second, the Working Group recommended an amendment to prohibit any device or service intended to circumvent copyright owners' technological protection mechanisms.[17]

Copyright advocacy has evolved its own tactical conventions over the years. The arguments that were deployed in this effort didn't look very different from the shape of very similar arguments that were raised in the 1980s, when the gods invented personal computers; or in the 1970s, when they invented videocassette recorders; or the 1960s, when they invented cable television; or the 1920s, when they invented commercial broadcasting and talkies. Arguing that Congress already considered a question, and resolved it in one's favor then, is a common tactic in the history of copyright lobbying, because it bypasses the problem of persuading Congress to consider the question and resolve it in one's favor today.[18] Sometimes it works; other times it fails. In evaluating these claims, it is always useful to inject a note of realism: would Congress have adopted such-and-such language if it believed at the time the legislation was enacted that this language would be interpreted to mean what is now being claimed? Whether a platonic Congress would have made that call or not, in view of what we now know about how the world has evolved, is that choice a good one, in policy terms? People are going to differ on the answers to both of these questions, but at least their differences are on the table; we aren't making information policy by sleight of hand.

The Lehman Working Group's characterization of extant law was dubious, and the majority of copyright scholars criticized it as skewed. [19] Even if it were not, however, its endorsement of what it presented as well-settled law deserves examination. If a bargain between the public and the authors and producers of copyrighted works were negotiated at arm's length and drafted up today, it might include a reproduction right, but it surely wouldn't include a "reading" right. It might include a performance right but not a "listening" right; it might have a display right, but it wouldn't have a "viewing" right. From the public's vantage point, the fact that copyright owners are now in a position to claim exclusive "reading," "listening," and "viewing" rights is an accident of drafting: when Congress awarded authors an exclusive reproduction right, it did not then mean what it may mean today.

NOTES

1. The president's task force was charged to come up with "comprehensive telecommunications and information policies aimed at articulating and implementing the administration's vision for the NII." *See* 58 Fed. Reg. 53917 (October 19, 1993). With the exception of the Working Group on Intellectual Property, however, the various working groups issued documents suggesting, in essence, that there was no need for precipitous government action. Thus, the task force's ultimate position on privacy was that privacy was a good thing, and proprietors of databases collecting private information should be reminded that members of the public preferred respect for privacy over the alternative. *See* Information Infrastructure Task Force Information Policy Committee Privacy Working Group, *Privacy and the Information Infrastructure: Principles for Providing and Using Personal Information* (June 6, 1995), URL: <http://www.iitf.nist.gov/ipc/ipc/ipc-pubs/niiprivprin_final.html>; National Telecommunications and Information Administration, *Privacy and the NII: Safeguarding Telecommunications-Related Personal Information* (1995), available at URL: <http://www.nita.doc.gov/ntiahome/privwhitepaper.html>. The task force's ultimate position on technical standards came down to an assertion that interoperability was good, and private industry, acting in accord with private firms' business plans, might choose to adopt interoperable technology to some degree. *See, e.g., IITF Committee on Applications and Technology Working Group on Technology Policy Charter,* URL: <http://nii.nist.gov/ cat/tp/tpwg_charter.html>. Most documents emanating from the IITF cautioned against undue haste, suggesting that the value of permitting the private sector to thrash things out and work toward consensus could not be overemphasized.

2. *See* United States Department of Commerce U. S. Patent & Trademark Office, National Information Infrastructure Task Force Working Group on Intellectual Property, *Public Hearing on Intellectual Property Issues Involved in the National Information Infrastructure Initiative* (Thursday, November 18, 1993); *see also Request for Comments on Intellectual Property Issues Involved in the National Information Infrastructure Initiative,* 58 Fed. Reg. 53917 (October 19, 1993).

3. *See, e.g.,* United States Department of Commerce U. S. Patent & Trademark Office, *National Information Infrastructure Task Force Working Group on Intellectual Property, Public Hearing on Intellectual Property Issues Involved in the National Information Infrastructure Initiative 14* (Testimony of Steven J. Metalitz for Information Industry Association); ibid. at 201 (Testimony of Mark Traphagen for Software Publishers Association).

4. Information Infrastructure Task Force, *Intellectual Property and the National Information Infrastructure: A Preliminary Draft of the Report of the Working Group on Intellectual Property Rights* (1994) [Hereinafter Lehman Working Group Green Paper].

5. *See Mai Systems Corp.* v. *Peak Computer, Inc.,* 991 F.2d 511 (9th Cir. 1993); *Triad*

Systems Corp. v. *Southeastern Express Co.*, 1994 U.S. Dist. LEXIS 5390 (N.D. Cal. 1994); *Advanced Computer Services* v. *MAI Systems Corp.*, 845 F. Supp. 356 (E.D.Va 1994).

6. See *Mai Systems* v. *Peak Computer*, 1992 US Dist. LEXIS 21829 (C.D. Cal. 1992), *aff'd*, 991 F.2d 511 (9th Cir. 1993).

7. See *Triad Systems Corp.* v. *Southeastern Express*, 31 U.S.P.Q. 2d (BNA) 1239 (N.D. Cal. 1994); *Advanced Computer Services* v. *MAI Systems Corp.*, 854 F. Supp. 356 (E.D. Va 1994). Congress overruled this reading of the law, as applied to computer maintenance and repair services, in 1998. See Digital Millennium Copyright Act, P.L. 105-304, Title III, § 302, 112 Stat. 2887 (1998) (codified at 17 U.S.C. § 117(c)).

8. See Lehman Working Group Green Paper, above at note 4, at 35–37.

9. The Lehman Working Group recommended that an amendment "reflect that copies of a work can be distributed to the public by transmission, and such transmissions fall within the exclusive distribution right of the copyright owner." Lehman Working Group Green Paper, above at note 4, at 121. This recommendation drew the ire of composers, who typically retain control over music public performance rights. Composers' performing rights societies were looking forward to collecting performance royalties for digital transmissions and weren't at all happy to see the potential income transferred to music publishers, who typically control the exercise of distribution rights.

10. See Lehman working Group Green Paper, above at note 4, at 39.

11. See NII Copyright Protection Act of 1995: *Joint Hearing on H.R. 2441 and S. 1284 Before the Subcommittee on Courts and Intellectual Property of the House Judiciary Committee and the Senate Judiciary Committee,* 104th Cong., 1st sess. (November 15, 1995) (testimony of Bruce Lehman, Commissioner of Patents):

> Since I've been in this government job, I've had to realize, and go through what all of you have to go through. And that is, it's simply humanly impossible to please everybody in a society of 250 million people. It's hard to please 500,000 constituents in a congressional district. It's impossible to please 250 million people. I think we did the best job we could. We listened to everybody. There's never been a more open process than this.

12. See Information Infrastructure Task Force, *Intellectual Property and the National Information Infrastructure: The Report of the Working Group on Intellectual Property Rights* 19–130 (1995) [hereinafter White Paper].

13. White Paper, above at note 12, at 212.

14. I am both a lawyer and a law professor. These tools are my stock in trade, and I make my living teaching them to my students. I have no quarrel with lawyers' tools, used responsibly. Because their primary purpose is to make arguments more persuasive, however, some skepticism may be appropriate. In particular, it is useful to recognize the work that lawyers' tools are doing. When convenient for its argu-

ment, for example, the White Paper relied on the expressed intent of congressional committees to buttress its analysis of current copyright law, *see, e.g.,* White Paper, above at note 12, at 226; when express language in the congressional Committee Reports was less convenient, the White Paper ignored it, *see, e.g.,* ibid. at 65, or characterized it as irrelevant, *see* ibid. at 72 note 226. Similarly, the report was highly selective in its citation of case authority. Some of the more egregious examples are detailed in James Boyle, *Overregulating the Internet,* Washington Times, November 14, 1995, at A17, and Pamela Samuelson, *The Copyright Grab,* Wired, January, 1996, at 137–38.

15. 17 U.S.C.§ 106(1) (1994):

> . . .the owner of copyright . . . has the exclusive right to do or authorize any of the following:
> (1) to reproduce the copyrighted work in copies or phonorecords

"Copies" are defined in 17 U.S.C. § 101 as
> material objects . . . in which a work is fixed by any method now known or later developed, and from which the work can be perceived, reproduced, or otherwise communicated, either directly or with the aid of a machine or device.

"Fixed" is also defined in section 101:
> A work is "fixed" in a tangible medium of expression when its embodiment in a copy or a phonorecord . . . is sufficiently permanent or stable to permit it to be perceived, reproduced or otherwise communicated for a period of more than transitory duration. . . .

16. White Paper, above at note 12, at 64–66. This particular piece of revisionist interpretation is irresponsible. The legislative materials accompanying the 1976 Copyright Act make it clear that Congress intended to assimilate the appearance of a work (or portions of a work) in a computer's random-access memory to unfixed, evanescent images rather than "copies." *See* H.R. Rep. No. 1476, 94th Cong., 2d sess. 52–53, 62 (1976); Jessica Litman, *The Exclusive Right to Read,* 13 Cardozo Arts & Entertainment Law Journal 29 (1994); Pamela Samuelson, *Legally Speaking: The NII Intellectual Property Report,* 37 Communications of the ACM (December 1994): 12.

17. White Paper, above at note 12, at 230–34. The Working Group dismissed any objection predicated on fair use:

> It has been suggested that the prohibition is incompatible with fair use. First, the fair use doctrine does not require a copyright owner to allow or to facilitate unauthorized access or use of a work. Otherwise, copyright owners could not withhold works from publication; movie theatres could

not charge admission or prevent audio or video recording; museums could not require entry fees or prohibit the taking of photographs. Indeed, if the provision of access and the ability to make fair use of copyrighted works were required of copyright owners—or an affirmative right of the public—even passwords for access to computer databases would be considered illegal.

Ibid. at 231.

18. *See* Jessica Litman, *Copyright Legislation and Technological Change*, 78 Oregon Law Review 275, 353–54 (1989); *see, e.g., Home Video Recording: Hearings Before the Senate Judiciary Committee*, 99th Cong., 2d sess. 3 (1987) (testimony of Jack Valenti, Motion Picture Association of America); ibid. at 84–94 (statement of Charlie Ferris, Home Recording Rights Coalition); *Home Audio Recording Act: Hearing on S. 1739 before the Senate Committee on the Judiciary*, 99th Cong., 1st and 2d sess. (1986).

19. The crux of the criticism was that the Working Group had exaggerated the scope of copyright owners' rights while minimizing users' rights and privileges, and ignoring or mischaracterizing judicial opinions that undermined the Working Group's analysis. *See, e.g.,* James Boyle, *Shamans, Software, and Spleens: Law and the Construction of the Information Society* 135–39 (Harvard University Press, 1996); Leslie A. Kurtz, *Copyright and the National Information Infrastructure in the United States,* 18 European Intelligence Prop. Review 120 (1996); Pamela Samuelson, *The Copyright Grab,* Wired 4.01 (January 1996): 134, 137; Diane Leenheer Zimmerman, *Copyright in Cyberspace: Don't Throw Out the Public Interest with the Bath Water,* 1994 Annual Survey of American Law 403.

SEVEN

CREATION AND INCENTIVES

T HE WHITE PAPER ARGUED THAT its proposed enhancement of copyright owner's rights was without question in the public interest, because it was a necessary first step in the creation of the Information Superhighway. This was the central justification for further enhancing the rights in the copyright bundle: without strong copyright protection, there would be no National Information Infrastructure. The public might believe that what it wanted was unfettered access to copyrighted works in return for reasonable royalty payments to authors, but, if we let the public set the freight charges, we would risk underproduction of freight. If authors and publishers could not reliably control their works, they would decline to make them available at all. The working group put it this way:

> Thus, the full potential of the NII will not be realized if the education, information and entertainment products protected by intellectual property laws are not protected effectively when disseminated via the NII. Creators and other owners of intellectual property rights will not be willing to put their interests at risk if appropriate systems—both in the U.S. and internationally—are not in place to permit them to set and enforce the terms and conditions under which their works are made available in the NII environment. Likewise, the public will not use the services available on the NII and generate the market necessary for its success unless a wide variety of works are available under equitable and reasonable terms and conditions, and the integrity of those works is assured. All the computers, telephones, fax machines, scanners, cameras, keyboards, televisions, monitors, printers, switches, routers, wires, cables, networks and satellites in the world will not create a successful NII, if there is no *content*. What will drive the NII is the content moving through it.[2]

If the public wished an NII, the argument went, it must offer strong copyright protection as a bribe to those it hoped to persuade to create enough stuff to make an NII worthwhile. Relying on a hope that if the public only built the infrastructure, the information to travel it would come was said to be naive; of course the owners of protectible works would refuse to permit those works to be exploited unless their ownership rights were secure.

To the extent that authors were willing to make content available on the Internet under existing law, the argument continued, it was because the material was so low in quality as to have little value except to its author. We would need to ensure that the authors of the future had control over the uses of their creations, so that they would feel secure in distributing their works over the Information Infrastructure—that's why so much of the content that was already there was material that nobody would want to steal.[3]

Only a few years later, that assertion seems incredible. Well before the enactment of the Digital Millennium Copyright Act, there was plenty of professionally created and formatted commercial content out there on the World Wide Web. The *New York Times*, the *Washington Post*, and the *Wall Street Journal* launched hypertext versions of their newspapers.[4] CNN and ABC news both opened Web sites that allowed browsers to read material that had been broadcast earlier.[5] *Wired* magazine and c|net did them one better with news sites on the Web that were updated continuously.[6] It still isn't clear to me whether all these businesses will end up making money from their sites, but it seems evident that they think there's a good possibility that they will figure out a way to do so.[7] The fact that a wealth of commercial content flooded the Web, even as the Lehman Working Group insisted that commercial content producers would withhold their material, suggests that the argument was based on flawed assumptions. Still, the fact that there were some daring entrepreneurs who were willing to take big risks in the interest of gaining market share, on the theory they would worry about making a profit later, is not necessarily news. That's our history: it happened with radio, television, and cable television; why not the Internet? What's more damaging to the Lehman Working Group's account is the extraordinary variety and innovativeness of the expression available over the Net that isn't professionally created and formatted commercial content, but that explores some of the new possibilities of the medium.

Before the deployment of the World Wide Web, the Internet contained a wealth of useful and entertaining material. Individuals posted files containing interesting information, data, software, or text. Gopher software enabled others to search the Internet for those files and retrieve them. Usenet news, a free-floating collection of more than twenty thousand subject-specific online discussion groups, offered virtual conversation on any imaginable topic. A second-year law student put together a six-part FAQ (collection of frequently asked questions)[8] about copyright law that was superior to all study aids I've seen and to most of the copyright treatises.[9] I recommend it to my students—and it's free. A software design professor I ran into amused himself for a time by writing reviews of classic science-fiction books and posting them to Usenet news.[10] Now, I would buy a book of these reviews just to have it on my shelf. They are elegantly written, perceptive, clever, worth reading in their own right. I'm embarrassed to admit that early in our electronic acquaintance, I suggested that he write such reviews professionally. Silly me—after all, he was a software design professor who was doing this for fun.

These are just two examples of work that, in my judgment, is of better quality than I already pay cash for in stores. In addition to that kind of material, there is the whole-is-greater-than-the-sum-of-its-parts stuff—the works that have enormous value precisely *because* they're collaborative. As a middle-aged parent, I feel as if I have acquired a lot of expertise on the usefulness of many of the sources of "How-to-be-a-parent" advice out there. All my friends gave me their favorite parenting books, and I've spent a lot of time in the childcare sections of a large number of bookstores. Perhaps the most useful collection of parenting advice I've ever run into, though, is a series of assemblages, without evaluative editorial comment, of wisdom on any parenting topic you could name from subscribers to the Usenet newsgroup misc.kids.[11] It isn't that any of the individual posters to misc.kids is so wise a parent, as that the online dialogue among many parents (and some of their children) allows a great deal of common wisdom to emerge.

Usenet news and gopher services had undeniably clunky interfaces, and their audiences were accordingly small. The World Wide Web enabled the transformation of the Internet into a mass medium. The siren call of e-commerce should not obscure the fact that much of the most compelling content available on the Web today was originally created by volunteers who made it freely available. Yahoo!® is rated the second most popular site on the Web by Neilsen/Netratings,[12] with reported net revenues of $270,116,000 for the second quarter of 2000. The service originated with a directory created in 1994 by two Stanford graduate students, who posted it on Stanford University's Web server. Traffic was overwhelming, and the following year Yahoo! moved to a commercial Web server.[13] The Internet Movie Database (IMDB) at <www.imdb.com> is a highly rated (and highly addictive) advertising-supported Web site that offers comprehensive information on movies, video, and television shows. It began in 1990 as lists of FAQs assembled through collaboration among movie fans and posted to the Usenet news group rec.arts.movies. The individual who went on to found the Web site created a computer program that permitted the lists to be searched. Volunteers created enhanced search software and added items and categories to the database. In 1993, the database was posted on the Web, again hosted on a university server. In 1996, IMDB incorporated and began to sell advertising. Two years later, Amazon.com saw an opportunity to market videotapes, and purchased the company.[14]

Both of these applications, like much of the content on the Internet, began as someone's hobby before evolving into significant businesses, and were initially made freely available without any notion of an ultimate business plan. Napster is a system that allows individual Internet users to search one another's computers for music files, and to copy music files directly from other people's hard drives. Napster began when a college freshman designed the software and posted a beta version on the Internet for free downloading. The application's popularity was nearly instantaneous, and its creator dropped out of college to pursue the project full time.[15] It accumulated forty million subscribers in less than a year. Napster itself provides no content. Its forty million subscribers sign on to take advantage of its software, which permits them to share content with each other. Indeed the World Wide Web itself was developed to enable high energy physicists to share information.[16] That design was and continues to be freely available to anyone with an Internet connection. Most fundamentally, lots of people continue to make material available on the Internet because they enjoy sharing it. The Internet makes collaboration and sharing easy.[17]

The fact that authors are willing to create new works in the absence of strong copyright protection should hardly be surprising. Of course many authors write much of what they write because they will get paid for it. If payment were the most important consideration, though, most of them would probably not write anything at all—they'd be doing something more remunerative with their talents and their time. We have always needed copyright, rather, because publishers and distributors publish and distribute to make money. We have needed copyright as an incentive to bribe publishers to invest in finding the authors, and their works, and printing, reprinting, publishing, and vending that work to end users.

But one of the miracles of modern technology is that publishing over a digital network needn't be expensive. The ease of copying that poses the threat to copyright also makes it possible for works to be widely distributed at very low cost. People who have created, or wish to create, works that for one reason or another would not be likely to find a conventional publisher are able to make those works available very cheaply via the Internet, and less incentive is needed to inspire such distributions, since the cost and trouble involved in distributing is nominal.

© © ©

Imagine for a moment that some upstart revolutionary proposed that we eliminate all intellectual property protection for fashion design. No longer could a designer secure federal copyright protection for the cut of a dress or the sleeve of a blouse. Unscrupulous mass-marketers could run off thousands of knockoff copies of any designer's evening ensemble, and flood the marketplace with cheap imitations of haute couture. In the short run, perhaps, clothing prices would come down as legitimate designers tried to meet the prices of their freeriding competitors. In the long run, though, as we know all too well, the diminution in the incentives for designing new fashions would take its toll. Designers would still wish to design, at least initially, but clothing manufacturers with no exclusive rights to rely on would be reluctant to make the investment involved in manufacturing those designs and distributing them to the public. The dynamic American fashion industry would wither, and its most talented designers would forsake clothing design for some more remunerative calling like litigation. All of us would be forced either to wear last year's garments year in and year out, or to import our clothing from abroad.

Or, perhaps, imagine that Congress suddenly repealed federal intellectual-property protection for food creations. Recipes would become common property. Downscale restaurants could freely recreate the signature chocolate desserts of their upscale sisters. Uncle Ben's® would market Minute® Risotto (*microwavable!*); the *Ladies' Home Journal* would reprint recipes it had stolen from *Gourmet* magazine. Great chefs would be unable to find book publishers willing to buy their cookbooks. Then, expensive gourmet restaurants would reduce their prices to meet the prices of the competition; soon they would either close or fire their chefs to cut costs; promising young cooks would either move to Europe or get a day job (perhaps the law) and cook only on weekends. Ultimately, we would all be stuck eating Uncle Ben's Minute Risotto® (*eleven yummy flavors!!*) for every meal.

But, you've heard all of this before. It's the same argument motion picture producers make about why we needed to extend the duration of copyright protection another twenty years; the same argument software publishers make about what will happen if we permit other software publishers to decompile and reverse-engineer their software products; the same argument database proprietors make about the huge social cost of a failure to protect their rights in their data. Perhaps the most important reason why we have intellectual property protection is our conclusion that incentives are required to spur the creation and dissemination of a sufficient number and variety of intellectual creations like films, software, databases, fashions, and food.

Of course, we don't give copyright protection to fashions or food.[18] We never have.

©   ©   ©

The link between production and dissemination of valuable, protectible works and the degree of available intellectual property protection is equivocal. History teaches that whenever we have discovered or enacted a copyright exception, an industry has grown up within its shelter. Player piano rolls became ubiquitous after courts ruled that they did not infringe the copyright in the underlying musical compositions;[19] phonograph records superseded both piano rolls and sheet music with the aid of the compulsory license for mechanical reproductions;[20] the jukebox industry arose to take advantage of the copyright exemption accorded to "the reproduction or rendition of a musical composition by or upon coin-operated machines."[21] Composers continued to write music and found ways to exploit these new media for their works.

The videotape rental business swept the nation shielded from copyright liability by the first sale doctrine.[22] The motion picture industry predicted that if Congress failed to rush in to correct the problems posed by the invention and marketing of the videocassette recorder, American television would slowly be destroyed, and American motion picture production would sustain grave injury.[23] In 1982, Howard Wayne Oliver, Executive Secretary of the American Federation of Television and Radio Artists (AFTRA), told a House subcommittee:

> Unless we do something to ensure that the creators of the material are not exploited by the electronics revolution, that same revolution which will make it possible for almost every household to have an audio and video

recorder will surely undermine, cripple, and eventually wash away the very industries on which it feeds and which provide employment for thousands of our citizens.[24]

Notwithstanding all of the gloom and doom, however, both the motion picture and television industries discovered that the videocassette recorder generated new markets for prerecorded versions of their material.

Cable television began spreading across America with the aid of a copyright exemption;[25] it eclipsed broadcast television while sheltered by the cable compulsory license.[26] Yet, there is no dearth of television programming; indeed, as recently as the early 1990s, the popular media image of the "Information Superhighway" included five hundred television channels to accommodate it all.

Even an erroneous assumption of copyright immunity can stimulate a nascent industry. The commercial photocopy shop prospered in part because of the university course-pack business[27] made possible by a supposed fair use privilege.[28] Commercial and noncommercial subscriptions to services providing access to the Internet increased geometrically in the early 1990s, when much of the activity on the net seemed to take place on the (false) assumption that any material on the Internet was free from copyright unless expressly declared to be otherwise. Nonetheless, there were scores of electronic magazines and news services developed specifically for electronic distribution, even then, and many commercial publishers had begun to release their works over the Internet despite the absence of effective coercive means of protection.

Without regard to legal rules, there is already a wealth of incentives that seem to suffice for the production and distribution of a great deal of authorship over the Internet. I find some of that authorship to be of extraordinary quality. Lots of it I would pay cash for in stores if I could find it in stores. That suggests that even without any improvement in the incentives for authors or the control authors have over their works, there will be many interesting things available over the Information Infrastructure—but that those things may not come to us from the entities who have been supplying content to the conventional media. This last fact, while of crucial importance to the folks who have been supplying content to the conventional media, is not really a problem for the rest of us. Indeed, it may be a positive good from our perspective. The new players who are entering the game now are exploring the possibilities and idiosyncracies of the new digital medium and inventing new sorts of copyrightable authorship leading to works not currently available in stores.

The narrow focus on threats to copyright owners' control of their works can lose sight of the potential value, to authors as well as to readers, of a digital network permitting high-speed transmission of a variety of material with few constraints. That network can both encourage creation and dissemination by reducing the costs associated with it, and can enhance the value of material made available over the network because of the ease with which it can be linked to other valuable material.

The most exciting possibilities offered by networked digital technology aren't its potential to allow the instant distribution of books, music, and movies, but, rather, its capacity to generate new classes of *un*books, *un*music, and *un*movies. If we try to restructure this market to impose the pattern that has worked so well for the purveyors of current books, music, and movies, we risk driving the new unbooks out. That would be a terrible loss.

NOTES

1. Portions of this chapter are adapted from two previously published articles: *The Exclusive Right to Read*, 13 Cardozo Arts & Entertainment Law Journal 29 (1994), and *Copyright Noncompliance (or Why We Can't "Just Say Yes" to Licensing)*, in *Symposium: The Culture and Economics of Participation in an International Intellectual Property Regime*, 1-2 New York University Journal of International Law and Politics 29 (1997).

2. Information Infrastructure Task Force, *Intellectual Property and the National Information Infrastructure: The Report of the Working Group on Intellectual Property Rights* 10–11 (1995).

3. *See, e.g., Copyright Protection on the Internet: Hearing Before the Courts and Intellectual Property Subcommittee of the House Committee on the Judiciary*, 104th Cong., 2d sess. (February 7, 1996) (testimony of Barbara A. Munder, McGraw Hill Co., for the Information Industry Association); *see also* Bruce A. Lehman, *Copyright Fair Use and the National Information Infrastructure* (address delivered at George Mason University, February 23, 1996).

4. *See* URL: <http://www.nytimes.com>; URL: <http://www.washingtonpost. com/>; URL: <http://interactive.wsj.com/>. *See also, e.g.,* URL: <http:// www.epicurious. com> (*Gourmet* and *Bon Appetit* magazines).

5. *See* URL: <http://www.cnn.com>; URL: <http://www.abcnews.com>; *see also* URL: <http://www.npr.org> (National Public Radio).

6. *See* URL: <http://www.wired.com>; URL: <http://www.news.com>.

7. Many Web sites sell advertising, although the value of (and appropriate

price for) Web advertising is still unclear. Other sites sell subscriptions, *see, e.g.,* URL: <http://interactive.wsj.com/subinfo.html> (Wall Street Journal).

8. "FAQ" stands for "answers to Frequently Asked Questions" and is a common format for reference works disseminated through Usenet news or over the World Wide Web.

9. *See* Terry Carroll, *Copyright F.A.Q.,* URL: <http://www.tjc.com/copyright/>.

10. *See* Dani Zweig, *Belated Reviews,* URL: <http://sf.www.lysator.liu.se/sf_archive/sub/belated.html>. Dr. Zweig is the source of the turns of phrase used by the imaginary client in chapter 4. He has given up the joys of academia for a private-sector job in the software industry.

11. *See, e.g.,* URL: <http://www.familyweb.com/faqs/> (a collection of child-rearing and related reference material assembled from original contributions by misc.kids subscribers).

12. Neilsen/Netratings, *Netratings Top Properties, June 2000,* at URL: <http://209.249.142.27/nnpm/owa/NRpublicreports.toppropertiesmonthly>.

13. *See Yahoo Company History,* URL: <http://docs.yahoo.com/info/misc/history.html>.

14. *See* Internet Movie Database, *IMDB history,* URL: <http://us.imdb.com/Help/Oweek/history>.

15. *See* Napster | Company | About Us, URL: <http://www.napster.com/company/>.

16. *See* World Wide Web Consortium, *About the World Wide Web,* URL: <http://www.w3.org/WWW/>.

17. Another whole realm of content on the Internet is represented by works that explore the features of the new media in ways that lead to works of authorship that are different from conventional works in fundamental ways. Authors have only begun to exploit the ways that hypertext linking can transform the ways people write and the ways that they read. The variety of hypertext-enhanced compilations on the World Wide Web is mind-boggling. Hypertext fiction challenges conventional notions of plot progression. *See, e.g.,* Isabel Chang (aspergillum gently), URL: <http:// doxa.net/168/> (2000); Judd Morrisey, w.i.p., URL: <http://www.the-jewsdaughter.com/> (2000). Hypertext markup language makes possible new species of visual puns. Such puns are easy to find on the World Wide Web, but tend to be fleeting. One of my favorite examples was the mock Bob Dole for President Home Page, which once existed at URL: <http://www. dole96.org />, and was probably removed in response to a protest from the Dole Pineapple Company. The parody superimposed the candidate's image over the Dole Company's logo, and the slogan "the ripe man for the job!" The site included links to real and mock Web pages for other politicians and other fruits and vegetables.

18. *See, e.g.,* Malla A. Pollack, Note, *Copyright Protection for the Creative Chef, or How to Copyright a Cake: A Modest Proposal,* 12 Cardozo Law Review 1477 (1991);

Malla Pollack, *A Rose Is a Rose Is a Rose, but Is a Costume a Dress? An Alternative Solution in Whimsicality, Inc. v. Rubie's Costume Co.*, 41 Journal of the Copyright Society of the USA 1 (1993).

19. See *Kennedy* v. *McTammany*, 33 F. 584 (CC MA 1888); *White-Smith Music Publishing* v. *Apollo Co.*, 209 U.S. 1 (1908).

20. Copyright Act of March 4, 1909, § 1(e), 35 Stat. 1075. *See* U.S. Library of Congress, Second Supplementary Report of the Register of Copyrights on the General Revision of the U.S. Copyright Law: 1975 Revision Bill, ch. IX (1975).

21. Copyright Act of March 4, 1909, § 1(e), 35 Stat. 107. *See* U.S. Library of Congress, Second Supplementary Report of the Register of Copyrights on the General Revision of the U.S. Copyright Law: 1975 Revision Bill, ch. X (1975).

22. *See* 17 U.S.C. § 109. The first sale doctrine allows the owner of any lawful copy of most works to dispose of that copy as she pleases.

23. *See Video and Audio Home Taping: Hearing on S. 31 and S. 175 Before the Subcommittee on Patents, Trademarks and Copyrights of the Senate Committee on the Judiciary*, 98th Cong., 1st sess. 276–306 (1983) (testimony of Jack Valenti, Motion Picture Association of America); ibid. at 307–309 (testimony of Kay Peters, Screen Actors Guild); *Home Recording of Copyrighted Works: Hearings on H.R. 4783, H.R. 4794, H.R. 4808, H.R. 5250, H.R. 5488, and H.R. 5705 Before the Subcommittee on Courts, Civil Liberties and the Administration of Justice of the House Committee on the Judiciary*, 97th Cong., 2d sess. 4–16 (1982) (testimony of Jack Valenti, Motion Picture Association of America).

24. *Home Recording of Copyrighted Works: Hearings on H.R. 4783, H.R. 4794, H.R. 4808, H.R. 5250, H.R. 5488, and H.R. 5705 Before the Subcommittee on Courts, Civil Liberties and the Administration of Justice of the House Committee on the Judiciary*, 97th Cong., 2d sess. 142 (1982).

25. *See Teleprompter Corp.* v. *Columbia Broadcasting System*, 415 U.S. 394 (1974); *Fortnightly Corp.* v. *United Artists Television*, 392 U.S. 390 (1968).

26. *See* 17 U.S.C. § 111; Jessica Litman, *Copyright Legislation and Technological Change*, 68 Oregon Law Review 275, 342–46 (1989).

27. "Course packs" are photocopied collections of reading materials assigned for particular courses. Instructors frequently assemble course packs comprising journal articles and excerpts from published books to use in university courses in lieu of anthologies. Commercial photocopying services began in the 1980s to duplicate and bind course packs and then sell them to students.

28. See *Basic Books, Inc.* v. *Kinko's Graphics Corp.*, 758 F. Supp. 1522 (SDNY 1991); *Princeton University Press* v. *Michigan Document Services*, 1996 U.S. App. LEXIS 29132 (6th Cir. 1996) (en banc). The popularity of the course-pack services provided by commercial photocopy shops eventually enabled publishers to establish a lucrative course-pack photocopy licensing business. *See* ibid.

EIGHT

"JUST SAY YES
TO LICENSING!"[1]

"I'm *so* glad I'm a Beta."[2]

OST INDIVIDUAL END USERS DO not observe copyright rules in their daily behavior. The phenomenon is not new. It has captured so much recent attention because networked digital communications threaten and promise to revolutionize the way people interact with information and works of authorship in ways that make the behavior of individual end users far more crucial than it has been in the past. Our copyright laws have, until now, focused primarily on the relationships among those who write works of authorship and disseminate those works to the public. The threat and promise of networked digital technology is that every individual with access to a computer will be able to perform the twenty-first-century equivalent of printing, reprinting, publishing, and vending. If the vast majority of them do not comply with the copyright law, then the copyright law is in danger of becoming irrelevant.

The Lehman Working Group addressed this problem in its White Paper Report in three different ways. First, if the root of the problem was that individual end users didn't bother with extant copyright rules because they believed that the copyright rules in the statute don't apply to them, the White Paper offered a solution: it advanced an interpretation of the current statute under which all of the current rules apply with full force to individual end users. Second, if the reason that individual end users didn't bother with extant copyright rules was that they realized that those rules were difficult to enforce against them, the White Paper suggested a variety of measures to beef up enforcement, ranging from enhanced penalties to new legal protection for technological anticopying tools. Finally, if individual end users didn't bother with extant copyright rules because they didn't understand them, the White Paper argued that an ambitious education program modeled around the theme "just say *yes*" (to licensing) would bring the American public around.[3]

Whether those proposals are likely to work depends on why it is that the public believes that extant copyright rules don't apply to individual end users; why it might be that the public thinks the rules are, or should be, unenforceable; why the public might have some trouble understanding the way the current rules work. The answers to these questions must influence the determination whether the good old rules should be the rules we devise to govern the behavior of individual end users, or whether we ought instead to try to fashion a legal regime that the general public finds more hospitable.

I have complained more than once in this book that the copyright law is complicated, arcane, and counterintuitive, and the upshot of that is that people don't believe the copyright law says what it does say. People do seem to buy into copyright norms, but they don't translate those norms into the rules that the copyright statute does; they find it very hard to believe that there's really a law out there that says the stuff the copyright law says.

Of course we have lots of laws that people don't seem to believe in. Think of the laws prohibiting consensual sodomy, for instance.[4] I learned about those laws from my father, and I had a tough time believing that he wasn't making them up. Think about the late national 55-mile-an hour speed limit law. These are laws that people don't believe actually say what they do say. And, since people don't think that familiar sexual activities, or driving at 70 miles an hour, are really against the law, they don't refrain from doing those things just because some law on the books says they can't.

People don't obey laws that they don't believe in. I'm not claiming that they behave lawlessly, or that they'll steal whatever they can steal if they think they can get away with it. Most people try to comply, at least substantially, with what they believe the law to say. If they don't believe the law says what it in fact does say, though, they won't obey it—not because they are protesting its provisions, but because it doesn't stick in their heads. Governments stop enforcing laws that people don't believe in. Laws that people don't obey and that governments don't enforce get repealed, even if they are good laws in some other sense of the word. The national 55 miles-an-hour speed limit, for instance, (had it been followed) would have conserved fuel and saved lives, but it wasn't, so it didn't, and now it's history. Congress repealed it.[5]

People are nonetheless attached to the symbolic significance of some of these laws. "They're good," people say, "because they make a statement. They express the norms of civilized society." You hear that sort of thing a lot when people talk about the war on drugs. Many people agree that the laws against drugs aren't working, indeed, are doing as much harm as good, but they are unwilling to give up the symbolic force of the prohibitions. That's one good reason to keep a law around even though nobody seems to be obeying it. It can be very expensive to cling to a law that is unenforced and unenforceable, but sometimes, with some laws, some people feel that it is worth the price for the symbolism.

But laws that we keep around for their symbolic power can only exercise that power to the extent that people know what the laws say. If nobody knew that we had a law against selling cocaine, it wouldn't be serving much of a symbolic function. (To go back to the laws against consensual sodomy for a moment, they stopped performing whatever symbolic function they were supposed to perform once people stopped believing that there were real laws out there that made things like that illegal.) The reason people don't believe in the copyright law, I would argue, is that people persist in believing that laws make sense, and the copyright laws don't seem to them to make sense, because they don't make sense, especially from the vantage point of the individual end user.

We know quite a bit about the problems that inhere in educating the public about copyright law, because copyright owners have been expending huge sums of energy, time, and money with that goal in mind. The music-performing rights societies have been trying to educate a recalcitrant public for the past eighty-five years, and the effort has hardly made a dent in the psyches of their customers or the people who patronize them. Restaurateurs wouldn't think of selling their patrons stolen food, or sitting them in stolen chairs, but they think nothing of selling them stolen music; many of those who buy performing rights licenses from ASCAP, BMI, and SESAC say that they do so only because they're afraid of the copyright police.[6]

The performing rights situation is straightforward: if you run an establishment open to the public, you need to buy a license to perform music unless your performances fit into one of the exceptions.[7] Licenses are sold relatively cheaply, but compliance is grudging at best.[8] People perceive the law to be grossly unfair, partly because enforcement is incomplete and uneven, so there's no guarantee that the business down the street is licensed, and who wants to be a chump? Then there are all of the exceptions in the statute, which don't make any sense. Copyright lawyers might understand that the reason for various privileges is that particular lobbyists insisted on them, but there is nothing intuitively appealing about the statutory distinctions. Some prospective licensees fail to buy licenses because they believe the law could not possibly have been intended to apply to their situations; others find its complex provisions arbitrary, and incomprehensible, and therefore unfair. And, every single year, despite the fact that the liability of unlicensed commercial establishments is well settled, people choose to litigate rather than pay up. And, of course, they lose. Their lawyers could have told them they would lose at the beginning, but they go through the painful and expensive litigation process anyway.

The moral of the story: some things are easier to teach than others. The current copyright statute has proved to be remarkably education-resistant. One part of the problem is that many people persist in believing that laws make sense. If someone claims that a law provides such and such, but such and such seems to make no sense, then perhaps that isn't really the law, or wasn't intended to be the way the law worked, or was the law at one time but not today, or is one of those laws, like the sodomy law, that it is okay to ignore. Our current copyright statute has more than merely a provision or two or three or ten that don't make a lot of sense; it's chock-full of them.

The current crisis has been precipitated by the widespread adoption of new digital technology, which enables members of the general public to print, reprint, publish, and vend, and communicate with a vast audience without resorting to publishers, record companies, motion picture studios, or television networks. By the summer of 1998, estimates pegged the number of Internet users in the United States at about 70 million people, and those numbers keep growing.[9] By November of 1999, the total number of U.S. Internet users had reached 110 million; the world total was estimated at 259 million.[10] By June of 2000, the United States had an estimated 137 million Internet users.[11] If 137 million members of the general public copy, save, transmit, and distribute content without paying attention to the written copyright rules, those rules are in danger of becoming irrelevant.

Current stakeholders, who are used to the current rules, would of course prefer that the rules that apply to the general public engaging in these activities be the current rules, or ones that work as much like them as possible.[12] They have been seeking ways to maintain what they see as the appropriate balance in the law, by reinvigorating and extending their version of the current rules.

I have urged that this version of the copyright balance is ahistorical. Copyright law never gave copyright owners rights as expansive as those that they have recently argued were their due. I would surely argue that my claim to defend the old balance is the more authentic one. But, the truth is, we *all* need to give it up. That balance is gone. Whatever approach we choose, we will need to find a different balance. The new players whom we are trying to account for—hundreds of millions of consumers of networked digital technology who dwarf the current stakeholders on the basis of numbers alone—are too big an elephant to travel the length of a boa constrictor without permanently distorting its shape.[13]

In a spectrum of possible strategies, the solution supported by current stakeholders is at one extreme: let's first reinterpret the current statute to define as an actionable copy every appearance of a work in the temporary memory of any computer anywhere. Then, let's make the good old rules (as reinterpreted) apply with full force to these 259 million new printers, reprinters, publishers, and vendors, essentially by fiat. We'll simply say it does, and then we'll try to ensure that *they* see it that way by teaching them to "just say yes" in elementary school, by encouraging the widespread use of technological controls that compel them to comply with whatever terms copyright holders elect to impose, and by pursuing a subtle but decided shift toward criminal enforcement of extant copyright rules.[14]

The trouble with the plan is that the only people who appear to actually believe that the current copyright rules apply as written to every person on the planet are members of the copyright bar.[15] Representatives of current stakeholders, talking among themselves, have persuaded one another that it must be true, but that's a far cry from persuading the 137 million new printers and reprinters. The good old rules were not written with the millions of new digital publishers in mind, and they don't fit very well with the way end users interact with copyrighted works. If you say to an end user, "You either need permission or a statutory privilege for each appearance, however fleeting, of any work you look at in any computer anywhere," she'll say, "But there can't really be a law that says that. That would be silly." Even copyright lawyers, who have invested years in getting used to the ways the copyright law seems arbitrary, have had to engage in several pretzels' worth of logical contortions to articulate how the good old rules do and should apply to end users without any further exemptions or privileges.

Instead of polling the old guard for its version of good rules to constrain the individual end users who, after all, are now threatening to compete as well as consume, and then foisting those rules on the public in a "just say yes—to licensing" campaign, it might be worthwhile to take a step back. I take it that a law that folks complied with voluntarily would be superior on many counts to one that required reeducation campaigns, that depended on technological agents to be our copyright police, and that relied on felony convictions to be our deterrents. Nobody has proposed a law that might meet this description because the members of the copyright bar have all looked around and concluded that consumers will not voluntarily comply with the current collection of copyright rules. Stop and think about it for a minute. We can't rely on voluntary compliance because the great mass of mankind will not comply voluntarily with the current rules.

Well, why not? Is it that consumers are lawless, or ignorant? Is it, in other words, the consumers' fault? Or might there instead be some defect in the current rules—at least from the consumers' standpoint? To recast the question, can we look at the dilemma from the opposite direction? Are there rules that we believe consumers would comply with voluntarily? Do those rules potentially supply sufficient incentives to authors and their printers, publishers, and vendors to create new works and put them on the Global Information Infrastructure, and, if not, can we tweak them so that they do?

More than ever before, our copyright policy is becoming our information policy. As technology has transformed the nature of copyright so that it now applies to everybody's everyday behavior, it has become more important, not less, that our copyright rules embody a bargain that the public would assent to. The most important reason why we devised and continue to rely on a copyright legislative process whereby the copyright rules are devised by representatives of affected industries to govern interactions among them is that it produced rules that those industries could live with. Now that it is no longer merely the eight major movie studios, or the four television networks, or the six thousand radio stations, or the two-hundred-some book publishers, or the fifty-seven thousand libraries in this country[16] who need to concern themselves about whether what they are doing will result in the creation of a "material object . . . in which a work is fixed by any method," but hundreds of millions of ordinary citizens, it is crucial that the rules governing what counts as such an object, and what the implications are of making one, be rules that those citizens can live with.

The Lehman Working Group's White Paper suggested that we invest in citizen reeducation to persuade everyone that the current copyright rules are right, true, and just. I am less distressed by this suggestion than I might be if I thought it were likely to work. There's something profoundly un-American about the campaign, at least as the White Paper described it.[17] But, instead of trying to change the minds of millions of people, instead of trying to persuade them that a long, complicated, counterintuitive, and often arbitrary code written by a bunch of copyright lawyers is sensible and fair, why don't we just replace this code with a set of new rules that more people than not think *are* sensible and fair?

Of course, that approach would force us to confront the knotty question of how we figure out what set of rules more people than not would think were sensible and fair. I don't want to minimize the difficulties of the problem, but let me suggest that a plausible first step might be to ask people. There is very little survey evidence to tell us what the general public thinks about copyright matters, but the survey evidence that's out there is intriguing.[18] It accords with anecdotal evidence: members of the general public seem to attach quite a bit of significance to intellectual property, but they also seem to believe very firmly in a "free use zone,"[19] or an area of use for which individual users don't need to ask permission. That makes a great deal of sense, even to copyright lawyers, since U.S. copyright law has always had fairly substantial free use zones. On the other hand, it's less easy to account for this: according to more than one study conducted for the Office of Technology Assessment (back when we still had an Office of Technology Assessment[20]), most people seem to believe that the copyright law draws a distinction between exploitation of a work for commercial purposes and consumption of a work for personal purposes, and makes the first actionable and the second privileged.[21] People believe this despite the fact that that's never been the law, and despite eighty-five years of concerted educational efforts by ASCAP, and a somewhat shorter, if more intense, educational campaign by the Software Publishers Association.[22]

It may be that we can come up with a copyright law that incorporates that principle without doing too much damage to copyright incentives. I think we could, and I explore one such proposal in chapter 12, but I know there are a lot of people out there who disagree. If we are committed to the course of applying a single set of rules to both commercial film studios and high school students, though, we can't assess the feasibility of doing so merely by asking what the commercial film studios think of the idea—there are, after all, far more high school students than film studios out there.

With all of the pollsters pounding the streets these days to try to find out who the American public wants to elect as its next president, it's difficult to argue that asking the public what *it* thinks is somehow not feasible. We just haven't committed the resources to it before, because the answers to the questions didn't strike many people as very important. Let me suggest that today they are very important.

NOTES

1. Portions of this chapter are adapted from an essay published as *Copyright Noncompliance (or Why We Can't "Just Say Yes" to Licensing)*, in *Symposium: The Culture and Economics of Participation in an International Intellectual Property Regime*, 1–2 New York University Journal of International Law and Politics 29 (1997).

2. Aldous Huxley, *Brave New World* 18 (Bantam Classic 1958) (emphasis in original).

3. *See* Information Infrastructure Task Force, *Intellectual Property and the National Information Infrastructure: The Report of the Working Group on Intellectual Property Rights* 203–10 (1995) [hereinafter White Paper]. I am not making this up. The Working Group was concerned that "copyright education should not be a series of 'thou shall nots.' Instead, education should carry a 'just say yes' message. . . ." Ibid. at 208. The White Paper suggested that the "just say yes" copyright awareness campaign should focus on the minimal difficulties associated with seeking permission before gaining access to or making use of a work. Ibid.

4. *See, e.g.*, Ark. Stat. § 5-14-122 (1995); Kentucky Rev. Stat. § 510.00 (Michie 1995).

5. Pub. L. 104-59, Title II § 205(d)(1)(B), 109 Stat. 577 (1995). Traffic deaths have apparently increased substantially in the years since the law was repealed. Another example is provided by the law that requires household employers to pay Social Security taxes for babysitters, housekeepers, and other in-home employees. Until 1994, the law required Social Security taxes to be paid on behalf of any employee who earned more than $50 in any quarter of the year, and was apparently widely ignored. In 1992, President Bill Clinton's first nominee for the office of Attorney General disclosed that she had failed to pay taxes for her son's babysitter; her nomination was withdrawn. An official White House policy requiring nominees to have complied with the law soon foundered when it turned out that a significant number of nominees had failed to pay the required FICA taxes. *See* Ruth Morris, *Clinton Delays Announcement on Court Choice; Breyer Tax Issue Disclosed*, Washington Post, June 13, 1993, at A1. The White House settled on a modified policy requiring high-level appointees to tender back taxes and penalties to the IRS and say they were sorry. *See* Editorial: *Again the Social Security Taxes*, Washington Post, December 22, 1993, at A20. Two years later, Congress amended the law to ease its requirements. *See* Editorial, *Nanny Tax Change, Not Repeal*, Washington Post, October 8, 1994, at A18.

6. In 1994, the House held oversight hearings on the performing rights societies. Restaurateurs, bar owners, and the proprietors of small businesses complained bitterly about the unfairness of the societies' royalty demands, and insisted that the law simply couldn't say what ASCAP, BMI, and SESAC said it did. *See generally Music Licensing Practices of Performing Rights Societies: Oversight Hearing Before*

the Subcommittee on Intellectual Property and Judicial Administration of the House Committee on the Judiciary, 103d Cong., 2d sess. (February 23–24, 1994) [Hereinafter Music Licensing Hearing]; Ralph Oman, *Source Licensing: The Latest Skirmish in an Old Battle,* 11 Columbia-VLA Journal of Law and Arts 251 (1987).

7. The statute has a variety of limited exceptions that apply in specified circumstances, including privileges that permit some public performances in connection with classroom teaching, distance education, religious services, agricultural fairs, record stores, and consumer appliance stores. The law also permits reception of radio or television broadcasts on the premises of restaurants, bars, and small retail businesses. *See* 17 U.S.C. § 110. Some of the privileges are not entirely logical. Section 110(7) of the statute, for instance, permits stores selling televisions to perform musical works on their in-store televisions to permit television sales. The exemption, however, does not extend to showing any pictures on those televisions. Presumably, therefore, the stores infringe the copyrights in the visual portions of the programming they play, but not in the accompanying music.

In addition to the exemptions, the law has a number of complicated statutory licenses, including those covering cable and satellite television.

8. The music performing rights situation is exemplary; I choose it because of the long-standing campaigns waged by ASCAP, BMI, and SESAC to educate the public. Organizations like the Software Publishers' Association have been in the public education business for far fewer years, with no more success. On compliance with the copyright law as it concerns software, John Perry Barlow wrote:

> The laws regarding unlicensed reproduction of commercial software are clear and stern. . .and rarely observed. Software piracy laws are so practically unenforceable and breaking them has become so socially acceptable that only a thin minority appears compelled, either by fear or by conscience, to obey them. When I give speeches on this subject, I always ask how many people in the audience can honestly claim to have no unauthorized software on their hard disk. I've never seen more than 10 percent of the hands go up.
>
> Whenever there is such profound divergence between law and social practice, it is not society that adapts. Against the swift tide of custom, the software publishers' current practice of hanging a few visible scapegoats is so obviously capricious as to only further diminish respect for the law.

John Perry Barlow, *The Economy of Ideas: A Framework for Rethinking Patents and Copyrights in the Digital Age (Everything You Know about Intellectual Property Is Wrong),* Wired, March, 1994, at 84, 88.

9. *See, e.g., The Commercenet/Neilsen Internet Survey,* URL: <http://www.commerce.net/nielsen/index.html>.

10. *See Computer Industry Almanac, U.S. Tops 100 Million Internet Users According to Computer Industry Almanac* (November 4, 1999), at URL: <http://www.c-i-a.com/199911iu.htm>.

11. Nielsen/Netratings, *Average Web Usage-Month of June 2000, U.S.*, at URL: <http://209.249.142.27/nnpm/owa/NRpublicreports.usagemonthly>.

12. Indeed, they're happy to say so on the record. *See, e.g., Copyright Protection on the Internet: Hearing Before the Courts and Intellectual Property Subcommittee of the House Committee on the Judiciary*, 104th Cong., 2d sess. (February 7, 1996) (testimony of Jack Valenti, MPAA); ibid. (testimony of Gary McDaniels, Software Publishers Association).

13. *See* Antoine de Saint-Exupery, *The Little Prince* 8 (New York: Harcourt Brace & Co., 1943). Saint-Exupery begins the book with the tale of how, as a little boy, he had seen an illustration of a boa constrictor swallowing a rodent and had been inspired to draw a picture of a boa constrictor which had swallowed and was trying to digest an elephant.

14. *See* White Paper, above at note 3, at 177–200, 203–208, 228–36.

15. I mean to include, here, copyright lawyers in government and academia as well as those in private practice or in corporate positions. My argument is that we who live with and interpret copyright rules every day have simply forgotten how counterintuitive those rules are to people who don't. We frequently neglect to factor that aspect of reality into our constructions of the meaning of copyright rules.

16. The sources of the numbers in text are World Wide Web pages published by industry trade association. The number of major movie studios comes from the Motion Picture Association of America, *see* URL: <http://www.mpaa.org>. The book publishers count comes from the Association of American Publishers, *see* URL: <http://www.publishers.org>. The number of radio stations comes from the Web page of the National Association of Broadcasters, *see* URL: <http://www.smpte.org/sustain/nab.html>; and the number of libraries is derived from the Web page of the American Library Association, *see* URL: <http://www.ala.org>.

17. The White Paper outlined a "Copyright Awareness Campaign," *see* White Paper, above at note 3, at 201–10, that emphasized the excellence of intellectual property ownership at every opportunity and left no room for contradiction. It is reminiscent of nothing so much as the sort of educational propaganda campaigns one can read about in older science fiction novels about totalitarian states.

18. *See* Office of Technology Assessment, U.S. Congress, *Copyright & Home Copying: Technology Challenges the Law* 163–65 (1989); Office of Technology Assessment, U.S. Congress, *Intellectual Property Rights in an Age of Electronics and Information* 121–23, 208–209 (1986).

19. The phrase is Professor Marci Hamilton's. *See* Marci A. Hamilton, *The TRIPS Agreement: Imperialistic, Outdated, and Overprotective*, 3 Vanderbilt Journal of Transnational Law 613 (1996).

20. Congress established the Office of Technology Assessment (OTA) in 1972, to provide nonpartisan, in depth technical analysis of legislative and policy questions implicating science and technology. The OTA prepared reports for Congress on subjects ranging from environmental and health issues to military and space issues, and included evaluations of the effectiveness of government science and technology policy in connection with particular questions. During the twenty-three years it operated, the OTA proved unusually resistant to political and industry pressure. Congress abolished it in 1995.

21. *See Copyright & Home Copying,* above at note 18, at 163–65; *Intellectual Property Rights in an Age of Electronics and Information,* above at note 18, at 121–23, 208-209; The Policy Planning Group, Yankelovich, Skelly & White, Inc., *Public Perceptions of the "Intellectual Property Rights" Issue* (1985) (OTA Contractor Report).

22. Until recently, however, the public's impression was not a bad approximation of the scope of copyright rights likely, in practice, to be enforced. If copyright owners insisted, as sometimes they did, that copyright gave them broad rights to control their works in any manner and all forms, the practical costs of enforcing those rights against individual consumers dissuaded them from testing their claims in court. *See, e.g., Audio Home Recording Act of 1991: Hearing on H.R. 3204 before the Subcommittee on Intellectual Property and Judicial Administration of the House Committee on the Judiciary,* 102d Cong., 2d sess. (1993). In a small number of recent cases, copyright owners joined allegedly representative individuals as nominal parties defendant to lawsuits challenging the sale of goods or services said to facilitate infringement, but neither sought nor received relief against them. *See, e.g., Universal City Studios* v. *Sony Corp. of America,* 480 F. Supp. 429 (C.D. Cal. 1979), *aff'd in part, rev'd in part,* 659 F.2d 963 (9th Cir. 1981), *rev'd,* 464 U.S. 417 (1984); Edwin McDowell, *Ideas and Trends: College "Copy Mills" Grind Quickly, So Publishers Sue,* New York Times, December 19, 1982, §4, at 18, col. 1; *but cf. Demetriades* v. *Kaufmann,* 690 F. Supp. 289 (SDNY 1988) (individual home buyers sued for hiring builder to construct look-alike house).

NINE

THE BARGAINING TABLE

W HEN THE GOVERNMENT RELEASED THE White Paper in September 1995, it looked as if the White Paper's recommendations were all but a done deal. Immediately after the report's release, implementing legislation was introduced in both houses of Congress with bipartisan support, and Commissioner Lehman confidently predicted easy enactment before spring. It didn't turn out that way. Library groups, online service providers, consumer organizations, writers' organizations, computer hardware manufacturers, Internet civil liberties groups, telephone companies, educators, consumer electronics manufacturers, and law professors registered early and fervent objections. They collaborated with one another in opposing the legislation, and used a tool that the supporters of the White Paper were not yet in a position to exploit: they organized, planned, and lobbied using the Internet.

The digital copyright enhancement legislation introduced at the administration's request in the wake of the White Paper was minimalist in form if not effect. It would have added about one thousand words to the existing statute. The new words would have expanded copyright owners' exclusive rights to distribute their works to encompass transmission, and would have protected copyright owners' ability to use mechanisms to prevent or discourage infringement. The bill would have made it illegal for anyone, for any reason, to make, sell, or give away a product designed to enable people to get around such a mechanism, even when that product had legitimate uses. Precisely what protective mechanisms the bill contemplated was unclear. The White Paper mentioned the use of passwords to restrict access to works, the distribution of copies of digital works with encoded information limiting the uses that might be made of them, and the introduction of systems for tracking and monitoring all uses of copyrighted works.

The effect of the bill, had it been enacted, would have been more far reaching than initially appeared. Historically, as I've explained earlier, statutory copyright rights have been phrased broadly, but made subject to a variety of broad and narrow exceptions, limitations, and privileges. The new statutory rights, however, were subjected to no exceptions, limitations, or privileges.[1] Defeating a monitoring and tracking system by using a false name, for example, to conceal your interest in reading information about hemorrhoids, or herpes, or HIV would have violated the bill's anticircumvention provisions.

Because computer-mediated uses of works in digital form can be subjected to extensive restrictions using software tools, the upshot would have been to give copyright owners far more control over use of any works in digital form than they had ever had over analog uses. But the language of the bill was not limited to digital works. Libraries objected that the bill was phrased broadly enough to cover any system purporting to limit the uses consumers might make of conventional books or music.

In the weeks following the release of the White Paper and the introduction of its implementing legislation, Peter Jaszi, a law professor at American University in Washington, held informal consultations with like-thinking law professors and representatives of library organizations to see whether there was any possibility of mounting an effective opposition to the White Paper's proposals. (I confess to being one of the law professors.[2]) The copyright owner lobbies had responded to the White Paper with a flurry of supportive press events. Naysayers were few: a large number of copyright law professors, most of the library organizations, cyber-libertarians, and some computer scientists had registered quiet opposition without getting much attention from politicians or the press. Adam Eisgrau, the newly hired lobbyist for the American Library Association, suggested to Jaszi that Congress regularly ignored the efforts of nonprofit and educational organizations. What it would take to get serious congressional attention, Eisgrau believed, was the opposition of commercial and business interests.

Jaszi asked likely White Paper opponents to come to a meeting at American University billed as a roundtable discussion of the White Paper's recommendations. The purpose of the meeting was to organize a coalition among business and nonprofit entities unhappy with the White Paper, to combine their efforts into an effective opposition. Jaszi had invited representatives of library organizations, online service providers, telephone companies, computer hardware and software manufacturers, consumer electronics companies, and civil rights and consumer protection organizations. All of them, he believed, ought to find something objectionable in the White Paper's proposals. Copyright-holder lobbies had perfected a strategy of working out their differences privately and then presenting Congress with a united front. The interests of the White Paper's likely opponents were probably too dissimilar to enable them to stand together in the long term, Jaszi thought, but, so long as they shared the short-term goal of preventing the enactment of the White Paper's recommendations in their current form, they might be able to accomplish more working together than in their individual capacities.

By the end of the afternoon, several of the invitees had agreed to a temporary, informal alliance, and had settled on a name: the Digital Future Coalition, or DFC for short. At Eisgrau's suggestion, the group's early efforts emphasized the commercial and business interests among its members. Nonetheless, onlookers perceived DFC to be essentially a library and law professor effort, and with reason. In its early months, DFC was a two-man show. Eisgrau and Jaszi coordinated its activities out of the American Library Association's Washington office, and, with the help of members of the library and law professor communities, wrote or assembled all of its materials. In fact, however, while the DFC's early funding relied largely on a private foundation grant, a large chunk of its eventual operating budget and the majority of its legislative strategy derived from the Home Recording Rights Coalition (HRRC).

The Home Recording Rights Coalition styles itself a grass-roots lobby organized to protect consumers' right to private home audio- and video-taping. It represents consumer electronics manufacturers, wholesalers, and retailers: makers and sellers, in other words, of recording devices, whose business depends on consumers' legal ability to record. Operating through the HRRC, the consumer electronics industry had used the public's desire to make free copies of music and movies as a tool to block copyright owner's efforts to prevent unauthorized copying, while making bundles of money selling devices that facilitated it. Organized in the early 1980s in response to the *Sony Betamax* litigation, in which movie studios unsuccessfully sued the manufacturer of the Betamax VCR for copyright infringement, the HRRC established itself as a player entitled to sit at the copyright bargaining table. It lobbied to prevent the enactment of bills prohibiting videotape rental, or the manufacture and sale of dual-deck recording devices. It blocked enactment of the Audio Home Recording Act until copyright owners made a variety of concessions to equipment manufacturers.

The professors knew the law, knew the White Paper, and could criticize it to their peers[3] and write mainstream critiques for the popular press.[4] The library groups had a geographically dispersed membership who took copyright law extremely seriously, and could easily be brought up to speed on the threat posed by the legislation. The HRRC had a sophisticated lobbying and public relations machine already in place, and a significant commercial interest in the outcome.

The DFC gained significant initial credibility when it recruited representatives of the technical community. A significant portion of the opposition to the White Paper came from people and groups who were Internet-savvy. The supporters of the legislation, by and large, were not. Much of the early opposition to the bill was effective precisely because opponents knew the Internet and could use it to get the word out—to scientists, to journalists, to writers and students, and lawyers and cyber-libertarians. Initial press coverage of the White Paper Report had ranged from deferential to reverential. As more criticism hit the Internet, the press treatment got nastier. Popular press accounts accused copyright-holder interests of grabbiness,[5] and the atmosphere became decidedly less pleasant. At one point in the debate, Commissioner Lehman was widely reported to have privately threatened one of his high-profile detractors with grievous bodily injury.[6]

Soon, supporters of the implementing legislation began to back away from the White Paper's analysis, and suggest that everyone ignore the White Paper and focus exclusively on the language of the bills. The Patent Office, the Copyright Office, and key senators and members of Congress encouraged private negotiations among opposing interests to reach compromise solutions, but compromises were hard to come by. Copyright owner groups, having been promised the moon by Commissioner Lehman, were unwilling to settle for a smaller chunk of some asteroid; opponents of the bills, for their part, had little to lose by delaying the legislation, and therefore had no incentive to compromise on unattractive terms. An additional complication was that the White Paper's strategy of claiming that existing copyright law already gave copyright owners all the additional rights they were seeking had generated a heated argument over the deceptiveness of that description, and that fight had quickly gotten ugly. The resulting atmosphere of mistrust made good faith negotiations difficult.

If the world of legislative politics were a more sensible place, perhaps the supporters of the digital copyright enhancement legislation could have added privileges, limitations, and exceptions to the new provisions that were analogous to the ones in the extant law, and everyone could have gone home early. What happened instead was what always seems to happen: intensive negotiations among supporters and detractors of the bill led to a proliferation of narrow, stingy, conditional privileges and exceptions that apply to the folks who insisted on them, but not to you and me.

As soon as it became clear that the White Paper implementing bills would not merely sail through Congress unopposed, supporters of the legislation began negotiating with opponents in a variety of fora. The "serious" negotiations—the ones perceived to be necessary to ensure the enactment of legislation—involved the motion picture industry, the music recording industry, the book publishers and the software publishing industry on behalf of the "content owners," and the online and Internet service provider industry, the telephone companies, the television and radio broadcasters, computer and consumer electronics manufacturers, and libraries representing the "user interests."

The consumer electronics and library groups were perhaps less equal opponents than the others. Long negotiating experience had led the content owners to view consumer electronics groups as manufacturers with the souls of pirates. The Home Recording Rights Coalition had proved unwilling to settle on terms acceptable to the content owners in the past, and could mobilize significant grass-roots opposition working through local distributors of tape and video recorders. From the content owners' vantage point, it may have seemed more profitable to try to discredit the consumer electronics groups than to negotiate with them. Playing on xenophobic themes that had served them well in the past, representatives of content owners dismissed the Home Recording Rights Coalition as a front for Japanese manufacturers eager to make a buck off of American material.

A long copyright history of negotiations with libraries may also have persuaded content owners that library groups were easily marginalized and not a significant threat. Library groups had a history of settling for very little. Commissioner Lehman had no compunction about criticizing as out of line and out of touch libraries' demand that in a digital age their patrons should continue to have essentially free use of valuable material. The effort made to accommodate library interests was accordingly modest, and seemed to focus primarily on first dividing libraries from the commercial opposition and then buying them off cheaply. Thus, Commissioner Lehman initially suggested that libraries' fair use concerns should be addressed by encouraging them to meet with publishers to negotiate a mutually satisfactory solution, and that Congress therefore need not take up any of the libraries' objections. When those negotiations failed to produce any agreement, Lehman offered a modest amendment expanding a library's established privilege to make a single facsimile copy in order to preserve or replace an out-of-print work. Lehman's proposal would have permitted the library to make up to three copies of a single work—a necessary expansion if the Working Group's position that RAM copies were actionable should prevail.

The folks who make tape recorders and run libraries have many altruistic motives, but they also have their own agendas. Their interests may often accord with the public's, but where they diverge, the electronics industry and the libraries will look out for themselves. They are not, in other words, effective substitutes for a public advocate. In earlier legislative sagas, public interest groups had not been interested enough in copyright to try to get involved. This time it could have been different. Thanks largely to the early efforts of the DFC, consumer groups, public interest organizations, and Internet civil liberties groups had weighed in in opposition to the White Paper's proposals. The Consumer Project on Technology suggested that the bill would require Internet service providers to monitor their subscribers' private electronic mail and to censor content passing through their systems. The Electronic Privacy Information Center objected that the anticircumvention provisions would undermine privacy and impede computer system administration. The National Education Association warned that the bill would gravely impede distance learning. The Electronic Frontier Foundation complained that the White Paper's recommendations would inhibit browsing on the World Wide Web and make encryption research illegal. Mobilized by DFC and library group action alerts, a variety of organizations with no prior investment in copyright issues advised their members that the legislation would make browsing the Internet illegal, and would subject computer system operators to ruinous liability.[7] It made little difference. Public interest groups weren't regulars at the copyright negotiating table. Supporters of the legislation essentially ignored them. Many of the groups participated to a greater or lesser degree in the DFC's efforts, but were never invited to participate in the private negotiations over the legislation. Nor, for that matter, did the DFC ever gain its own seat at the table. Its efforts were limited to behind-the-scenes coordination of its members' activities.

That left the Internet and online service providers, the telephone companies, the broadcasters, and the manufacturers of computer hardware to deal with. The White Paper had suggested that service providers and phone companies would be liable under current law whenever their facilities were used to transmit or reproduce infringing content. It recommended that no change in the current liability standard should be made. The clear implication was that henceforth, this sort of liability would give content owners a deep pocket to sue; fear of liability would drive service providers to agree to a variety of measures designed to choke off, deter, or avenge infringement by their customers. While the content owner groups insisted that fears of ruinous liability were speculative and any move to relax the traditional strict liability standard was premature, one content owner proved them wrong. The Church of Scientology brought suit against a variety of service providers for transmitting the contents of church documents that their subscribers had posted.[8] (The documents revealed secret church teachings explaining that human beings were in fact the reincarnation of dead space aliens who had been kidnapped to earth many millennia ago and then murdered by an intergallactic tyrant. For some reason, the church was upset that the documents had been revealed to the general public.) The church sought orders compelling the removal or destruction of all unauthorized copies. As those cases worked their way through the courts, companies in the Internet and online service business started paying attention. Finding some compromise that was minimally satisfactory to service providers and telephone companies soon emerged as a necessary precondition to enacting legislation.

Copyright owners remained unwilling to let service providers off the hook, and the providers and telephone companies were determined that the bill not move until their interests were addressed. As the legislation got into trouble, proponents of other unrelated copyright reforms came forward to decorate the administration bill with their own additions, seeking a twenty-year extension to the copyright term, or a broad privilege to play copyrighted music in restaurants and bars, or a narrow privilege to enable computer service businesses to fix broken computers.[9] A variety of different actors tried to broker deals, but nobody was yet willing to settle. By the summer of 1996, the effort to enact NII copyright legislation in the 104th Congress was stalled.

Meanwhile, Commissioner Lehman's initial confidence that the United States would have the project wrapped up before spring had led him to press for an international diplomatic conference in Geneva hosted by the World Intellectual Property Organization (WIPO),* which administers the major

---

*The World Intellectual Property Organization is an agency of the United Nations responsible for administering more than twenty international intellectual property treaties.

international copyright treaties. Lehman hoped to use the conference to persuade the rest of the world to make the United States approach the basis for a new world copyright treaty. He had spent enormous time and energy to assure that any draft treaty presented to the conference for adoption would embody the reforms proposed by the White Paper. The diplomatic conference was scheduled for December; a draft that reflected the White Paper's recommendations was about to be distributed. The domestic legislation, however, was not moving. The commissioner, therefore, decided to attack the problem the other way around. He focused his attention on getting his agenda adopted by the WIPO member nations, reasoning that when the United States signed the treaty, Congress would be obliged to adopt implementing legislation in accord with the White Paper's recommendations.

Lehman therefore pushed a draft of the new treaty that would have required signatory nations to implement the controversial elements of the White Paper's recommendations. One proposed article would have defined actionable reproductions to include all temporary RAM copies. Another would have guaranteed a comprehensive right to communicate works to the public, which would have incorporated Lehman's proposal for a broad transmission right. A third article would have required countries to prohibit the manufacture or distribution of any devices or services designed to defeat technological copy-protection measures. In addition, the draft included a provision requiring nations to prohibit removal or alteration of "electronic rights management information," that is, digital code identifying a work, its author, and the owner of rights in the work. All of these proposals echoed similar substantive elements of the original White Paper legislation. Finally, the draft contained a proposed article limiting the scope of fair use or other exceptions to copyright.[10]

Opponents of the White Paper legislation perceived the effort to foist the substance of the White Paper on the United States in the form of a new intellectual property treaty as a sneaky trick. A number of them shifted their lobbying efforts to the international arena in the hope of influencing the treaty process. Meanwhile, developing nations were unenthusiastic about the more expansive proposals. When the treaty conference convened, the majority of nations proved unwilling to sign on to the U.S. delegation's vision of fortified copyright in cyberspace, and a number of the most controversial parts of the package were voted down in Geneva. Ultimately, the treaty text adopted by the conference incorporated few of Lehman's ambitious proposals, and even those were substantially diluted. The proposal on temporary copies was eliminated. The new right of communication to the public was limited; delegates adopted language exempting any firm that acted as a mere conduit by providing transmission facilities. The broad technological protection proposal was weakened: while the proposal supported by the United States had prohibited the manufacture, sale, or distribution of devices or services to circumvent technical protections, the ultimate treaty language required only that signatory nations offer effective legal remedies for circumvention in connection with activities that themselves violate the copyright laws. The proposal limiting fair use and other exceptions was transformed into a proposal authorizing the extension of privileges like fair use in order to ensure their effective exercise in the digital environment. The United States signed the treaty adopted by the conference.

Treaties in the United States are not self-executing. They require Congress to enact laws that implement them. Back in the United States, therefore, negotiations shifted to the shape and language of treaty-implementing legislation. Copyright owners, disappointed by the circumscribed provisions included in the final treaty, nonetheless hoped to use the treaty as a platform to achieve more expansive objectives. At the same time, the controversy surrounding the White Paper legislation suggested that the approach most likely to result in expeditious treaty ratification was to introduce a "clean" or minimal bill that effected the legal changes prescribed by the treaty without a bunch of extra stuff. The U.S. Department of Commerce preferred the "clean bill" approach. The Clinton administration had committed itself to a general game plan in connection with all Internet regulation that required it to identify what needed to be done to facilitate electronic commerce, to do that, and to do as little as possible except for that. After the bruising copyright fight in the last Congress, it wanted to satisfy the Hollywood and Silicon Valley communities but did not want to have to expend significant political capital to do so.

If copyright owners wanted major improvements on the treaty's prescriptions, then, they would need to be clever about how those improvements were framed. The White Paper had predicated its expansive rendition of copyright owner control on a broad interpretation of the classic reproduction right and a proposal for a new transmission right, but both of those elements of the draft treaty had been watered down considerably in the final version. Rather than expending further effort on shoring up the reproduction and transmission rights as a step in implementing the treaty, it seemed more prudent to retreat to the position that U.S. copyright law already provided expansive rights to control all transmissions and temporary reproductions.[11] At the same time, the new anticircumvention provisions adopted as part of the treaty might be used as a basis for greatly enhanced copyright owner control.

The original White Paper legislation would have prohibited the importation, manufacture, or distribution of any device or service whose primary purpose or effect was to circumvent any technological measure that prevented copyright infringement.[12] The actual treaty language was narrower: it required only that the signatory nations "provide adequate legal protection and effective legal remedies against the circumvention of effective technological measures that are used by authors . . [to] restrict acts . . . which are not authorized by the authors concerned or permitted by law." Arguably, United States law met that standard. Copyright infringement accomplished through circumvention was already actionable as copyright infringement. In addition, courts imposed liability for knowing facilitation of copyright infringement on producers of devices that had no substantial noninfringing application.[13] Such liability was narrow: In the *Sony Betamax* case, the United States Supreme Court had refused to hold the manufacturer of a VCR liable merely because the machine could be used to make illegal copies, given that it was also "widely used for legitimate, unobjectionable purposes." The manufacturer should be liable, the Court explained, only where a device was incapable of substantial noninfringing uses.[14]

The availability of infringement actions against circumventers who succeeded in violating copyright owners' rights, together with the possibility of suing makers of devices that had no legitimate use, met the standard set by the treaty. Copyright owners maintained, however, that the obligation to provide "effective legal remedies" required the United States to give them the legal ability to prevent circumvention of technological protection measures from occurring *at all*, by first prohibiting any circumvention of technological protection, without regard to the reason for it, and second, by making any devices or services that facilitate circumvention illegal—regardless of whether the devices or services were used for legitimate purposes.

This would give copyright owners even more extensive control over the use of their works than had been proposed by the White Paper. Once a work was protected by a technological defense, the copyright owner could prohibit and prevent unauthorized use of that work, even where the use would be legal under the copyright law. If circumvention was illegal whatever the reason, it would be illegal to circumvent technological protection to make fair use of a work, or to extract uncopyrightable ideas or facts. If a work were distributed with a password that functioned to limit access, selling or loaning the work along with the necessary password could be deemed illegal circumvention. If the copyright in a work enclosed within a technological protection measure expired, users could still not circumvent the protection to gain access to the unprotected work—even if doing so were legal, the prohibition on devices or services that facilitated circumvention would make circumvention impossible for all but the most expert hackers.

User interests responded with alarm. After all, expansive anticircumvention language had been rejected by the international convention in favor of a provision that promised effective legal remedies only against those acts of circumvention committed in connection with copyright infringement. Indeed, they argued, the treaty expressly invited signatory nations to expand exceptions like fair use to ensure that they continued to be meaningful in a world in which many important copyrighted works were digitally encrypted. Armed with those treaty concessions, the coalition opposing the bill insisted that attacking devices or services was inappropriate and unwise. All the treaty required, and all that made policy sense, was to give copyright owners remedies against people who circumvented technological protection in aid of infringement and redress against others—including device makers and sellers—who deliberately facilitated circumvention for an infringing purpose. Moreover, the DFC suggested, in view of the provisions in the treaty supporting the extension of appropriate copyright limitations, the implementing legislation ought to include language extending fair use to any prohibition on circumvention. If the reason a person circumvented a copy protection measure was to make fair use of the protected work, then that circumvention should itself be legal.

The White Paper had dismissed any call for a fair use exception to anticircumvention legislation with the observation that "the fair use doctrine does not require a copyright owner to allow or to facilitate unauthorized access or use of a work."[15] Copyright owners expanded on that theme. Fair use, they suggested, might permit some use to be made of an authorized copy of a work in very special cases, but it didn't permit the theft of a copy. If someone wanted to buy a book, or borrow it from a library that had purchased it, he could then make fair use of it, but fair use didn't authorize him to break into the author's house to steal her personal copy. Breaking into technological protection, they argued, was like breaking into a home or stealing a book, and had never been permitted by the fair use doctrine.

The housebreaking metaphor proved effective. It was also misleading. The thing about houses is that property laws give homeowners legal control over who gets to come in. A homeowner may therefore say: "My painting may be in the public domain but I don't have to let you into my locked home to see it." Backed up by that legal control, she can use protective devices—locks, burglar alarms, electrified fences, vicious attack dogs—to keep outsiders out of her home and away from her painting. The property laws about home ownership are what gives the locks and other devices their legitimacy.

Without those property rights, however, the metaphor collapses. Imagine, for example, that somebody used a lock or other protection measure (a well-trained attack dog, say) to prevent strangers from viewing some painting she didn't own in some place she didn't own. If I were to set my vicious attack dog to keep folks away from the Mona Lisa in the Louvre Museum, the guards would simply shoot it. The housebreaking metaphor, therefore, was inapt to support legal recognition of technological protection measures designed to prevent uses that did not invade anyone's property rights. Using the housebreaking metaphor allowed proponents of unconditional protection against circumvention to skip right past the question whether what was inside that lock was something they were entitled to prevent people from seeing.

The United States Department of Commerce, which was superintending the task of drafting a treaty implementing bill, came up with what appeared to it to be a compromise: It would reformulate circumvention to encompass two different things. First, there was circumvention of technological protection in order to gain unauthorized access to a work. That, the department reasoned, corresponded to stealing a book or breaking into a house. It should be flatly illegal. Not only should the law prohibit trafficking in devices or services designed to facilitate that sort of circumvention, but the law should impose liability on any individual consumer who circumvented technology to gain unauthorized access. Second, there was circumvention of technological protection on a copy of a work that the circumventer was entitled to gain access to, in order to make use of the work in some way that might turn out to be copyright infringement or might turn out to be fair use. In that circumstance, it would be excessive to impose criminal liability for circumvention on individual infringers, because they would already be subject to stiff liability for copyright infringement. It was still necessary, however, to prohibit the making and selling of devices or services to facilitate this kind of circumvention, in order to prevent the widespread marketing of piracy devices under the pretext that they had some noninfringing purposes. The department apparently did not stop to wonder how consumers could engage in circumvention of copy controls for non-infringing purposes, if all devices and services to facilitate that circumvention were illegal.

The Department of Commerce incorporated its two-pronged approach into its draft treaty implementing bill. In its original formulation, circumvention to gain unauthorized access was intended to be limited to *initial* access: hacking into a work one had no right whatsoever to read, view, or hear. User interests pressed the administration to make that limitation explicit, and copyright owners balked. What about pay-per-view? If a copyright owner chose to distribute a digital version of a movie along with an electronic license to view the work once, and sell licenses for further viewing, someone who had bought a single view should not be permitted to hack the password protection and obtain unlimited viewings free of charge. The more that user interests pressed for some limitation on the copyright owners' control of access, the more adamant content lobbyists became that any limitation would be unfair and intolerable.

The bills introduced at the administration's request at the beginning of the 105th Congress were styled treaty implementation bills; they were about twice as long as the bills introduced in 1995, but contained many similar substantive provisions. Commissioner Lehman insisted that the failure of the WIPO conference to adopt his more expansive proposals demonstrated the need for United States leadership on these issues.[16] The commissioner suggested that the United States had a narrow window of opportunity to exercise world leadership by showing our trading partners, through the enactment of potent implementing legislation, that the United States interpreted the treaties to require them to take effective steps to prevent piracy of American property. Lehman argued to Congress that other nations would not act to prevent piracy of United States works until the U.S. Congress demonstrated leadership by enacting tough antipiracy laws, that, for example, made it illegal to defeat copy protection (or to market devices or services that do so) for any purpose whatsoever. Representatives of the motion picture and recording industries backed up the commissioner's arguments with prophecies of widespread international piracy unless Congress acted quickly. The world's eyes, they said, were on America.

Telephone companies, commercial Internet service providers, libraries, and schools insisted that an agreement setting up a safe harbor for online service providers was a precondition to the enactment of implementing legislation. Content owners, however, resisted linking the expansion in digital copyright with relief for Internet service providers. Not only were the two subjects legally unrelated, they argued, but content owners' only meaningful weapon against online pirates was their ability to use the risk of strict liability (liability imposed regardless of fault) for subscribers' copyright infringement to persuade Internet service providers to assist their enforcement efforts. It soon became clear to content owners, however, that the legislation could not move without a solution to the problem of Internet service provider liability. With House and Senate staffers acting as intermediaries, content-owner groups traded proposals with telephone companies and commercial Internet service providers. Early on in this series of negotiations, a staffer suggested incorporating a privilege for individual consumers who unwittingly viewed material that turned out to be infringing. Neither content owners nor service providers thought that that would be a good idea. Finally, after more than three months of intensive bargaining, the content owners and commercial service providers and telephone companies engaged in a last burst of direct negotiations. They reached a deal.

Content owners agreed that Internet service providers should not be liable for their subscribers' infringing transmissions so long as the provider had no reason to suspect infringement was taking place, on the condition that the service provider agreed to shut down copyright violators and remove infringing material as soon as a content owner notified it of a violation. The deal did not require complaining copyright owners to substantiate their claims of infringement. Service providers agreed to turn identifying information about accused copyright violators over to complaining copyright holders, and received a complete exemption from liability in suits by subscribers complaining that their material had been improperly removed in response to a copyright holder's complaint, or that their access had been unreasonably terminated for material wrongly alleged to be infringing. Both sides pronounced themselves satisfied.

The agreement was incorporated into a new WIPO copyright bill to be introduced in the Senate. The new bill was provisionally scheduled for markup by the Senate Judiciary Committee even before the language of its provisions took final form. Interest groups that had opposed the legislation were told by its supporters and by House and Senate staff that if they wanted to reach a bargain they needed to do so immediately, because the bill would be sent to the Senate floor either with them or without them. Most of them dealt. The form the bargains took was the addition of a variety of narrow carve-outs for interests that agreed that, in return for them, they would support the bill.[17]

The Digital Millennium Copyright Act, introduced in the Senate as S. 2037, followed the basic structure of earlier digital copyright bills, prohibiting any "circumvention" of a "technological protection measure that effectively controls access to a work" for any reason, and the manufacture or provision of "any technology, product, service, device, or component" designed to assist in circumventing technological protection. The technology, product, or service prohibition extended to both access-control protection systems and copy-control protection systems.[18] A second provision prohibited unauthorized alteration of "copyright management information"—information identifying a work, its author, its copyright owner, and any terms and conditions of use.[19]

There were narrow exemptions added for law enforcement activities, radio and television broadcasters, and cable systems. Computer software publishers received a narrow exemption that allowed them to circumvent access protection in order to analyze a computer program to enable the creation of a compatible program. Case law held that fair use permitted technical copyright infringements committed in the course of analyzing or reverse-engineering a computer program, even if the reason for the analysis were to permit the creation of a competing product, but the anticircumvention exemption was intentionally drafted to permit reverse engineering only in far more limited circumstances. Libraries received an un-asked-for and unwanted privilege to circumvent access controls for the sole purpose of browsing a protected work to decide whether to purchase it. (The exception thus neatly implied that ordinary citizens had no privilege to browse.) The portion of the bill imposing civil and criminal penalties for trafficking in technology designed to aid in circumvention, however, included no exceptions permitting such technology to be supplied to libraries or law enforcement officers in order to enable them to take advantage of their statutory privileges. Oddly, there was an exception permitting trafficking in technology to assist software designers in the exercise of their limited circumvention privilege, despite the fact that they were the only privileged group likely to have the expertise to do so without outside help. Everyone else entitled to circumvent was apparently expected to develop the facility to do so in-house.[20] The Senate Bill, introduced as S. 2037, was reported favorably by the Senate Judiciary Committee on the same day it was introduced. It went to the Senate floor a week later, where it passed 99-0.

If you've been keeping score as you read, you will have noticed that the interests who had not yet made a deal were the consumer electronics companies, libraries, universities and schools, and civil liberties and consumer organizations. Stymied in the Senate, they went back to the House. Representative Rick Boucher (D-Va.), who had introduced an alternative WIPO implementation Bill that opponents of S. 2037 viewed as more responsive to their concerns,[21] had been unsuccessful in persuading the rest of the House Judiciary Committee to amend the administration's bill to answer their objections. Boucher, however, also sat on the House Commerce Committee. The Commerce Committee, which had long exercised jurisdiction over all telecommunications legislation, had expanded its jurisdiction over the past several years to embrace the Internet and electronic commerce. Since those issues were at the heart of the WIPO bill, the Commerce Committee might be persuaded to interest itself in the legislation. The consumer electronics lobby approached Commerce Committee leadership. Commerce normally left copyright matters to the Judiciary Committee, but the WIPO bill reported out of the House Judiciary Committee went far beyond copyright, containing prohibitions against the manufacture or sale of devices. Shouldn't such provisions be under the jurisdiction of the Commerce Committee? Committee chair Tom Bliley (R-Va.) and ranking member John Dingell (D-Mich.) agreed that they should, and asked the House leadership to refer the WIPO bill to the Commerce Committee.

The content community didn't like that idea. Things had gone well for them over in the Senate, and they'd hoped for a quick rubber stamp by the House. At best, a referral to the Commerce Committee would delay the enactment of the WIPO bill; at worst it might result in changes to it. Mitch Glazier, chief counsel for the House Judiciary Committee Subcommittee on Courts and Intellectual Property, didn't like the idea either. Glazier had been in charge of the House digital copyright legislation since the first bill was introduced in 1995. He had very warm relations with the content community,[22] the confidence of subcommittee chair Howard Coble (R-N.C.), and the ear of Judiciary Chairman Henry Hyde (R-Ill.). After two years of further negotiations, and the help of Senate staff, he had finally reached a compromise that Glazier felt ought to satisfy any legitimate objections. He was concerned that the request for a referral had been made in the interest of delaying action on the legislation, and was impatient for the bill he had worked so hard on to become law.

Glazier persuaded Coble and Hyde that the request for a referral was a power grab by the Commerce Committee, and the congressmen raised objections. The upshot was that the House leadership agreed to make the referral to Commerce for a limited period of a few weeks, but, by the time the Commerce Committee got hold of the bill, it was already annoyed at the effort expended to prevent it from doing so. The Subcommittee on Tele-communications, Trade, and Consumer Protection scheduled an immediate hearing. During the hearing, supporters of the bill suggested gently but repeatedly that the members of the subcommittee should leave the business of making copyright law to their colleagues in the Senate and in the House judiciary committees, who understood it. Even a minor change in the text of the bill passed by the Senate, they warned, would cause the entire edifice to come crashing down, and would destroy America's best chance to prevent widespread Internet piracy of its valuable intellectual property.

Subcommittee members made it clear that they did not want to do anything that would prevent the bill's enactment. Nonetheless, they insisted, the bill's opponents had raised some serious concerns that needed to be addressed. The crux of the problem was the issue of fair use. There seemed to be a difference of opinion as to whether fair use would survive the enactment of the anticircumvention provisions. The legislation passed by the Senate forbade individuals to circumvent access or copy protection systems, regardless of their reasons for doing so. Would the privilege of fair use permit circumvention in order to make fair use of a work? Would fair use allow circumvention in order to gain access to unprotected material bundled with protected expression inside of a single copy protection envelope?

Content owners responded that the anticircumvention provisions would have no effect on fair use. They resisted any suggestion that a fair use privilege be written into the legislation, however, insisting that any privilege to circumvent, even for fair use purposes, would "provide a roadmap to keep the purveyors of 'black boxes' and other circumvention devices and services in business" and would "reduce the legal protection for these key enabling technologies to an inadequate and ineffective level."[23]

In the face of the impasse, Commerce Committee members indicated that the content community was being unreasonable. Perhaps in the week remaining before the Commerce Committee's jurisdiction expired, they suggested, the content community might sit down with consumer electronics groups, libraries, universities, civil liberties and consumer organizations, and encryption researchers to see whether the problems could be solved.

The bill's supporters took a calculated risk: they decided not to negotiate any further. Content owners had many powerful friends in the House and Senate leadership. Ultimately, they believed, the Commerce Committee was unlikely to have the stomach to block the legislation. If the content community made a deal, it might have to stick with it. If, on the other hand, it stood firm, then any unwanted amendments attached by the Commerce Committee could be removed either on the way to the House floor or in conference with the Senate.

When the subcommittee met the following week to mark up the bill, therefore, nothing had changed except for the feelings of Commerce Committee leadership. What had been mild irritation at the content community's disregard of obvious Commerce Committee jurisdiction had grown into exasperation with what seemed to committee leadership to be unmitigated arrogance. Content was sending the Commerce Committee the message that it, and what it chose to do to the bill, didn't matter. The committee leadership suggested that the content community think again. Having made their exasperation clear, however, committee leaders were unwilling to monkey with anything fundamental; they put their stamp on the bill by tinkering around the edges. The subcommittee approved amendments to permit circumvention for the purpose of protecting personal privacy and to relieve manufacturers of consumer electronics of any obligation to implement any and all technological protection measures a copyright owner might devise. The subcommittee adopted an amendment requiring the secretary of commerce to make annual reports to Congress on whether the enactment of anticircumvention measures was impairing individual users' access to copyrighted works. More basic amendments to privilege encryption research and to make circumvention suits subject to traditional copyright defenses, including fair use, were introduced but not put to a vote. If the parties could reach a mutually agreeable solution to those problems before the full committee markup the following week, well and good. If not, the amendments would be considered.

Software publishers were initially reluctant to engage in further negotiations, but ultimately they were able to reach a deal on encryption research. Publishers, motion picture producers, and record companies, on the other hand, were unwilling to compromise on fair use, and trusted Senate Judiciary Chairman Orrin Hatch (R-Utah) to get them out of any uncomfortable amendments attached by the House Commerce Committee during markup. That attitude didn't do anything to assuage the irritation of Commerce Committee leadership. In view of the content community's demonstration of disdain for the Commerce Committee's jurisdiction, Chairman Tom Bliley and ranking member John Dingell asked for and got a four-week extension.

But the content community, which felt as if it had been forced to reach too many deals it wasn't thrilled with, did not want to bargain any further. Allen Adler, the chief lobbyist for the book publishers group, was frankly resentful that the Commerce Committee had dared to insist on exercising jurisdiction in the first place. He found it outrageous that Commerce Committee members, who had far less experience on copyright bills than their colleagues on the House and Senate judiciary committees, would insist that the content community make a deal that would satisfy libraries, universities, or consumer electronics manufacturers. Adler insisted that it was time for the House leadership to put an end to this turf battle between the Commerce and Judiciary committees before it jeopardized the legislation's chances of enactment in the current session of Congress.[24] Lobbyists for Hollywood requested an urgent meeting with Speaker of the House Newt Gingrich (R-Ga.), and reported that they had received his personal assurance that the WIPO bill would pass Congress that year. Meanwhile, content lobbyists made the rounds, characterizing library, university, and consumer electronics proposals as scandalous, unprecedented, and unabashedly greedy. Under pressure from Commerce Committee staff, content owners agreed to sit down at the table with libraries and universities, but refused to make any substantive concessions. By the day before the full committee markup, no deals had been reached and further talks seemed fruitless. Commerce Committee staff circulated the text of amendments it would recommend for committee adoption in the event no compromise emerged. At that point, talks finally began in earnest.

The markup was scheduled for 10:00 A.M. Thursday, July 17. As negotiations continued, the Commerce Committee postponed its markup until 2:00 P.M., and then until 4:00 P.M. and then, finally, until 10:00 the following morning. Talks persisted throughout the evening, with staffers pressuring parties to reach some sort of deal on fair use. Content owners continued to refuse to consider subjecting the anticircumvention provisions to traditional copyright defenses. After midnight, libraries and content owners reached a compromise that nobody liked, but everyone agreed to live with.

The compromise on fair use nowhere mentioned the phrase "fair use." Devices and services that facilitated circumvention would still be made illegal, and trafficking in them willfully or for commercial gain would still be made criminal, but the provision prohibiting end users from circumvention would be replaced with one directing the Department of Commerce to promulgate regulations forbidding any person to circumvent technological protection measures. The Commerce Department was to be instructed to conduct biennial studies directed toward identifying classes of copyrighted works that should be exempted from the regulations because of adverse impact on users of those classes of works. Significantly for members of the Commerce Committee, the Commerce Department negotiations would fall under the continuing oversight jurisdiction of the House and Senate commerce committees, although copyright matters would in general remain the business of the judiciary committees.

At 10:00 A.M., when the full Commerce Committee met officially to mark up the Digital Millennium Copyright Act, no further important opposition to the bill remained. The Commerce Committee adopted language incorporating the bargain, and voted unanimously to send the newly amended bill to the House floor. That set the stage for a turf battle between the Judiciary Committee, which had adopted one version of the legislation back in March, and the Commerce Committee, which had just voted out a significantly revised one. At stake were not only the character and shape of digital copyright law, but also the disposition of enormous sums of lobbying and campaign contribution money expended by the major copyright-affected industries.

As part of the Commerce Committee understanding, all parties had agreed to support the Commerce Committee version of the legislation in preference to any earlier versions. The initial reaction to the details on the Commerce Committee deal from those not party to the bargain, however, was negative, and the content owner organizations started backing away from the deal. House and Senate Judiciary Committee members objected to vesting decision-making authority in the controversial Department of Commerce, which Republican leaders had recently tried to abolish.[25] The onerous prescribed rule-making procedure drew criticism from all sides; under the newly drafted compromise, the Commerce Department was to precede each biennial rule making with a lengthy trial-type hearing before an administrative law judge, in which each of the myriad affected parties could call witnesses to testify and could cross-examine the witnesses called by others. The elaborate proceedings could easily have taken years. Crucial ambiguities in the agreed-upon text of the bill inspired attacks laced with worst-case scenarios.

Mitch Glazier, chief intellectual property counsel for the House Judiciary Committee, took charge of the negotiations, determined to restore the legislation to something closer to the version his committee had approved. With the support of House Republican leadership, he spoke with affected parties as well as the staff of both House committees with an eye to getting the bill back into shape and through a vote on the floor of the House before Congress broke for its summer vacation in early August.

Copyright bills never seem to get shorter, clearer, or less complicated when "improved" through the negotiation process. As initially introduced, H.R. 2281 and its companion Senate Bill were both about three thousand words long. The version of H.R. 2281 adopted by the Judiciary Committee in March had grown to more than four thousand words. By the time that the Digital Millennium Copyright Act passed the Senate, the legislation had ballooned to something in the neighborhood of ten thousand words. After the House Commerce Committee had finished its work, the bill comprised more than twelve thousand words. The version of the legislation that Mitch Glazier prepared for vote of the full House contained more than twenty-five thousand words. As the legislation passed through his hands, Glazier succumbed to the temptation to load it up with a variety of unrelated measures pending before the Judiciary Committee, including a provision to, for the first time, give federal intellectual property protection to the facts and data contained in databases and a measure to give copyright-like protection to boat-hull designs. The legislation had been assembled in a hurry, and was riddled with ambiguities, internal inconsistencies, contradictions, and obfuscatory prose. On purely aesthetic grounds, it was an ugly piece of work. It retained the procedure requiring rule making by the Department of Commerce, and thus allowed the Commerce Committee to exercise oversight jurisdiction, but it gutted many of the safeguards that the library and education communities had bargained to make part of that procedure. Glazier had come up with a formulation that satisfied both House Commerce Committee members and his friends in the content community, without giving in to libraries, universities, or consumer groups. It passed the House essentially without debate.

Glazier's solution did not please the Senate leadership, who objected to any role for the Department of Commerce. The Senate refused to pass the House bill, insisting instead on the version of the bill that it had passed four months earlier. The end of the 105th Congress was only weeks away, and, somehow, the House and Senate needed to agree to enact the same version of the legislation. The bill's proponents focused on ensuring that the right Senators and Representatives were appointed to sit on a House-Senate Conference Committee, so that a reconciled and improved version could be rushed through both Houses of Congress in the final days of the session. The bill's opposition concentrated on strategies that might delay the appointment of a conference committee or ensure that it included members unlikely to accept the revisions that the content community demanded.

By the time the conference committee met, only a few weeks remained before the election recess, and committee members from both parties were in a hurry to get a deal done and passed before they left town. The bill they put together was a hodgepodge, incorporating bits and pieces of both versions. The conference committee jettisoned some of Glazier's late additions, but added other last-minute bargains. In final form, the Digital Millennium Copyright Act included nearly thirty thousand words and ran to more than fifty pages.[26]

As signed by the president on October 28, 1998, the DMCA incorporated two key provisions and a host of private side deals. The first key provision was the Internet service provider safe harbor, which spelled out the conditions under which service providers could avoid liability when infringing material passed through their systems. The statute identified distinct categories of problematic events that *might* be able to qualify for a privilege: transitory communications, system caching, hosting of subscribers' files, and technical infringements committed through the use of search engines and other information location tools.[27] It set different rules and conditions for absolution, depending on which category the offending conduct fit into. There were further special rules and conditions for nonprofit educational institutions. None of the categories, rules, and conditions made much sense on their own terms. Rather, each set gave the wary Internet service provider an opportunity to jump through a long, complicated series of hoops and thereby avoid liability.[28]

The second major part of the law was the anticircumvention provisions. Effective immediately, it became illegal to "manufacture, import, offer to the public, provide, or otherwise traffic in any technology, product, service, device, component, or part thereof" designed to circumvent copy-protection or access-protection technology. Effective October 2000, it would be illegal for any individual to circumvent access-protection technology—that is, measures preventing unauthorized *access* to a work. Borrowing your brother's password so that you can read a publication he subscribes to but you don't is now illegal. So is using a widely distributed software utility that would permit you to view a DVD movie you purchased on a player manufactured and sold in a different region of the world and licensed to play only DVDs from that region. The statute did not prohibit individual consumers' circumvention of copy-protection technology—that is, measures that prevent infringement of the copyright in a work. Individuals may still, if their purpose is otherwise lawful, devise a trick to defeat Macrovision, which seeks to prevent copying of commercial videotapes. They may try to save material that is posted on the Web in a hard-to-save format. They must, however, come up with ways to do this on their own. Distributing technology designed to help people circumvent copy-protection technology, whatever their reason for needing it, is illegal and in some cases criminal.[29]

The statute leaves it unclear how far the access-anticircumvention prohibition extends. That presents a problem: If "access" is understood to refer only to *initial* access, the statute's distinction between circumvention of access-protection technology and circumvention of copy-protection technology (almost) makes sense. If, however, "access" includes all subsequent actions to gain access to a work, the ban on circumvention of access-protection swallows up circumvention of copy-protection as well, since one will normally need to gain access to a work in order to engage in any use of it, fair or not.

The reason for delaying the effective date of the provision prohibiting individual circumvention to gain access was to permit the rule making—now to be conducted by the Librarian of Congress in consultation with the Copyright Office and Commerce Department (thus preserving both Commerce and Judiciary Committee jurisdiction and the associated generous campaign contributions)—to identify classes of works, if any, that should be temporarily exempt from the prohibition. It would remain illegal, however, to distribute devices or perform services designed to permit individuals to engage in circumvention of access-control technology even for works ruled exempt in the rule-making proceeding.[30]

I've described the process in mind-numbing detail because it appears to be inexorable. Copyright legislation written by multiparty negotiation is long, detailed, counterintuitive, kind to the status quo, and hostile to potential new competitors. It is also overwhelmingly likely to appropriate value for the benefit of major stakeholders at the expense of the public at large. There is no overarching vision of the public interest animating the

Digital Millennium Copyright Act. None. Instead, what we have is what a variety of different private parties were able to extract from each other in the course of an incredibly complicated four-year multiparty negotiation. Unsurprisingly, they paid for that with a lot of rent-seeking at the expense of new upstart industries and the public at large.

Even when interest groups start out with the high-minded intention of not only using the rhetoric of the public interest but actually fighting for the public interest, they end up settling for something that sells the public short. When the groups involved in the DFC agreed to withdraw their opposition to the Digital Millennium Copyright Act in return for modest concessions, most importantly the periodic government rule making that was the act's substitute for fair use, they believed the deal they had made was the best deal that they could get. By that point in the process, it probably was. Ironically, the resulting law is substantially more pernicious than the bill originally proposed by the Lehman Working Group's infamous White Paper. The original Lehman bill granted copyright owners sweeping new rights, but its silence on available exceptions invited the courts to apply copyright's traditional limitations. The DMCA also grants copyright owners sweeping new rights. Its laundry list of narrow exceptions, however, discourages the inference that the classic general exceptions and privileges apply. The original Lehman bill was breathtakingly expansive but it was short. It didn't improve the copyright law's general level of incomprehensibility, but it didn't greatly exacerbate it either. The DMCA is long, internally inconsistent, difficult even for copyright experts to parse and harder still to explain. Most importantly, it seeks for the first time to impose liability on ordinary citizens for violation of provisions that they have no reason to suspect are part of the law, and to make noncommercial and noninfringing behavior illegal on the theory that that will help to prevent piracy.

NOTES

1. *See* H.R. 2441, 104th Cong., 1st sess (1995); S. 1284, 104th Cong., 1st sess. (1995).

2. Other professors involved in the initial efforts included Pamela Samuelson, then at the University of Pittsburgh; James Boyle, then at American University; Lolly Gassaway from the University of North Carolina; Bob Oakley at Georgetown; Julie Cohen, also at Pittsburgh; and David Post, then at Georgetown. *See* Peter Jaszi, *Roundtable on the White Paper* (October 13, 1995).

3. *See, e.g.,* James Boyle, *Shamans, Software, and Spleens: Law and the Construction of the Information Society* (Harvard University Press, 1996); Laura Gassaway, *Growing Pains: Adapting Copyright for Libraries, Education and Society* (Fred B. Rothman, 1997); Julie E. Cohen, *A Right to Read Anonymously: A Closer Look at "Copyright Management" in Cyberspace,* 28 Connecticut Law Review 98 (1996); Peter Jaszi, *Caught in the Net of Copyright,* 75 Oregon Law Review 299 (1996); Jessica Litman, *Revising Copyright for the information Age,* 75 Oregon Law Review 19 (1996); Pamela Samuelson, *Technological Protection for Copyrighted Works,* 45 Emory Law Journal (1997).

4. *See* James Boyle, *Overregulating the Internet,* Washington Times, November 14, 1995, at A17; Pamela Samuelson, *The Copyright Grab,* Wired, January 1996, at 137–38.

5. *See, e.g.,* Andrea A. Lunsford and Susan West Schantz, *Copyright Bill Pending in Congress Threatens Free Exchange,* Columbus Dispatch, March 26, 1996, at 7A (op-ed); Denise Caruso, *Digital Commerce; Global Debate Over Treaties on Copyright,* New York Times, December 16, 1996, at D1.

6. *See* Cindy Skrzycki, *The Regulators: A Controversial Rules Rewrite,* Washington Post, March 8, 1996, at F1.

7. *See* Consumer Project on Technology, Comments on H.R. 2441: NII Copyright Protection Act of 1995 Before the Subcommittee on Courts and Intellectual Property of the House Committee on the Judiciary, 105th Cong., 2d sess. (February 15, 1996); Carolyn Breedlove, Statement on Behalf of the National Education Association, Digital Future Coalition Press Conference (June 11, 1996); Shari Steele, Letter to Keith M. Kupferschmid, Commissioner of Patents and Trademarks, on behalf of the Electronic Frontier Foundation (November 22, 1996); *Action Alert: Tell Legislators "No!" on Harmful NII Copyright Bill,* 9 EFFector Online No. 6 (May 17, 1996).

Other organizations registering early opposition to the proposed amendments included the Computer Professionals for Social Responsibility, the Consumer Federation of America, and the United States Catholic Conference.

8. *See Religious Technology Center* v. *Netcom,* 907 F. Supp. 1361 (N.D. Cal. 1995); *Religious Technology* v. *Lerma,* 908 F. Supp. 1353 (E. D. Va. 1995); *Religious Technology Center* v. *F.A.C.T.N.E.T., Inc.,* 907 F. Supp. 1468 (D. Colo. 1995). The *Netcom* case generated an opinion holding that the Internet service provider was not directly liable for copying and transmitting the material through its computers, but could be held liable as a contributory infringer for facilitating the copying if it knew that infringing material was posted on its server. Ultimately, the service provider defendants settled with the church. Two of the individuals who had originated the posts were held liable for copyright infringement; the individual defendants in the third case settled.

9. *See, e.g.,* S. 1137, Fairness in Musical Licensing Act of 1995, 104th Cong., 1st sess. (1995); S. 483, 104th Cong., 1st sess. (1995).

10. In some respects, the language proposed by the United States for the WIPO Treaty went further than that of the NII copyright bills. The draft defined copyright owners' control over reproductions to include ". . . direct and indirect reproduction of their works, whether permanent or temporary, in any manner or form," and limited the permissible exceptions to "cases where a temporary reproduction has the sole purpose of making the work perceptible or where the reproduction is of a transient or incidental nature, provided that such reproduction takes place in the course of use of the work that is authorized by the author or permitted by law." That language would have given copyright owners control over all temporary copies, even those never fixed in tangible form and those that under United States law would be deemed legal fair use. The proposed treaty draft further required signatory countries to prohibit "importation, manufacture or distribution of protection-defeating devices, or the offer or performance of any service having the same effect." *See* Proposed WIPO Treaty text, above at note 10 , art. 7; ibid. at art. 12; ibid. at art. 13.

11. *See, e.g.,* USIA-Text: *Bruce Lehman on New Intellectual Property Treaties* (April 4, 1997), at URL: <http://www.hri.org/news/usa/usia/97-04-04_1.usia.html>; *Copyright Legislation: Hearing Before the Subcommittee on Courts and Intellectual Property of the House Judiciary Committee,* 105th Cong., 1st sess. (September 16, 1997) (testimony of Robert W. Holleyman II, Business Software Association).

12. S. 1284 § 1201.

13. *See A&M Records* v. *Abdallah,* 948 F. Supp, 1449 (C.D. Cal. 1996).

14. *Sony* v. *Universal City Studios,* 464 U.S. 417 (1984). The VCR met that standard because, while some VCR recordings might infringe, others were authorized by the copyright owner and still others were excused by the fair use privilege.

15. *See* Information Infrastructure Task Force, *Intellectual Property and the National Information Infrastructure: The Report of the Working Group on Intellectual Property Rights* 231 (1995).

16. *See Hearing on H.R. 2281 and H.R. 2180 Before the Subcommittee on Courts and Intellectual Property of the House Judiciary Committee,* 105 Cong., 1st sess. (September 16, 1997) (testimony of Bruce Lehman, Commissioner of Patents).

17. Consumer electronics manufacturers, for example, received a provision that declared that the new law would not require them to redesign their products every time a copyright owner deployed a new protection system. Groups without the clout to insist on statutory exceptions were promised helpful language in the legislative history accompanying the bill. Parties negotiated language for insertion in the Senate Committee Report, only to discover that they had been working with a version of the text of the bill itself that differed from the version prepared by Senate Judiciary Committee staff. At the last minute, the Report language had to be reworked to incorporate the bargains reached while nonetheless reflecting the text and section numbers of the actual Senate bill.

18. I use "copy-control" here as shorthand for what the statute called "a tech-

nological protection measure that effectively protects a right of a copyright owner under this title in a work or a portion thereof"—in other words, a system that prevents unauthorized copying, adaptation, distribution, public performance, or public display. *See* 17 U.S.C. § 1201(b)(1)(A).

19. 17 U.S.C. § 1202.

20. The bill also included a couple of peculiar exceptions. There was some circular language, included in an unsuccessful attempt to mollify consumer electronics manufacturers without making any real concessions, that assured them that the statute didn't require them to design any device to implement any particular technological protection measure unless not doing so would cause the device to violate the prohibition of circumvention devices. There was an exception that purported to permit parents to do what they needed to do to protect minors from Internet pornography. There was also some language touted as disposing of any privacy concerns:

> Nothing in this chapter abrogates, diminishes, or weakens the provisions of, nor provides any defense or element of mitigation in a criminal prosecution or civil action under, any federal or state law that prevents the violation of the privacy of an individual in connection with the individual's use of the Internet.

Since there were *no* federal laws that had been read to prevent the violation of an individual's privacy in connection with her use of the Internet, the language must have struck even the most ardent supporters of copyright expansion as harmless.

21. Digital Era Copyright Enhancement Act, H.R. 3048, 105th Cong., 2d sess. (1998).

22. Shortly after the enactment of the Digital Millennium Copyright Act, Glazier left his position as chief counsel to take a new job as a lobbyist for the Recording Industry Association of America.

23. *Copyright Treaties Implementation Act: Hearing Before the Subcommittee on Telecommunications, Trade and Consumer Protection of the House Committee on Commerce,* 105th Cong., 2d sess. (June 5, 1998) (testimony of Steven J. Metalitz on behalf of the Motion Picture Association of America).

24. Mr. Adler expressed these sentiments publicly at a panel discussion entitled "Lobbying—For Copyright and Other Matters" held in Washington, D.C., on June 28, 1998, at the 1998 annual meeting of the Association of American University Presses.

25. *See* H.R. 1756, 104th Cong., 1st sess. (1995); H.R. Rep. No. 260, 104th Cong., 1st sess. (1995).

26. The Senate adopted the conference committee's version on October 8; the House was expected to follow suit the same day. At the last minute, however, Repub-

lican members of Congress decided to take H.R. 2281 off the calendar in a fit of pique. The Electronic Industries Alliance, which represents a number of groups that have been involved in negotiations over the provisions of the bill, selected former Democratic Representative Dave McCurdy as its president instead of any of the retiring Republican lawmakers that it had interviewed. House leaders decided to delay the vote on H.R. 2281 in order to signal their displeasure. After the story of the delay hit the wire services, the House leadership restored H.R. 2281 to the suspension calendar, and passed the bill on Monday, October 12.

27. *See* DMCA § 202 (codified at 17 U.S.C. § 512).

28. *See* United States Copyright Office, *The Digital Millennium Copyright Act of 1998: Copyright Office Summary* (December 1998), URL:<http:// www.loc.gov/copyright/legislation/dmca.pdf>, at 8-14; *A&M Records* v. *Napster,* Inc., 2000 U.S. Dist. LEXIS 6243 (N.D. Cal. 2000).

29. The Copyright Office explained the reason for treating the two differently this way:

> The distinction was employed to assure that the public will have the continued ability to make fair use of copyrighted works. Since copying of a work may be fair use under appropriate circumstances, Section 1201 does not prohibit the act of circumventing a technological protection measure that prevents copying. By contrast, since the fair use doctrine is not a defense to the act of gaining unauthorized access to a work, the act of circumventing a technological protection measure in order to gain access is prohibited.

Copyright Office Summary, above at note 28, at 4.

30. In October 2000, the Copyright Office completed the first rule making, and identified two narrow classes of works eligible for an exemption. Lists of World Wide Web sites blocked by Internet-content filtering software are one class of works whose access protection may lawfully be circumvented. In other words, if you want to find out whether Cyber Patrol® allows your children, your library's patrons, or your school's students to look up information about condoms, you may legally hack the access-protection system—if you can. Providing a software tool to reveal the hidden list, or even defeating access protection to reveal the list for someone else remains illegal. The other class of exempt works is literary works whose access-protection system is malfunctioning so that it fails to permit licensed users to gain access to the works despite their having obtained a license to use it. Again, the licensed user will need to figure out how to get around the access controls herself, since helping her would be providing an illegal "service. . .for the purpose of circumventing protection. . . ." A number of interests asked for a more expansive exception permitting circumvention of any sort of work, including movies and

music, protected by a malfunctioning access-protection system that denies access to licensed users. The Copyright Office, however, saw no need for so broad an exemption and suggested that Congress had not authorized it to grant exceptions except to very narrow categories of works. *See* Library of Congress, *Exemption to Prohibition on Circumvention of Copyright Protection Systems for Access Control Technologies*, 65 Federal Register 64555 (October 28, 2000).

TEN

THE COPYRIGHT WARS

This is a very profound moment historically. This isn't just about a bunch of kids stealing music. It's about an assault on everything that constitutes the cultural expression of our society. If we fail to protect and preserve our intellectual property system, the culture will atrophy. And corporations won't be the only ones hurt. Artists will have no incentive to create. Worst-case scenario: The country will end up in a sort of cultural Dark Ages.
—Richard Parsons, President, Time-Warner[1]

A profound moment, indeed. Indeed, it is an assault on everything that has stifled the cultural expression of our society. It's an assault on the system that stole every dime the Chambers Brothers ever made while grotesquely enriching Britney Spears.
—John Perry Barlow[2]

THE ENACTMENT OF THE DMCA seemed to give the content industries the security they were seeking. So long as they encased their content in technological protection envelopes, they could set and enforce any restrictions they chose on access and use. People would be forbidden to circumvent, and, because of the prohibition of circumvention devices and services, only the most talented teenage hackers would have the capability to circumvent in any event. Motion picture studios and record companies believed that they controlled the rights in content people wanted to see and hear, so they could pretty well write their own technological protection ticket—consumers would have to go along.

Technological protection standards have historically been hammered out in negotiations between representatives of copyright owners and organizations representing consumer electronics manufacturers. Consumer electronics companies are resistant to demands that they disable their machines, or install devices likely to impair viewing, listening, or recording performance. They have, however, been willing to install copy-protection devices so long as the technology is not too costly and every manufacturer agrees or is legally required to install precisely the same device. This removes the threat to compliant manufacturers that other manufacturers will compete by using less effective devices. It also removes the threat to copyright owners that some consumers will insist on purchasing noncompliant equipment.

Motion picture studios had some experience with technological protection. All of the mainstream studios used copy protection technology to prevent copying of videocassettes. In March of 1997, the digital video disc, or DVD, hit the market. It was slow to catch on. DVDs were themselves protected by a content scrambling system (CSS) that controlled access by restricting the play of all commercially released DVDs to licensed DVD players. The content on DVDs was scrambled, and the studios licensed DVD player manufacturers to build CSS descrambling software into their DVD players. The CSS license incorporated a host of conditions and specifications that the studios wanted to be sure were built into the players, and could easily be modified to mandate additional specifications as technology developed. Some of those specifications involved copy protection; others were attempts to preserve some of the profitable features of the pre-digital distribution market. The studios insisted, for example, that DVD players incorporate hardware or software that disabled them from playing DVDs released in different geographic regions, or that permitted DVD producers to include unskippable commercials. CSS did not prevent copying of DVDs, though, and pirate DVDs hit the market almost immediately. Since CSS operated to restrict access (that is, play), infringers simply copied the DVDs without playing them. The resulting copies worked exactly like the authorized ones, complete with CSS access-protection.

Some studios had been reluctant to release their films on DVD because of the potential for massive unauthorized digital copying, but had endorsed a more secure format, "Digital Video Express," or "Divx," which implemented pay-per-view. Divx discs were encoded to restrict access, and were playable only in Divx-compatible players. Consumers could buy a Divx disc for a small sum, watch it once, and would then be required to pay and gain reauthorization for subsequent viewings. Electronics retailer Circuit City announced the debut of the Divx format in the fall of 1997. Divx discs and players hit the stores in the summer of 1998. Some people bought them, but not many. A year later, Circuit City announced it was abandoning the format entirely.

Meanwhile, consumers had begun to complain about being unable to watch a DVD legally purchased in one country on a DVD player purchased in another country, and about having to watch the commercials every time they watched the feature. The motion picture industry took the position that since it controlled the content, it was entitled to condition access on any terms it chose, and since the new statute prohibited circumvention of access controls, any device or service that permitted consumers to evade those terms, regardless of the reason, violated the law. When a couple of amateurs reverse-engineered CSS in order to write DVD player software for the Linux operating system, and posted a CSS decryption program (dubbed "DeCSS") on the Internet, the motion picture industry filed three different lawsuits against sites posting the code for the utility or linking to sites that posted it, contending that the availability of the program raised a massive piracy threat.[3]

The DeCSS litigation poses the access question squarely. If "access" means only initial access, then it is clear that DeCSS should not violate the access-control-circumvention provisions of the DMCA. DeCSS is useless to people who do not already have a DVD in hand, and all of those people are authorized to gain access to the content in order to view it. On the other hand, if access means each act of viewing, listening, or using, then use of DeCSS would violate the access-control-circumvention provisions notwithstanding one's reason. It simply wouldn't matter that one wanted to employ a device to play a DVD one had purchased on a computer the Motion Picture Association has not licensed, or to play a DVD purchased in the UK on the DVD player one owned in the United States, or to keep one's six-year-old from seeing a salacious preview. The motion picture industry interpreted the law to bar circumvention of access control for any reason except the narrow and conditional exceptions explicitly enumerated in the statute. In the first judicial decision to interpret the DMCA, a court agreed.[4] The defendants argued that creating and posting the utility came within the fair use exemption. The motion picture studios responded that fair use was no defense to an anti-circumvention charge, and, again, the court agreed:

> The policy concerns raised by defendants were considered by Congress. Having considered them, Congress crafted a statute that, so far as the applicability of the fair use defense to Section 1201(a) claims is concerned is crystal clear. In such circumstances, courts may not undo what Congress

has so plainly done by "construing" the words of the statute to accomplish a result that Congress rejected.[5]

The story involving the music and recording industries is more complicated, in part because of longstanding social attitudes favoring free use of music, attitudes which the law had previously accommodated.[6] Record companies had not yet developed a copy-protection standard when the DMCA took effect. The recording industry insisted on technology as nearly leak-proof as possible, and had not yet found one. Instead, a variety of software companies had developed their own incompatible, proprietary technologies and were trying to persuade record companies and Web sites to adopt them. In 1998 the recording industry had a lock on most of the recorded music consumers wanted to listen to. All it needed to do was to hang on to consumers' ears long enough to get its piracy-resistant format up and running. It failed to appreciate how narrow its time window would be in Internet time.

By the time the Digital Millennium Act took effect in October, a small but significant number of music enthusiasts had discovered music recorded in MP3 format. MP3 is a patented file-compression format that permits near-CD quality recordings to be reproduced in files of manageable size. Freely available software allows consumers to translate the musical recordings on commercial CDs to MP3 files on a computer hard disk, and play the music through the computer's speakers. Because MP3 files have been compressed, it is feasible to store large numbers of files on a typical computer hard disk, and to transmit high-quality recordings over the Internet. Consumers can download entire music libraries over their telephone lines. By 1998, independent bands had begun to distribute their music directly to consumers in MP3 format, some for free and others for money. Bigger bands posted files containing free samples. Web sites sprung up devoted to MP3 hype and MP3 tips and MP3 files. In the summer of 1998, Diamond Multimedia announced that it would introduce a new portable MP3 player that would allow consumers to carry thirty minutes of music with them.

MP3 is just a file format. It most certainly can be used for unauthorized and infringing recordings; it may also be used for legitimate recordings, and in 1998 it was seeing both sorts of use. From the record companies' perspective, the problem with the MP3 format was that it was insecure: because the format incorporated no copy-protection standard, files could be copied, and copies could be copied and copied again. (In that respect, it was not appreciably different from the commercial CD format,[7] but because MP3 files are smaller than the music data files fixed on a commercial CD, making and trading MP3 files is more convenient than making and trading copies of commercial CDs.) The existence of an insecure digital format threatened the industry's ability to impose its own secure format on consumers and consumer electronics manufacturers. Perhaps even more frighteningly, the digital distribution of MP3 files held the potential for new paradigms for the distribution of music and new possibilities for making money from music. Some of the new paradigms incorporated conventional music publishers and record companies, but others bypassed the conventional business models. If everyone could be her own publisher on the Internet, every musician could be her own record company, and a small group of musicians were trying to do just that.

The recording industry responded to the growing popularity of music in the MP3 format by trying to shut the entire phenomenon down. All of it—the industry was determined to elbow both illegal trafficking in MP3 files and legitimate distribution of music in MP3 format out of the online market.[8] Record companies insisted that MP3 was a tool for pirates, and that all or at least most of the MP3 files sitting on consumers' hard disks were pirated recordings. Bands who posted MP3 files on their Web pages were ordered to take them down or lose their recording contracts.[9] When the first portable MP3 player came out, the recording industry filed suit to stop it.[10] The Recording Industry Association used its infringement lawsuit against the manufacturer of the Rio portable MP3 player as a threat against all consumer electronics manufacturers, and demanded that no business market a portable device capable of playing MP3 files. Instead, the Recording Industry Association insisted, portable digital players should be compatible only with secure, encrypted recording formats.

In December of 1998, the recording industry announced that it had formed a consortium of record companies, software companies, and consumer electronics companies to devise a new, secure digital music file format to enable record companies to distribute digital music over the Internet without surrendering control over their copyrighted material. The members of the Secure Digital Music Initiative (SDMI) then got together in secret monthly meetings to talk and talk and talk about what the new secure standard would look like. Companies that had already invested in some proprietary formats understandably pushed their formats. Copyright owners wanted something that was both impregnable and incompatible with MP3—indeed, they spent more time in the first months of the initiative demanding that devices be unable to play MP3 files than they did focusing on the specifics of a secure format. Consumer electronics manufacturers were unwilling to commit to manufacture equipment unless it seemed likely consumers would buy it. They talked and talked for months—not long in conventional time but an eon in Internet time. Six months later, the SDMI consortium had not yet come up with a secure digital specification. That's when the U.S. Court of Appeals for the Ninth Circuit ruled that the industry's lawsuit against the manufacturer of the Rio portable MP3 player was meritless.[11] The copyright law, the court held, entitled consumers to make MP3 recordings of their CDs, and it entitled manufacturers to make devices intended to help consumers play these recordings. Other manufacturers announced they would bring out their own portable MP3 players.

By engaging in a scorched-earth campaign, the recording industry squandered some truly awesome assets. If it had managed to keep its audience devoted long enough to get its piracy-resistant format up and running, it might well have been able to build the pay-per-listen world the DMCA seemed to promise it. There were two sensible ways to go about it: one was to rush lots of secure music and portable devices that could play that secure music into the market, and rely on the fact that, by controlling the music that people wanted to hear, conventional record companies were well-positioned to compete with MP3 in a head-to-head battle. There were lots of proprietary secure formats being tested and any one of them would have done for a start. The second possibility was to take more time to design a good secure format, but meanwhile to release product in MP3 format to keep hold of the public's ears. As business plans go, this one would not have been crazy. Music is still being released on CDs, and CD-to-MP3 is a trivial and legal transformation once one has the necessary software installed on one's computer. The recording industry, however, was unwilling to subject its current catalog to possible piracy, and was unwilling to commit itself to an insecure digital standard that might become entrenched. Instead, it fought about whose patented security algorithm would become the new standard, and it focused on herding all MP3 music off the Internet.

As the 1999 holiday buying season wound down, there was still no complete SDMI specification, and no SDMI music had been released. Meanwhile, consumers downloaded MP3 software, bought MP3 machines, and collected a slew of MP3 files. The granddaddy of MP3 Web sites was an

MP3 music portal at www.MP3.com. mp3.com, launched in 1996 by entrepreneur Michael Robertson, originally offered free MP3 downloads of non-major label music, MP3-related software, MP3 commentary and how-to articles, and MP3 discussion bulletin boards. The site also offered new bands and those not yet signed to recording contracts an opportunity to reach potential fans. Artists could sign up, upload an MP3 file or several, and any pictures or promotional material they wanted to. MP3.com would announce the artists and songs on its new songs list, and allow individuals to listen to or download a copy of the song. MP3.com also made and marketed CDs. MP3.com would sell consumers a digital automatic music (DAM) CD, containing songs in both conventional and MP3 format. A full-length DAM CD went for about half the price of a major label CD, and MP3.com split the price fifty-fifty with the artist. (Contrast that with a typical royalty of 6 percent of the suggested retail price for major label recordings: If a typical CD costs $15.99, and an MP3.com DAM CD costs $7.99, then even after earning back any cross-collateralized advances, an artist would earn less than a dollar per CD sold on a major label. She'd earn $3.99 outright per DAM CD sold via MP3. Of course, major label recordings sell many more CDs than MP3.com will; artists without major label record contracts, however, didn't have that option.)

Despite the legitimate services, the recording and music industries viewed MP3.com as a site that gave aid and comfort to pirates. Robertson received letters from lawyers in response to postings offering links to software enabling consumers to get around copy-protection mechanisms, or analyzing the weaknesses of particular copy-protection schemes, demanding that he remove the offending items from the MP3.com site. Robertson cultivated this "bad boy" image to enhance his site's appeal to an audience of young hacker wanna-bes. Armed with a large audience to sell to potential advertisers, Robertson bought performing rights licenses from ASCAP and BMI, permitting him to play hit songs on his Web site. He then announced an initial public offering, and a host of enhanced services including "MyMP3.com."

Robertson's MyMP3.com service allowed subscribers to listen to (but not save) music cuts copied from any CD in their possession, from any remote location. A subscriber would demonstrate possession of a CD by putting the CD in a computer CD-ROM drive and transmitting the CD's identifying information to MP3.com over the Internet. MP3.com provided a password-protected virtual music "locker" permitting access to exactly the same music the locker would have contained if the subscriber had translated each cut on the CD to MP3 format and then uploaded the MP3 file over the Internet. Actually uploading the music would have taken hours. By using its own library of MP3 recordings created from CDs it had purchased, and requiring transmission only of proof of consumers' possession of corresponding CDs, MP3.com made the process of assembling a private online music library quick and convenient. Robertson figured that the service was legal: consumers, after all, were legally entitled to make noncommercial recordings of music, and he had licensed from ASCAP and BMI the right to transmit the music over the Internet. The music and recording industries disagreed, and filed several lawsuits.

Although Robertson had negotiated licenses with composers to perform their music, he hadn't obtained licenses from record companies to perform their *recordings* of that music, and he hadn't even thought he might need licenses from record companies or composers' music publishers to *copy* recordings of their music, since he was relying on consumers' legal privileges to make copies for their own personal use. The court refused to permit MP3.com to stand in its subscribers' shoes, noting that MP3.com was a commercial business and made its recordings for purely commercial purposes.[12]

While the MP3.com suit was pending, a college freshman named Shawn Fanning, who enjoyed trading MP3 music files and talking about them with other music fans, invented Napster, designed to make it easier to do both. Napster permitted individuals to locate and share MP3 files across the Internet, and it automated the transfer of files from fans who want to share their music libraries to fans who want to listen to or copy particular recordings.

Fanning posted Napster on the Internet for free download. Millions of consumers installed Napster and began to trade MP3 files with one another. The recording industry filed suit against Napster even before the company could officially launch the product.[13] If the campaign was meant to chill Napster subscriptions, it didn't work. Within several months, Napster had accumulated twenty million subscribers, and estimated its probable subscriber base at seventy million by the time it reached its first birthday.

As an adjunct to its lawsuit, the RIAA had sent letters to universities urging them to block Napster access from their servers—hundreds complied. The popular rock band Metallica upped the ante by filing its own lawsuit against Napster and three universities. Two of the universities, Yale and the

University of Southern California, had declined to disable Napster access, citing academic freedom. The third defendant, Indiana University, had initially blocked Napster because it consumed too great a share of the system's bandwidth, but had restored access in response to student protests. Yale surrendered first, blocking Napster a week after being served with Metallica's complaint. Indiana caved next, disabling access the next day. The University of Southern California followed suit a few days later. Metallica, meanwhile, had an answer to Napster's insistence that, since it didn't monitor or control its subscribers' downloads, it had no information indicating that any subscriber was infringing the band's copyrights. Metallica hired a consultant to analyze Napster traffic and assemble a list of subscribers trading Metallica songs. It then dumped thirteen boxes full of documents identifying 335,435 individual Napster subscribers who had allegedly downloaded Metallica music. Napster obligingly blocked the accounts.

Napster had a number of more than plausible arguments that it was not liable for copyright infringement. First, it argued, it posted or stored no music on its servers, and had no control over the content traded using its service, but merely facilitated transfers initiated and controlled by its subscribers. Napster provided none of the content; rather it supplied a directory service and assisted its subscribers in making connections between their computers, so that they could transmit material to each other. Therefore, it claimed, it acted as an Internet service provider and was entitled to invoke the service provider and directory service safe harbors in the DMCA. Thus, when Metallica provided it with lists of infringing subscribers, it had followed statutory procedures to cut off their access, and would gladly do so for any other aggrieved copyright owner. The record industry responded that the service provider and directory safe harbors were not intended to protect services like Napster, and were sufficiently narrowly defined to make Napster's activities an awkward fit with the statutory language. Even were that not the case, the record companies insisted, the service provider safe harbors incorporated a variety of conditions and procedural prerequisites that Napster had failed to comply with, so it was not entitled to invoke the safe harbors as a matter of law. The judge sided with the record companies.[14]

Second, Napster argued, it shouldn't be liable because the file transfers it facilitated were completely legal—individual consumers were making personal noncommercial copies of music, behavior permitted by the Audio Home Recording Act and by fair use. The judge sided with the record companies.

Finally, Napster argued, it shouldn't be liable because its service had legitimate as well as allegedly infringing uses: many of the music files transferred by its subscribers were authorized or licensed material. The record companies insisted that the chief and perhaps only reason users signed up with Napster was the lure of easy access to free pirate recordings, and that Napster had built its entire business model on promoting copyright infringement. The judge sided with the record companies, and ordered Napster to block access to major label recordings or shut down pending trial.

The court gave Napster two days to comply. Napster announced it would file an emergency appeal, but might have to shut down in order to comply with the judge's decision. In the next forty-eight hours, Napster traffic nearly doubled. Meanwhile, visitors to sites offering Napster-like functionality without the central server (and therefore without some obvious intermediary to sue) increased to the point of server overload. Hours before the deadline, the Court of Appeals for the Ninth Circuit stayed the injunction pending an expedited appeal.

The content industry continued to find new folks to sue. The motion picture industry filed two lawsuits against Web sites that purported to rely on statutory privileges to permit the retransmission of television signals. The recording industry sued a site named MP3board.com, claiming that, while the site hosted no infringing content itself, it posted extensive hyperlinks to sites that did host infringing content. Merely posting hyperlinks, the record companies argued, was itself egregious piracy. Both the motion picture and the recording industry filed a lawsuit against a site named Scour.com. Scour.com was an advertising-supported entertainment portal that included a search engine for music, video, image, and radio material on the Web, and a file-sharing utility that permitted the exchange of music, video, and audio files. Scour's search engine, like other search engines, did not differentiate between files made available on the Web under the authority of the copyright owner and files made available by unauthorized volunteers, and a Scour.com search would typically retrieve links to content of both sorts. That, said the content industry, amounted to promoting and enabling widespread piracy: "This is about stealing, plain and simple."[15]

But it wasn't plain or simple. In each of the cases, defendants had appealing arguments that their activities were legal. In each case, analogous behavior in the offline world was permitted by statute or caselaw. MP3.com's archive of recordings, for instance, was functionally indistinguishable from the recordings that television and radio broadcasters make of licensed material to facilitate the broadcast. Television and radio stations have never asked permission to make these copies, and in 1976 obtained an express statutory privilege to make "ephemeral" recordings incidental to licensed transmissions. There is no principled reason to distinguish webcasting.

MP3.com had permission from composers to perform their music, but had not secured permission from record companies to perform their recordings. Again, the radio and television analogy is instructive. Television and radio stations have never needed permission from record companies (as distinguished from composers) to perform their recorded music, because the owners of sound recording copyrights had no legal right to control public performances of their recordings. Here there *is* a principled reason to treat Webcasting differently: an Internet transmission could result in a saved digital file. Congress therefore amended the copyright law in 1995 to give record companies exclusive rights over some digital audio transmissions. MP3.com, however, was not engaging in that sort of transmission as part of its MyMP3.com service; instead it was streaming the music in a format that resisted reproduction. The DMCA had included a complicated deal that sought to address audio streaming, but where MyMP3.com's transmissions fell within the new scheme was far from clear.[16]

Napster was not itself actually doing anything that infringed music or record copyrights directly. It made no copies, created no adaptations, distributed no copies, and transmitted no files. Indeed, no MP3 files passed through Napster's servers. Instead, it distributed software that enabled it to maintain a directory of designated MP3 files on the computers of those of its subscribers who were actually online, that permitted subscribers to use that directory to find MP3 files, and that automated a subscriber-to-subscriber transfer. The suit against Napster sought to hold it liable as a contributory infringer for facilitating widespread unauthorized distribution of files copied from recorded music. Deciding whether contributory liability was warranted required answering the question whether individual consumers could legally engage in noncommercial online exchange of MP3 files. If Napster's subscribers were not breaking the law, then Napster was not breaking the law either.

Did individuals have a privilege to share MP3 files? No court had yet answered that question. The Ninth Circuit had held that consumers had a legal privilege to *make* MP3 files, just as they had a legal privilege to tape television programs on a VCR. Giving away or loaning legitimately made copies of copyrighted works in the offline world is legal under the first sale doctrine. Online, however, sharing files involves both transmission and the creation of additional copies. Posting MP3 files for the world to download would clearly violate the copyright owners' rights to control public performances. Was a Napster-mediated one-to-one file transfer a public performance or a private one?

iCraveTV, a Canadian Web site, permitted Canadian browsers to view Webcasts of free Toronto television signals, claiming that its activities were authorized by the Canadian copyright law's license for cable television.[17] In both Canada and the United States, cable television operators have a statutory license to retransmit broadcast programming. The motion picture studios argued that even if iCraveTV's interpretation of Canadian law were sound, the nature of the Internet made it impossible for iCraveTV to prevent viewers who weren't in Canada from gaining access to their site. Since U.S. residents (or Canadians vacationing in the United States) could claim to be in Canada and thus view iCraveTV's transmissions, iCraveTV was illegal in the United States, where Canadian copyright law didn't apply. The court ordered iCraveTV to shut down unless it could guarantee that no individual in the United States could gain access to iCraveTV's programming.[18]

David Simon started RecordTV.com, seeking to use the Internet as a virtual VCR, to solve the problem of people's learning they would miss their favorite TV shows at places and times that made it impractical to arrange to record them. Subscribers could log on to their private accounts from any location and place a request to record a particular TV show; after the show aired, they could sign back on within ten days and view (but not save) the show. Like MyMP3.com and iCraveTV, RecordTV tried to capitalize on Internet delivery by offering consumers more flexible and convenient access to works they were already permitted to see and hear. Simon believed that he was entitled to rely on individuals' privilege to record TV shows in order to watch them at different times. His site's performance of a recording of any particular program would be transmitted only to the subscriber who requested the recording. That would make it a private performance rather than a public one, and private performances do not violate the copyright law. The motion picture industry disagreed; twelve motion picture studios filed a lawsuit to shut RecordTV.com down.[19]

MP3Board.com deploys an automated search engine that searches the Internet for publicly accessible MP3-related material, and generates hyperlinks to the sites that it finds. The links are displayed on the MP3Board.com web pages. MP3Board does not review or monitor the links or the sites that they refer to. Hyperlinks are merely coded instructions giving the location of files on the Internet. They make it easy for Web browsing software to find a site on the Web in a way that's analogous to the way footnotes make it easy to find a cited source, or driving directions make it easy to find a street address. Hyperlinks are not copies, adaptations, distributions, performances, or displays of the sites they link to or the content those sites contain, and no court had held that posting a hyperlink constituted copyright infringement. When MP3Board received a letter from the Recording Industry Association of America demanding that MP3Board remove all links to sites containing infringing material or cease its operations, it filed a lawsuit asking the court to declare that its hyperlinks did not infringe RIAA's member copyrights.[20] The RIAA filed a counterclaim to shut MP3Board down, insisting that it was "an extensive and egregious link site that facilitates widespread copyright infringement on the Internet."[21]

The spring and summer of 2000 saw an explosion of Internet-related copyright litigation. Some cases involved straightforward piracy, but far fewer than the content industries claimed. Other cases revealed a different pattern: Innovators and upstarts sought to exploit the Internet's potential by creating an online analogue to an offline resource. They set up their sites believing their activities to be legal. Some of them relied on legal privileges that had permitted analogous activity in the offline world. Copyright owners insisted that even long-standing offline privileges didn't extend to online activities, and relied on statutory language drafted so narrowly that it had no elasticity at all. Meanwhile, though, content industries declined to make their material available for licensed download, fearing possible loss of control.

NOTES

1. Quoted in Chuck Philips, *Piracy: Music Giants Miss a Beat on the Web,* Los Angeles Times, July 17, 2000, at A1.

2. E-mail from John Perry Barlow to Dave Winer, July 18, 2000, posted at the Napster Weblog, URL: <http://napsterdiscuss.weblogs.com/stories/storyReader$48>.

3. *DVD Copy Control Association* v. *McLaughlin,* Case No. CV 786804 (Cal Super. Santa Clara, January 20, 2000); *Universal City Studios* v. *Reimerdes,* 82 F. Supp. 2d 211 (SDNY 2000); *Universal City Studios* v. *Hughes,* No. 300 CV 72 RNC (D.Conn., filed January 14, 2000). The cases quickly grew ugly. Plaintiffs sought an injunction against anyone who posted the code and anyone who linked to a site

that posted the code. The DVD Copy Control Association at one point amended its trade secrecy complaint to seek an injunction against an organization that sold a protest T-shirt displaying the DeCSS code.

4. *Universal Studios* v. *Reimerdes*, 82 F. Supp. 2d 211 (S.D.N.Y. 2000).

5. *Universal Studios* v. *Reimerdes*, 111 F. Supp. 2d 294, 324 (S.D.N.Y. 2000).

6. The specific statutory exemptions for public performances of music are broader than the exemptions for public performances of dramatic works or films. *See* 17 U.S.C. § 110. Although the performing rights societies—ASCAP, BMI, and SESAC—enforce composers' rights to license nonexempt public performances, they operate subject to antitrust consent decrees that constrain their ability to refuse to grant licenses or impose unreasonable terms. When Congress granted composers rights to make and license recordings of their music, it subjected those rights to a "compulsory license" that permitted artists to record and publish any previously recorded song upon payment of a statutory fee. 1909 Act § 1(e); 17 U.S.C. § 115. When Congress amended the statute to prohibit record rental, it was careful to leave consumers' rights to loan, give, and resell records undisturbed. Finally, in 1992, Congress enacted a provision exempting consumers from liability for copyright infringement for noncommercial copying of recorded music. 17 U.S.C. § 1008.

7. Although commercial digital recording technology incorporates a copy-protection scheme prescribed by the Audio Home Recording Act, 17 U.S.C. § 1001-1011, the CDs themselves include only identifying information. The serial copy prevention technology is contained in digital audio recorders that meet the act's definition. Computers are excluded from the definition, and do not incorporate SCMS.

8. *See Music Download Debate Continues*, C|Net News.Com, December 16, 1998, at URL: <http://www.news.com/News/Item/0,4,29980,00.html>. *See also* Electronic Frontier Foundation, *Electronic Frontier Foundation Digital Audio and Free Expression Policy Statement*, May 1999, at URL: <http://www. eff.org/cafe/eff_ audio_ statement.html>.

9. *See* Neil Strauss, *Free Web Music Spreads from Campus to Office*, New York Times, April 5, 1999, at A1.

10. *See Recording Industry Association* v. *Diamond Multimedia*, 29 F. Supp. 2d 624 (C.D. CA 1998), *aff'd*, 180 F.3d 1072 (9th Cir. 1999).

11. *Recording Industry Association* v. *Diamond Multimedia*, 180 F.3d 1072 (9th Cir. 1999), *aff'g* 29 F. Supp. 2d 624 (C.D. CA 1998).

12. *See UMG Recordings* v. *MP3.com*, 92 F. Supp. 2d 349 (S.D.N.Y. 2000).

13. *See A&M Records* v. *Napster, Inc.*, 54 U.S.P.Q.2D (BNA) 1746 (N.D. Cal. 2000).

14. *See* ibid. *See also A&M Records* v. *Napster*, 114 F.Supp. 2d 286 (N.D. Cal. 2000).

15. Jack Valenti, quoted in July 20, 2000, joint MPAA, RIAA, and NMPA press release, online at URL: <http://www.mpaa.org/Press/ScourPressRelease.htm>.

16. In November 2000, MP3.com settled the last of the record-company lawsuits, agreeing to pay millions of dollars in damages and license fees. MP3.com announced that it had reconfigured its MyMP3.com "Beam It" service as a paid subscription service, and would henceforth collect information about subscribers' demographics and music-listening preferences to market to its new friends.

17. The license is subject to statutory royalties. iCrave's founder testified before the U.S. Congress that the company had filed a petition with Canada's Copyright Board seeking an official tariff rate. See *Video on the Internet: iCraveTV.com and Other Recent Developments in Webcasting, Hearing Before the Subcommittee on Telecommunications, Trade and Consumer Protection of the House Commerce Committee*, 106th Cong., 2d sess. (February 16, 2000) (testimony of Ian McCallum, iCraveTV). As part of a settlement of a related lawsuit brought by Canadian broadcasters, iCraveTV reportedly agreed to withdraw the petition and to abandon all efforts to seek any ruling resolving the legality of Internet retransmission of broadcast programming. See Steven Bonisteel, *iCraveTV Settlement Leaves Legal Issues Open*, Newsbytes, February 29, 2000, reprinted in *BizReport*, February 29, 2000, at URL: <http://www.bizreport.com/news/2000/02/20000229-9.htm>.

18. *Twentieth Century Fox Film Corp.* v. *iCraveTV*, 53 U.S.P.Q.2D (BNA) 1831 (W.D. Pa. February 8, 2000).

19. *MGM Studios* v. *RecordTV.com*, No. CV-DO-06443 (C.D. Cal.).

20. *MP3Board, Inc.* v. *Recording Industry Association of America*, No. C-00-20606 (N.D. Cal., filed June 1, 2000).

21. RIAA, Press Release: "Important Facts about the Recording Industry's Lawsuit against MP3Board.com," June 28, 2000, online at URL: <http://www.riaa.org/News_Story.cfm?id=292>.

ELEVEN

COPYRIGHT LAW IN THE DIGITAL MILLENNIUM

I N THE WAKE OF THE enactment of the Digital Millennium Copyright Act, the content industries' chief strategy combined litigation with the threat of further litigation. They searched out, identified, threatened, and if necessary sued intermediaries who arguably facilitated individuals' unauthorized use. They used automated programs that roamed the Internet searching for signs of infringement to find suspicious sites, and the DMCA's expedited subpoena procedures to force service providers to identify alleged pirates. In many cases, a threat was all that was necessary. The Recording Industry Association sent scores of letters to universities demanding that student Web sites be shut down, and they were shut down. The RIAA demanded that Internet service providers terminate subscribers and subscribers were terminated.

The software industry had begun to sell its products online long before the enactment of the DMCA. Advertising-supported works like newspapers and magazines spawned online versions in the early 1990s. The motion picture, music, and book publishing industries, however, had maintained that until the DMCA's protections became law, they would not risk their valuable content on the Internet. After the DMCA's protections became law, they still declined to make their works available for download, concerned that existing technological protections were insufficiently leak-proof. Even after the popularity of MP3.com, Napster, MP3Board, iCraveTV, and Scour demonstrated the tremendous demand for digital music and television, the recording and motion picture industries remained reluctant to license Web distribution of their material. Instead, they pursued relentless campaigns designed to educate, deter, and avenge.

As individual offenders were shut down, others sprang up. The recording industry association's suit against Napster inspired a number of Napster-variants supplying similar functionality without Napster's vulnerabilities. A start-up introduced "Aimster"—a Napster-like add-on to America Online's Instant Messenger program that permitted file sharing within a small group of "buddies." Programs like Gnutella and Freenet supplied distributed search and file-sharing capability, bypassing a central server entirely, so that there would be no intermediary to sue and no records of who had transferred what files to subpoena.

As a comprehensive strategy, litigation works best against commercial actors. If it takes a lot of money to produce or distribute content, producers and distributors will need money, will have money, will be likely to hire lawyers, and will be vulnerable to weapons aimed at their pocketbooks. MP3.com and Napster have investors to keep happy. Universities have legislatures and donors to soothe. Thus it is completely understandable that the content industry focused its lobbying efforts on pinpointing intermediaries to sue. It eschewed the politically difficult course of seeking an amendment expressly imposing liability on individual consumers for noncommercial copying and private transmission. It sought instead to prevent individual infringement by securing a tough anticircumvention law. That focus turned out to be shortsighted. When producing and distributing content is cheap, commercial intermediaries are optional. The Internet permits individuals to share material with one another on an immense scale and at negligible cost. Stopping each of them is not the sort of task that litigation does best—especially when the basis for their liability is murky.

The strategy of making it impossible for millions of teenagers to engage in unauthorized uses by enacting legal protection for access controls has not worked particularly well either—at least so far. Content owners started pressing for anticircumvention laws as early as 1993. The Lehman Working Group recommended such a law in its Green Paper report in 1994. Multiple access-control technologies appeared under the name of "electronic rights management systems" in 1995, and commercial systems appeared early in 1996. Yet, in the spring of 2000, several generations later in Internet time, record companies had failed to secure their recordings, or to make them available for digital download. Had record companies begun encrypting their recordings in 1993, or even 1996, the vast majority of content traded on Napster would have been unavailable to the ordinary consumer with no hacker skills, because the source recordings would have been technologically protected. Having failed to deploy secure digital music, record companies have relied on courts to revise the bargain to insert a provision imposing liability on consumers for noncommercial copying, private performance, and private distribution. That's a hard sell, especially if the consumers don't go along.

Moreover, the music industry's reluctance to release product over the Internet undermined its campaign to persuade citizens to "say yes to licensing." The RIAA failed in its bid to marginalize MP3 software and keep portable MP3 players from the market. It failed to persuade consumer electronics manufacturers to make their portable digital music players MP3 incompatible. It promised consumers, repeatedly, that the availability of licensed major-label music for their SDMI-compliant portable players was imminent, and then it didn't deliver any. What did it imagine consumers were going to play on their portable MP3 players? If unlicensed major-label music was the only major-label music available, consumers didn't have the option to say yes to licensing.

Nor was the record companies' moral position appealing. The recording industry's insistence that unless musicians were fairly paid, there would be no music rang particularly hollow with fans given the industry's years of demonstrating that when musicians are not fairly paid, they continue to play, write songs, perform at concerts, and cut records. Record companies had collected the lion's share of record revenues for years, arguing that their part of the process of creating and selling records was the expensive part. They controlled the recording studios, record pressing and CD burning plants, and the distribution network, and if studios, pressing plants, and distributors don't get paid, they don't stay in business. The Internet makes much of that infrastructure optional. Yet not one major label proposed reallocating the share of revenue as between the record company and the artist. No major label has been willing to invest in models in which individuals pay artists and authors directly, even one obliging artists and authors to send the record companies their cut. Not one major label has announced that the money it won't spend burning, packaging, and shipping CDs would be shared with consumers in the form of lower prices. Instead, the recording industry suggested that when it did make its catalog available online, the consumer should pay the same $17.99 for an encrypted, downloaded digital file (protected from copying, sharing, lending, or resale) that she pays for an unencrypted, loanable, copyable, resalable CD. No wonder consumers aren't going along.

And they aren't. Napster has more than forty million subscribers despite the record industry's attempts to paint it as a pirate. In the forty-eight hours after the court ordered Napster to shut down, Napster traffic increased markedly. Napster subscribers checked out Gnutella and Freenet. Millions of people apparently decided that they would continue to share files without regard to the court's ruling. In the following weeks, several small start-ups announced their own file-sharing applications. Either they figured that they had incorporated some features that evaded Napster's legal problems, or they gambled that the legal ruling wouldn't last. If forty million people refuse to obey a law, then what the law says doesn't matter. It may be that people flout it because they're natural lawbreakers, or it may be, as I argue in chapter 8, that they don't comply because it doesn't make sense to them. Whatever the reason, the law is not going to work well in the real world.

Bandwidth constraints have so far limited both the demand for digital, downloadable movies and the unauthorized trading of feature films. Digitized movies comprise very large files; 56k modems are slow. The movie studios are even further from distributing encrypted product via download than their siblings in the recording industry. Although the motion picture industry distributes CSS-encrypted DVDs, it has limited its release of online product to low-resolution, video streaming of movie trailers. The ease with which DeCSS was created and disseminated, however, suggests that, as high-speed Internet connections become more common, the motion picture industry may face similar difficulties. Its litigation strategy, aimed in part at banishing unwanted links from the Internet, suggests that it insists on tighter control of the networked digital environment than the public is likely to allow it to exercise.

Beyond a very small number of well-publicized "e-books,"[1] the print publishers' forays into online publishing of technologically protected words has thus far been limited to a rudimentary and leaky subscription model. Online newspapers, magazines, technical publishers, and information services condition access to text on registration, payment (in money, personal data, or both), and clicking "I accept" to a long recital of restrictive terms of use. Subscribers who click seem to feel little compunction, however, about reposting access-protected texts to their friends, their acquaintances, and the world at large.[2] Again, the publishers' moral position is not especially appealing. At the same time newspaper publishers joined as plaintiffs in a copyright infringement suit to shut down a site encouraging individuals to repost copyrighted news stories,[3] many of them were posting or licensing others to post content online without permission from or payment to the individual copyright owners who had written it.[4] Digital print publishers are only beginning to deploy heavy encryption and disappearing digital ink to prevent authorized readers from saving what they read and passing it along. It remains to be seen how much control the public will be willing to let publishers exercise over reading.

Access controls and anticircumvention laws may yet enable the content industry to assert its control over audiences' eyes and ears, once it does get its encrypted content online. Or, the industry may need to return to the bargaining table and try to achieve yet another law to plug the perceived leak. There are noises being made in that direction already.[5] Unless the stakeholders do things very differently this time around, though, that law won't work either.

NOTES

1. *See, e.g.,* Stephen King's home page, <http://www.stephenking.com>.

2. *See Los Angeles Times* v. *Free Republic,* 54 U.S.P.Q.2D (BNA) 1453 (C.D. Cal. 2000).

3. *See* ibid.

4. *See, e.g., Tasini* v. *New York Times,* 192 F.3d 356 (2d Cir. 1999), *cert. granted,* 121 S.Ct. 425 (2000).

5. *See, e.g.,* Shane Ham and Robert D. Atkinson, *Napster and Online Piracy: The Need to Revisit the Digital Millennium Copyright Act,* Progressive Policy Institute Policy Report (May 2000).

TWELVE

REVISING COPYRIGHT LAW
FOR THE INFORMATION AGE[1]

W HEN WE EXAMINE THE QUESTION whether copyright needs redesign to stretch it around digital technology, we can look at the issues from a number of different vantage points. First, there is the viewpoint of current copyright stakeholders: today's market leaders in copyright-affected industries. Their businesses are grounded on current copyright practice; their income streams rely on current copyright rules. Most of them would prefer that the new copyright rules for new copyright-affecting technologies be designed to enable current stakeholders to retain their dominance in the marketplace.[2]

One way to do that is to make the new rules as much like the old rules as possible. Current copyright holders and the industries they do business with are already set up to operate under those rules: they have form agreements and licensing agencies and customary royalties in place. There are other advantages in using old rules: if we treat the hypertext version of the *New York Times* as if it were a print newspaper, then we have about two hundred years' worth of rules to tell us how to handle it. We can avoid the problems that accompany writing new rules, or teaching them to the people (copyright lawyers, judges, newspaper publishers) who need to learn them.

Using old rules, however, has the obvious disadvantage that the rules will not necessarily fit the current situation very well. Where the new sorts of works behave differently from the old sorts of works, we need to figure out some sort of fix. Here's a simple example: Newsstands turn out to be an effective way of marketing newspapers and magazines in part because it is difficult as a practical matter to make and distribute additional copies of newspapers and magazines that one buys from the newsstand. If one "buys" a newspaper by downloading it from the World Wide Web, on the other hand, it is pretty easy to make as many copies as one wants. The old rules, customs, and practices, therefore, will not work very well unless we can come up with a way to prevent most of those copies from getting made.

Relying on old rules encourages us to solve the problem that the World Wide Web is not like a newsstand by disabling some of its non-newsstand-like qualities. We could enact rules requiring the proprietors of Web pages to set them up to behave much more like newsstands; we could demand that they insert code in each of their documents that would prevent downloading or would degrade any downloaded copies; we could require modem manufacturers to install chips that disabled the transfer of digital data unless some credit card were charged first.

But why would we want to do that? Adopting rules that disable new technology is unlikely to work in the long term, and unlikely to be a good policy choice if it does work. We have tried before to enact laws that erect barriers to emerging technology in order, for policy reasons, to protect existing technology. The FCC did precisely that when it regulated cable television to the point of strangulation in order to preserve free broadcast TV. That particular exercise didn't work for very long.[3] Others have been more successful. Direct broadcast satellite television subscriptions still lag far behind cable television subscriptions in the United States, and no small part of the reason is that our current legal infrastructure makes it much more difficult for direct satellite broadcasters than for cable operators or conventional broadcasters.[4]

If our goal in reforming current law were to make things more difficult for emerging technology, in order to protect current market leaders against potential competition from purveyors of new media, then cleaving to old rules would be a satisfactory, if temporary, solution. Adhering to old rules might distort the marketplace for new technology for at least the short term (since that, after all, would be one of its purposes), which might influence how that technology developed in the longer term, which, in turn, might influence whether and how the affected industries would compete in the markets for those technologies in the future. It would probably delay the moment at which the current generation of dominant players in information and entertainment markets were succeeded by a new generation of dominant players in different information and entertainment markets.

If instead of looking at the situation from the vantage point of current market leaders, we imagined the viewpoint of a hypothetical benevolent despot with the goal of promoting new technology, we might reach an entirely different answer to the question. Such a being might look at history and recognize that copyright shelters and exemptions have, historically, encouraged rapid investment and growth in new media of expression.

As I described in chapter 7, player pianos took a large bite out of the markets for conventional pianos and sheet music after courts ruled that making and selling piano rolls infringed no copyrights; phonograph records supplanted both piano rolls and sheet music with the aid of the compulsory license for mechanical reproductions; the jukebox industry was created to exploit the 1909 act's copyright exemption accorded to the "reproduction or rendition of a musical composition by or upon coin-operated machines." Radio broadcasting invaded everyone's living rooms before it was clear whether unauthorized broadcasts were copyright infringement; television took over our lives while it still seemed unlikely that most television programs could be protected by copyright. Videotape rental stores sprang up across the country shielded from copyright liability by the first sale doctrine. Cable television gained its initial foothold with the aid of a copyright exemption, and displaced broadcast television while sheltered by the cable compulsory license.[5]

Why would a copyright exemption promote development? Conventional wisdom tells us that, without the incentives provided by copyright, entrepreneurs will refuse to invest in new media. History tells us that they do invest without paying attention to conventional wisdom. A variety of new media flourished and became remunerative when people invested in producing and distributing them first, and sorted out how they were going to protect their intellectual property rights only after they had found their markets. Apparently, many entrepreneurs conclude that if something is valuable, a way will be found to charge for it, so they concentrate on getting market share first, and worry about profits—and the rules for making them—later. The sort of marketplace that grows up in the shelter of a copyright exemption can be vibrant, competitive, and sometimes brutal. Some prospectors will seek to develop market share on a hunch; others from conviction. Still others may aim only to generate modestly valuable assets that will inspire some bigger fish out there to eat them. In any event, new products may be imagined, created, tested, and introduced, and new media may be explored. Fierce competition is not very comfortable, but it can promote the progress of science nonetheless.

In addition, by freeing content providers from well-established rules and customary practices, a copyright shelter allows new players to enter the game. The new players have no vested interest—yet—so they are willing to take more risks in the hope of procuring one. They end up exploring different ways of charging for value. Radio and television broadcast signals are given to their recipients for free; broadcasters have figured out that they can collect money based on the number and demographics of their audiences. Many valuable software programs obtained their awesome market share by being passed on to consumers at no extra cost (like Microsoft Windows®), or deliberately given away as freeware (like AOL® or Netscape®). Other software programs may well have achieved their dominant market position in part by being illicitly copied by unlicensed users. Indeed, industry observers agree that at least half of all of the copies of software out there are unauthorized, yet the software market is booming; it is the pride of the U.S. Commerce Department. Perhaps all of the unauthorized copies are part of the reason.

Our hypothetical benevolent despot, then, might propose a temporary period during which the Internet could be a copyright-free zone. Nobody seems to be making that sort of proposal these days, so perhaps I am mistaken about what a wise ruler would view as good policy. Or perhaps all the benevolent despots in the neighborhood are off duty, on vacation, or just simply hiding. Perhaps they've sought alternate employment.

A number of other viewpoints are possible. I'd like to focus on a third: the classic formulation of copyright as a bargain between the public and copyright holders.[6] In the efforts to enact the Digital Millennium Copyright Act, stakeholders focused almost exclusively on the copyright holders' side of that bargain. Copyright owners, however, have never been entitled to control all uses of their works. Instead, Congress has accorded copyright owners some exclusive rights, and reserved other rights to the general public. Commonly, copyright theorists assess the copyright bargain by asking whether it provides sufficient incentives to prospective copyright owners.[7] Yet, economists tell us that, at the margin, there is always an author who will be persuaded by a slight additional incentive to create another work, or who will be deterred from creating a particular work by a diminution in the copyright bundle of rights. If we rely on the simple economic model, we are led to the conclusion that every enhancement of the rights in the copyright bundle is necessary to encourage the creation of *some* work of authorship.

Asking "What should copyright holders receive from this bargain? What do they need? What do they want? What do they deserve?" then, may be less than helpful. We might instead look at the other side of the equation, and ask "What is it the public should get from the copyright bargain? What does the public need, want, or deserve?" The public should expect the creation of more works, of course, but what is it that we want the public to be able to do with those works?

The constitutional language from which Congress's copyright enactments flow describes copyright's purpose as "[t]o promote the Progress of Science and useful Arts." We can begin with the assertion that the public is entitled to expect *access* to the works that copyright inspires. That assertion turns out to be controversial. Public access is surely not necessary to the progress of science. Scientists can build on each others' achievements in relative secrecy. Literature may flourish when authors have the words of other authors to fertilize their own imaginations, but literature may thrive as well when each author needs to devise her own way of wording. If we measure the progress of science by the profits of scientists, secrecy may greatly enhance the achievements we find.

Still, if valuable works of authorship were optimally to be kept secret, there would be no need for incentives in the copyright mold of exclusive rights. Authors could rely on self-help to maintain exclusive control of their works. Copyright makes sense as an incentive if its purpose is to encourage the dissemination of works, in order to promote public access to them. It trades a property-like set of rights precisely to encourage the holders of protectable works to forgo access restrictions in aid of self-help. For much of this country's history, public dissemination was, except in very limited circumstances, a condition of copyright protection.[8] While no longer a condition, it is still fair to describe it as a goal of copyright protection.[9]

But why is it that we want to encourage dissemination? What is it we want the public to be able to do with these works that we are bribing authors to create and make publicly available? We want the public to be able to read them, view them, and listen to them. We want members of the public to be able to learn from them: to extract facts and ideas from them, to make them their own, and to be able to build on them. That answer leads us to this question: how can we define the compensable units in which we reckon copyright protection to provide incentives (and, since the question of how much incentive turns out to be circular, let's not worry about that for now) for creation and dissemination, while preserving the public's opportunities to read, view, listen to, learn from, and build on copyrighted works?

In 1790, Congress struck this balance by limiting the compensable events within the copyright owner's bundle of rights to printing, reprinting, publishing, and vending copyrighted works.[10] (That translates, in current lingo, into an exclusive right to make, distribute, and sell "copies."[11])

Public performances, translations, adaptations, and displays were all beyond the copyright owner's control. Courts' constructions of the statute supplied further limitations on the copyright owner's rights. The statutory right to vend was limited by the first sale doctrine.[12] The statutory right to print and reprint did not apply to translations and adaptations,[13] did not prevent others from using the ideas, methods, or systems expressed in the protected works,[14] and, in any event, yielded to a privilege to make fair use of copyrighted works.[15]

Congress, over the years, expanded the duration and scope of copyright to encompass a wider ambit of reproduction, as well as translation and adaptation, public for-profit performance, and then public performance and display. It balanced the new rights with new privileges: Jukebox operators, for example, enjoyed an exemption from liability for public performance for more than fifty years, and were the beneficiaries of a compulsory license for another decade after that.[16] Other compulsory licenses went to record companies, cable television systems, satellite carriers, and noncommercial television.[17] Broadcasters received exemptions permitting them to make "ephemeral recordings" of material to facilitate its broadcast; manufacturers of useful articles embodying copyrighted works received a flat exemption from the reproduction and distribution rights to permit them to advertise their wares. Libraries received the benefit of extensive privileges to duplicate copyrighted works in particular situations. Schools got an express privilege to perform copyrighted works publicly in class; music stores got an express privilege to perform music publicly in their stores; and small restaurants got an express privilege to perform broadcasts publicly in their restaurants.[18] Congress did not incorporate specific exemptions for the general population in most of these enactments because nobody showed up to ask for them.[19] At no time, however, until the enactment of the access-control anticircumvention provisions of the DMCA, did Congress or the courts cede to copyright owners control over looking at, listening to, learning from, or *using* copyrighted works.

The right "to reproduce the copyrighted work"[20] is commonly termed the fundamental copyright right. The control over the making of copies is, after all, why this species of intellectual property is called a *copy*right. So it is tempting, and easy, to view the proliferation of copying technology as threatening copyright at its core. However we revise the copyright law, many argue, we need to ensure that the copyright owner's control over the making of every single copy of the work remains secure. This is especially true, the argument continues, where the copies are digitally created and therefore potentially perfect substitutes for the original.[21]

Copyright holders have long sought to back up their legal control of reproduction with functional control. In the 1970s, copyright owners sought without success to prohibit the sale of videocassette recorders.[22] In the 1980s, copyright owners succeeded in securing a legal prohibition on rental of records or computer software to forestall, it was said, the unauthorized copying that such rental was likely to inspire.[23] In the 1990s, copyright owners and users groups compromised on the adoption of the Audio Home Recording Act,[24] which, for the first time, required that recording devices be technologically equipped to prevent serial copying. The Digital Millennium Copyright Act incorporated language prohibiting *any* devices or services designed to circumvent technological protection. Supporters of the anticircumvention provisions insisted that technological protection was the only feasible way to prevent widespread, anonymous digital copying.[25] The popular justification for giving copyright owners the legal right to control access to their works is that unauthorized access can lead to a ruinous proliferation of unauthorized copies. The underlying premise of the anticircumvention approach appears to be the notion that the right to make copies is central to the integrity of the copyright system, and must be protected by any available means.

The right to make copies, though, is not fundamental to copyright in any sense other than the historical one. When the old copyright laws fixed on reproduction as the compensable (or actionable) unit, it was not because there is something fundamentally invasive of an author's rights about making a copy of something. Rather, it was because, at the time, copies were easy to find and easy to count, so they were a useful benchmark for deciding when a copyright owner's rights had been unlawfully invaded. Unauthorized reproductions could be prohibited without curtailing the public's opportunities to purchase, read, view, hear, or use copyrighted works. They are less useful measures today. Unauthorized copies have become difficult to find and difficult to count. In addition, now that copyright owners' opportunities to exploit their works are as often as not unconnected with the number of reproductions, finding and counting illicit copies is a poor approximation of the copyright owners' injury.

The reasons that copyright owners might have for wanting to treat reproduction as a fundamental copyright right are obvious. By happenstance (at least from the vantage point of 1790, or 1870, or even 1909 or

1976), control over reproduction could potentially allow copyright owners control over every use of digital technology in connection with their protected works. This is not what the Congresses in 1790, 1870, 1909, and 1976 meant to accomplish when they awarded copyright owners exclusive reproduction rights. The photocopy machine was not invented until the baby boom. Printing presses used to be expensive. Multiple reproduction was, until very recently, a chiefly commercial act. Pegging authors' compensation to reproduction, therefore, allowed past Congresses to set up a system that encouraged authors to create and disclose new works while ensuring the public's opportunities to read, view, or listen to them; learn from them; share them; improve on them; and, ultimately, reuse them. Today, making digital reproductions is an unavoidable incident of reading, viewing, listening to, learning from, sharing, improving, and reusing works embodied in digital media. The centrality of copying to use of digital technology is precisely why reproduction is no longer an appropriate way to measure infringement.

As recently as the 1976 general copyright revision, the then-current state of technology permitted Congress to continue its reliance on the exclusive reproduction right by enacting a lot of arcane, hypertechnical rules and exceptions, at the behest of all of the stakeholders who argued that they required special treatment. That did not pose major problems because very few people needed to understand what the rules were, and many if not most of them could afford to hire lawyers. Unauthorized reproduction was illegal, said the rules, unless you were a "library or archives," a "transmitting organization entitled to transmit to the public a performance or display of a work," a "government body or other nonprofit organization," or a "public broadcasting entity"; or unless you were advertising "useful articles that have been offered for sale," "making and distributing phonorecords," or making pictures of a building "ordinarily visible from a public place."[26] Those entitled to exemptions knew who they were and knew what limitations their privileges entailed.

We no longer live in that kind of world. Both the threat and promise of new technology centers on the ability it gives many, many people to perform the twenty-first-century equivalents of printing, reprinting, publishing, and vending. Copyright owners all over want the new, improved rules to govern the behavior of all citizens, not just major players in the copyright-affected businesses. And, since anyone who watches citizen behavior carefully to detect copyright violations can easily find enough to fill up her dance card in an afternoon, copyright owners have taken to the argument that citizens must be *compelled* to obey the rules, by installing technology that makes rule breaking impossible for the casual user and difficult for the expert hacker. Otherwise, they've argued, there's no hope of everyone's obeying the law.

Well of course not. How could they? They don't understand it, and how could we blame them? It isn't a particularly easy set of rules to understand, and even when you understand it, it's very hard to argue that the rules make any sense—or made any sense, for that matter, when they were written. What nobody has tried, or even proposed, is that we either scrap the old set of rules, or declare the general citizenry immune from them, and instead devise a set of rules that, first, preserve some incentives for copyright holders (although not necessarily the precise incentives they currently enjoy); second, make some sense from the viewpoint of individuals; third, are easy to learn; and fourth, seem sensible and just to the people we are asking to obey them.

The first task, then, in revising copyright law for the new era, requires a very basic choice about the sort of law we want. We can continue to write copyright laws that only copyright lawyers can decipher, and accept that only commercial and institutional actors will be likely to comply with them, or we can contrive a legal structure that ordinary individuals can learn, understand, and even regard as fair. The first alternative will take of itself: The legislative proposal accompanying the White Paper inspired precisely the sort of logrolling that has achieved detailed and technical legislation in the past,[27] and culminated in the swollen DMCA. The second alternative is more difficult. How do we define a copyright law that is short, simple, and fair?

If our goal is to write rules that individual members of the public will comply with, we need to begin by asking what the universe looks like from their vantage point. Members of the public, after all, are the folks we want to persuade that copyright is just and good and will promote the progress of science. They are unlikely to think highly of the Lehman Working Group's argument that they need to secure permission for each act of viewing or listening to a work captured in digital form. They are unlikely to appreciate the relentless logic involved in concluding that, while copyright law permits the owner of a copy to transfer that copy freely, the privilege does not extend to any transfer by electronic transmission.[28] They are unlikely to be persuaded that the crucial distinction between lawful and unlawful activity should turn on whether something has been reproduced in the memory of some computer somewhere.

If we are determined to apply the copyright law to the activities of everyone, everywhere, then I suggest that the basic reproductive unit no longer serves our needs, and we should jettison it completely.[29] That proposal is radical: if we stop defining copyright in terms of reproduction, we will have to rethink it completely. Indeed, we will need a new name for it, since *copy*right will no longer describe it. What manner of incentive could we devise to replace reproduction as the essential compensable unit?

The public appears to believe that the copyright law incorporates a distinction between commercial and noncommercial behavior. Ask nonlawyers, and many of them will tell you that making money using other people's works is copyright infringement, while noncommercial uses are all okay (or, at least, okay unless they do terrible things to the commercial market for the work).[30] Now, that has never, ever been the rule but, as rules go, it isn't a bad start. It isn't very far from the way, in practice, the rules have actually worked out. Noncommercial users rarely get sued and, when they do, tend to have powerful fair use arguments on their side. Moreover, if it is a rule that more people than not would actually obey because it struck them as just, we would be a long way toward coming up with a copyright law that would actually work. So why not start by recasting copyright as an exclusive right of commercial exploitation? Making money (or trying to) from someone else's work without permission would be infringement, as would large-scale interference with the copyright holders' opportunities to do so. That means that we would get rid of our current bundle-of-rights way of thinking about copyright infringement. We would stop asking whether somebody's actions resulted in the creation of a "material object . . . in which a work is fixed by any method now known or later developed,"[31] and ask instead what effect those actions had on the copyright holder's opportunities for commercial exploitation.[32]

Such a standard is easy to articulate and hard to disagree with in principle. The difficulty lies in predicting how it would work out in practice. Routine free use of educational materials by educational institutions seems like a good example of the sort of noncommercial use that should be classed as "large-scale interference" with copyright holders' commercial opportunities. On the other hand, the fact that a particular individual's viewing or copying of a digital work might itself supplant the sale of a license to view or copy if such licenses were legally required should count neither as making money nor as large-scale interference with commercial opportunities.[33] Under this standard, individual trading of MP3 files would not be actionable, but Napster's activities would be, despite the fact that Napster collects no money for its service or software. Other uses, though, would need at least initially to be evaluated individually. So general a rule would necessarily rely on case-by-case adjudication for embroidery. One significant drawback of this sort of standard, then, is that it would replace the detailed bright lines in the current statute with uncertainty.[34] But the bright lines Congress gave us embody at least as much uncertainty, although it is uncertainty of a different sort. The detailed bright lines have evolved, through accident of technological change, into all-inclusive categories of infringers with tiny pockmarks of express exemptions and privileges, and undefined and largely unacknowledged free zones of people-who-are-technically-infringing-but-will-never-get-sued, like your next-door neighbor who duplicates his wife's authorized copy of Windows 98® rather than buying his own. The brightness of the current lines is illusory.

Giving copyright holders the sole right to exploit commercially or authorize the commercial exploitation of their works is a more constrained grant than the current capacious statutory language. It removes vexing (if rarely litigated) everyday infringements, like your neighbor's bootleg copy of Windows 98®, from the picture entirely. Is surgery that radical necessary? Probably not. It would, however, have some significant advantages.

First, to the extent that current constructions of the reproduction right have shown a rapacious tendency, their proponents commonly defend them on the ground that a single isolated unauthorized digital copy can devastate the market for copyrighted works by enabling an endless string of identical illegal copies. Sometimes they explain that a single harmless copy would never give rise to a lawsuit. If that's so, copyright owners lose nothing of value by trading in their reproduction rights for exclusive control over commercial exploitation. If the danger of an unauthorized copy is that it might ripen into a significant burden on the commercial market, then defining that harm as an actionable wrong will address the danger without being overinclusive.

Moreover, the common-law interpretive process we would necessarily rely on to explicate a general standard unencumbered by all of the detailed exceptions in the current statute is better set up to articulate privileges and limitations of general application than our copyright legislative process has proved to be. While judicial lawmaking may not succeed very well, very often, at arriving at sensible solutions, the process constrains it to try to draw lines that make sense. The public is more likely to accept lines drawn by drafters who are attempting to make sense. And the public's involvement, as jurors, in drawing these lines just might allow us to incorporate emerging social copyright norms into the rules we apply.

Finally, once we abolished the detailed, specific exemptions in the current law, the industries that have been able to rely on them would need to seek shelter within the same general limitations on which the rest of us depend. It is common for large copyright-intensive businesses to insist that they are *both* copyright owners and copyright users, and that they are therefore interested in a balanced copyright law.[35] They typically fail to mention that unlike the vast majority of copyright users, and unlike new start-up copyright-affected businesses, they were able to negotiate the enactment of detailed copyright privileges. In most cases, those privileges both gave them what they believed at the time they would need, and also, if they were clever or lucky, were drafted with enough specificity to prove unhelpful to new, competing media that might crawl out of the woodwork in the future. Eliminating current stakeholders' structural advantages from the copyright law would do much to restore a more durable balance.

In addition to separating copyright owners from a useful tool for overreaching, abandoning the reproduction right in favor of a right of commercial exploitation would have the benefit of conforming the law more closely to popular expectations. That would ease enforcement, and make mass education about the benefits of intellectual property law more appealing.

I don't suggest for a minute that limiting copyright's exclusive rights to a general right of dissemination for commercial gain will solve all of the problems I have raised for the public's side of the copyright bargain. Most obviously, copyright holders will rely, as they have in the past, on mechanisms outside of the copyright law to enhance their control over their works. The technological controls reified by the Digital Millennium Copyright Act are one such mechanism.[36] Adhesion contracts purporting to restrict users' rights as part of a license are another.[37] Indeed, one of the most important items on the content industry's continuing agenda seems to be the reinforcement of efforts to find contract law work-arounds for privileges that current copyright law accords to users.[38] Even if the copyright grant is narrowed in scope, the public will need some of *its* rights made explicit.

For example, the public has had, under traditional copyright law, and should have, a right to read. Until recently this wasn't even questionable. Copyright owners' rights did not extend to reading, listening, or viewing any more than they extended to private performances. The Lehman Working Group, though, seized on the exclusive reproduction right as a catch-all right that captures every appearance of any digital work in the memory of a computer. The White Paper insisted that it applied to private individuals as well as commercial actors.[39] The recording industry's recent litigation strategy reflects that view. Invocation of the fair use privilege to exempt private, temporary copying from the reach of the current statute is not much help, because one needs a hideously expensive trial to prove that one's actions come within the fair use shelter. More importantly, content owners are increasingly enclosing their works within technological copy protection, and have thus far succeeded in arguing that fair use can never be a defense to suits for circumvention.[40] Recasting copyright as a right of commercial exploitation will do much to solve that problem since consumptive or incidental use would almost never come within the scope of the redefined right. Still, principles are important, and it is easy to argue that facilitating individual consumptive uses significantly interferes with the copyright owner's opportunities to charge individuals for each incident of use. The public needs and should have a right to engage in copying or other uses incidental to a licensed or legally privileged use. So, let's make the right explicit. If temporary copies are an unavoidable incident of reading, we should extend a privilege to make temporary copies to all.

Further, the public has always had, and should have, a right to cite. Referring to a copyrighted work without authorization has been and should be legal. Referring to an infringing work is similarly legitimate. This was well settled until the world encountered hypertext linking. As I discussed in chapter 10, the fear that hypertext links enabled people to find and copy unauthorized copies inspired lawsuits claiming that linking to infringing works was itself piracy. Drawing a map showing where an infringing object may be found or dropping a footnote that cites it invades no province the copyright owner is entitled to protect even if the object is blatantly pirated from a copyrighted work. Posting a hypertext link should be no different. If the only way to offer effective protection for works of authorship is to prevent people from talking about infringing them, then we're finished before we even start.

Moreover, until the enactment of the DMCA, the public had, and the public should have, an affirmative right to gain access to, extract, use, and reuse the ideas, facts, information, and other public domain material embodied in protected works. That affirmative right should include a limited privilege to circumvent any technological access controls for that purpose, and a privilege to reproduce, adapt, transmit, perform, or display so much of the protected expression as is required in order to gain access to the unprotected elements.[41] Again, both long copyright tradition and case law[42] recognize this right, but the new prohibitions on circumvention of technological access protection threaten to defeat it. Copyright owners have no legitimate claim to fence off the public domain material that they have incorporated in their copyrighted works from the public from whom they borrowed it, so why not make the *public's* rights to the public domain explicit?

Finally, the remarkable plasticity of digital media has introduced a new sort of obstacle to public dissemination: Works can be altered, undetectably, and there is no way for an author to insure that the work being distributed over her name is the version she wrote. My proposal to reconfigure copyright as a right of commercial exploitation would certainly not solve this problem; indeed, it would exacerbate it. Authors of works adapted, altered, misattributed, or distorted in noncommercial contexts would have only limited recourse under a commercial exploitation right.[43] The fear of rampant alteration has inspired some representatives of authors and publishers to insist that the law give copyright holders more control over their digital documents, over access to those documents, and over any reproduction or distribution of them. Only then, they argue, will their ability to prevent alterations give them the security they need to distribute their works in digital form. That solution is excessive; as framed in current proposals, it would give copyright holders the means to prohibit access to or use of the contents of their works for any reason whatsoever. As sympathetic as we may find creators' interest in preserving their works from distortion, that interest is not so weighty that it impels us to sacrifice long-standing principles ensuring public access. Fortunately, there is a more measured alternative.

Most countries that belong to the Berne Union protect authors' interests in assuring the integrity of the works they create. American lawmakers have always found the notion hard to swallow. Although the United States, as a signatory to Berne, has undertaken the obligation to protect authors' interests in assuring the continuing integrity of their works,[44] it has followed up only in token ways.[45] Some copyright owners view integrity rights as a dangerous opportunity for individual authors to interfere with the exploitation of works by the copyright owners and licensees. Some copyright experts view integrity rights as yet another way that authors exert unwarranted control over the uses of their works.

The United States, however, could address the distinct problems posed by digital media while avoiding these concerns. We could adopt a narrowly tailored safeguard that framed the integrity right to meet the particular threats posed by digital technology. Authors have a legitimate concern, and that concern is often shared by the public. Finding the authentic version of whatever document you are seeking can in many cases be vitally important. Moreover, while traditional Berne integrity rights include the ability to prohibit mutilations and distortions, digital media gives us the opportunity to devise a gentler solution: any adaptation, licensed or not, commercial or not, should be accompanied by a truthful disclaimer and a citation (or hypertext link) to an unaltered and readily accessible copy of the original. That suffices to safeguard the work's integrity, and protects our cultural heritage, but it gives copyright owners no leverage to restrict access to public domain materials by adding value and claiming copyright protection for the mixture.

The most compelling advantage of encouraging copyright industries to work out the details of the copyright law among themselves, before passing the finished product on to a compliant Congress for enactment, has been that it produced copyright laws that the relevant players could live with, because they wrote them. If we intend the law to apply to individual end users' everyday interaction with copyrighted material, however, we will need to take a different approach. Direct negotiation among industry representatives and a few hundred million end users would be unwieldy (even by copyright legislation standards). Imposing the choices of the current stakeholders on a few hundred million individuals is unlikely to result in rules that the new majority of relevant players find workable. They will not, after all, have written them.

If the overwhelming majority of actors regulated by the copyright law are ordinary end users, it makes no sense to insist that each of them retain copyright counsel in order to fit herself within niches created to suit businesses and institutions, nor is it wise to draw the lines where the representatives of today's current stakeholders insist they would prefer to draw them. Extending the prescriptions and proscriptions of the current copyright law to govern the everyday acts of noncommercial, noninstitutional users is a fundamental change. To do so without effecting a drastic shift in the copyright balance will require a comparably fundamental change in the copyright statutory scheme. If we are to devise a copyright law that meets the public's needs, we might most profitably abandon the copyright law's traditional reliance on reproduction, and refashion our measure of unlawful use to better incorporate the public's understanding of the copyright bargain.

NOTES

1. This chapter is adapted from a paper presented at the 24th Annual Telecommunications Policy Research Conference in 1995 and originally published at 17 Oregon Law Review 19 (1996).

2. Note, here, that we are talking not only about author-stakeholders, or publisher-stakeholders, but also about collecting-agency-stakeholders. The Green Paper report issued in 1994 initially suggested that an electronic transmission of a musical recording should be treated as a distribution of a copy of that recording rather than as a performance of the recording. That recommendation proved to be the single most controversial proposal among conventional copyright-affected stakeholders. On one side of the dispute were the record companies and the Harry Fox Agency, which collects composers' royalties for the sale of recordings. On the other side were ASCAP, BMI, and SESAC, which collect composers' royalties for the public performance of music. The composer would have gotten the royalties either way, but the collecting entity's cut would have gone to a different stakeholder. See *Public Hearing at Andrew Mellon Auditorium Before the Information Infrastructure Task Force Working Group on Intellectual Property Rights*, September 23, 1994, at 19–22 (testimony of Stu Gardner, composer); ibid. at 25–28 (testimony of Michael Pollack, Sony Music Entertainment); ibid. at 28–31 (testimony of Marilyn Bergman, ASCAP); ibid. at 31–33 (testimony of Hillary Rosen, Recording Industry Association of America); ibid. at 33–38 (testimony of Frances Preston, BMI); ibid. at 38–43 (testimony of Edward Murphy, National Music Publishers' Association).

3. See Jonathan Weinberg, *Broadcasting and the Administrative Process in Japan and the United States*, 39 Buffalo Law Review 615, 694–700 (1991).

4. See Jessica Litman, *Copyright Legislation and Technological Change*, 78 Oregon Law Review 275, 342–46 (1989); *Hearing Regarding Copyright Licensing Regimes Covering Retransmission of Broadcast Signals Before the Subcommittee on Courts and Intellectual Property of the House Judiciary Committee*, 105th Cong., 1st sess. (October 17, 1997).

5. See above chapter 7 at pages 106–107.

6. See, e.g., *Sony Corp. of America v. Universal City Studios*, 464 U.S. 417, 429

and n.10 (1984) (quoting H.R. Rep. No. 2222, 60th Cong., 2d sess. [1909]). I discussed the model of copyright as bargain in chapter 3.

7. *See, e.g.,* Rochelle Cooper Dreyfuss, *The Creative Employee and the Copyright Act of 1976,* 54 University of Chicago Law Review 590 (1987); Jane C. Ginsburg, *Creation and Commercial Value: Copyright Protection of Works of Information,* 90 Columbia Law Review 1865, 1907–16 (1990); Wendy J. Gordon, *Fair Use as Market Failure: A Structural and Economic Analysis of the Betamax Case and Its Predecessors,* 82 Columbia Law Review 1600 (1982); Linda J. Lacey, *Of Bread and Roses and Copyrights,* 1989 Duke Law Journal 1532 (1989).

8. The 1976 Copyright Act extended federal statutory copyright to unpublished works. Before that, copyright protection was available for published works and for works, such as lectures or paintings, that were typically publicly exploited without being reproduced in copies. *See generally* 1 William F. Patry, *Copyright Law and Practice* 414–21 (1994).

9. *See* L. Ray Patterson, *Copyright and the "Exclusive Right" of Authors,* 1 Journal of Intellectual Property Law 1, 37 (1993).

10. Act of May 31, 1990, cg. 15, § 1, 1 Stat. 124.

11. *See* 17 U.S.C. § 106(1), (3) (1994).

12. *Bobbs Merrill v. Strauss,* 210 US 339 (1908); *Harrison v. Maynard, Merril & Co.,* 61 F. 689 (2d Cir. 1894). The first sale doctrine allows the owner of any lawful copy of a work to dispose of that copy as she pleases.

13. *Stowe v. Thomas,* 23 F. Cas. 201 (C.C.E.D. Pa 1853) (No 13,514); *Kennedy v. McTammany,* 33 F. 584 (C.C.D. Mass. 1888).

14. *Baker v. Selden,* 101 U.S. 99 (1879).

15. *See Folsom v. Marsh,* 9 F. Cas. 342 (C.C.D. Mass 1841)(No. 4,901).

16. *See* 2 Patry, above at note 8, at 971–87.

17. *See* 17 U.S.C. §§ 111, 115, 118, 119 (1994).

18. *See* ibid. §§ 108, 110 (1), 110(5), 110(7), 112, 113(c).

19. There is one, sort of. Section 1008 includes a provision, enacted as part of the Audio Home Recording Act of 1992, that bars infringement suits "based on the noncommercial use by a consumer" of an audio-recording device for making "musical recordings." 17 U.S.C. § 1008 (1994). *See* chapter 3, above at 59–70. The provision carefully omits any statement that such recordings are not infringement, and was demanded by the consumer electronics industry as a condition for supporting the Audio Home Recording Act.

20. 17 U.S.C. § 106(1).

21. *See* Jane C. Ginsburg, Essay: *From Having Copies to Experiencing Works: The Development of an Access Right in U.S. Copyright Law,* in Hugh Hansen, ed., *U.S. Intellectual Property: Law and Policy* (Sweet & Maxwell, 2000).

22. *See Sony Corporation of America v. Universal City Studios,* 464 U.S. 417 (1984); *Home Recording of Copyrighted Works: Hearings Before the Subcommittee on*

Courts, Civil Liberties and the Administration of Justice of the House Judiciary Committee, 97th Cong., 2d sess. (1982).

23. Record Rental Amendment of 1984, Pub. L. No. 98-450, 98th Cong., 2d sess., 98 Stat. 1727 (1984); Computer Software Rental Amendments of 1990, Pub. L. No. 101-650, 101st Cong., 2d sess, 104 Stat. 5089, 5134-37 (1990) (codified at 17 U.S.C. § 109 [1994]). *See generally* 2 Patry, above at note 8, at 842–62.

24. Audio Home Recording Act of 1992, Pub. L. No. 102-563, 102d Cong., 2d sess., 106 Stat. 4237 (1992). *See Audio Home Recording Act of 1991: Hearing on H.R. 3204 Before the Subcommittee on Intellectual Property and Judicial Administration of the House Committee on the Judiciary,* 102d Cong., 2d sess. (1993).

25. *See, e.g., NII Copyright Protection Act of 1995: Hearing on H.R. 2441 Before the Subcommittee on Courts and Intellectual Property of the House Committee on the Judiciary,* 104th Cong., 1st sess. (November 15, 1995) (testimony of Marybeth Peters, Register of Copyrights):

> The Copyright Office supports the concept of outlawing devices or services that defeat copyright protection systems. One of the most serious challenges to effective enforcement of copyright in the digital environment is the ease, speed, and accuracy of copying at multiple, anonymous locations. In order to meet this challenge, copyright owners must rely on technology to protect their works against widespread infringement. But every technological device that can be devised for this purpose can in turn be defeated by someone else's ingenuity. Meaningful protection for copyrighted works must therefore proceed on two fronts: the property rights themselves, supplemented by legal assurances that those rights can be technologically safeguarded.

26. *See* 17 U.S.C. §§ 108, 112(a), 112(b), 113(c), 115, 118, 120.

27. *Compare* S. 1121, 104th Cong., 1st sess. (1995) with S. 2037, 105th Cong., 2d sess. (1998).

28. The White Paper's explanation of why this should be so seems particularly unpersuasive:

> Some argue that the first sale doctrine should also apply to transmissions, as long as the transmitter destroys or deletes from his computer the original copy from which the reproduction in the receiving computer was made. The proponents of this view argue that at the completion of the activity, only one copy would exist between the original owner who transmitted the copy and the person who received it—the same number of copies at the beginning. However, this zero sum gaming analysis misses the point. The question is not whether there exist the same number of

copies at the completion of the transmission or not. The question is whether the transaction when viewed as a whole violates one or more of the exclusive rights, and there is no applicable exception from liability. In this case, without any doubt, a reproduction of the work takes place in the receiving computer. To apply the first sale doctrine in such a case would vitiate the reproduction right.

Information Infrastructure Task Force, *Intellectual Property and the National Information Infrastructure: The Report of the Working Group on Intellectual Property Rights* 93–94 (1995) [hereinafter White Paper].

29. The discussion in this chapter completely omits the immense practical difficulties in getting such a proposal enacted into law, over the presumed antagonism of current copyright stakeholders, and in apparent derogation of our obligations under international copyright treaties. Other copyright lawyers who have gone along with my argument thus far are invited to leave the bus at this station.

30. *See, e.g.,* Office of Technology Assessment, U.S. Congress, *Intellectual Property Rights in an Age of Electronics and Information* 121–23, 209 (1986); *see generally* The Policy Planning Group, Yankelovich, Skelly & White, Inc., *Public Perceptions of the "Intellectual Property Rights" Issue* (1985) (OTA Contractor Report). That ethos seems to be behind the public's ambivalent attitude toward Napster: sharing music files is cool, but the sheer scale of Napster has persuaded many that its operation must be illegitimate. *See, e.g.,* Catherine Greenman, *Taking Sides in the Napster War,* New York Times, August 31, 2000, at D1.

31. 17 U.S.C. § 101 (1994).

32. As an illustration, consider the case of Robert LaMacchia. Mr. LaMacchia was unsuccessfully prosecuted under the wire-fraud statute for providing a computer bulletin board where users uploaded and downloaded unauthorized copies of commercially published software. *See United States* v. *LaMacchia,* 871 F. Supp. 535 (D. Mass. 1994). *LaMacchia* had no commercial motive and gained no commercial advantage by this activity, but his bulletin board made it possible for some number of people who might otherwise have purchased authorized copies of software to obtain unauthorized copies for free. Congress has amended the copyright law to ensure that people like Robert LaMacchia can be successfully prosecuted for criminal copyright infringement from now on. *See No Electronic Theft (NET) Act,* Public L. 105-147, 111 Stat. 2678 (1997). Under the standard I propose, that activity would be infringement only if copyright holders demonstrated to the trier of fact that LaMacchia's BBS worked a large-scale interference with their marketing opportunities. Merely proving that if such activities were to become widespread (because of the similar activities of lots of individuals like LaMacchia) they would have potentially devastating marketing effects, on the other hand, would not satisfy the standard.

33. For a contrary view, *see* Jane C. Ginsburg, *Putting Cars on the "Information Superhighway": Authors, Exploiters and Copyrights in Cyberspace*, 95 Columbia Law Review 1466, 1478–79 (1995). Professor Ginsburg argues that because the private copying market has supplanted traditional distribution, even temporary individual copying in cyberspace will impair the copyright owner's rights, although she concedes that fully enforcing those rights may be impractical. Ibid. That copyright holders have recently begun to exploit the market for licenses to make individual copies, however, tells us little about the scope of their entitlement to demand such licenses under current law, and even less about whether a revised law should extend to such claims. *See Michigan Document Services v. Princeton University Press*, 74 F.3d 1512, 1523 (6th Cir. 1996) ("It is circular to argue that a use is unfair, and a fee therefore required, on the basis that the publisher is therefore deprived of a fee"), *vacated en banc*, 74 F.3d 1528 (6th Cir. 1996).

34. There is a substantial literature on the relative merits of rules and standards. *See, e.g.,* Jonathan Weinberg, *Broadcasting and Speech*, 81 California Law Review 1110 (1993).

35. *See, e.g., Public Hearing at University of California Los Angeles Before the Information Infrastructure Task Force Working Group on Intellectual Property*, September 16, 1994, at 22 (testimony of William Barwell, Times Mirror Company).

36. *See* Pamela Samuelson, *Intellectual Property and the Digital Economy: Why the Anti-Circumvention Regulations Need to Be Revised*, 14 Berkeley Technology Law Journal 519 (1999).

37. *See, e.g.,* Mark A. Lemley, *Intellectual Property and Shrinkwrap Licenses*, 68 Southern California Law Review 1239 (1995); Steven Metalitz, *The National Information Infrastructure*, 13 Cardozo Arts & Entertainment Law Journal 465, 469–72 (1995); Pamela Samuelson, *Legally Speaking: Software Compatibility and the Law*, 38 Communications of the ACM, August 1995, at 15, 20. The National Conference of Commissioners on Uniform State Laws has proposed that every state adopt a complicated uniform law to assist sellers of digital information products by permitting them to bind purchasers to the terms of form licenses that have, up until now, been deemed by many courts to be unenforceable. The Uniform Computer Information Transactions Act (UCITA) would make it possible for content owners to restrict consumers' uses of both copyright-protected and uncopyrightable material contained in digital works by denominating transactions related to those works as "licenses." Supporters of UCITA explain that it would make users' rights under copyright irrelevant by permitting sellers to require a waiver of those rights as a condition of access. *See generally* Symposium: Intellectual Property and Contract Law in the Information Age: The Impact of Article 2B of the Uniform Commercial Code on the Future of Transactions in Information and Electronic Commerce, 13 Berkeley Technology Law Journal 809 (1998) and 87 California Law Review 1 (1999).

38. *See* White Paper, above at note 28, at 49–59.

39. *See* ibid. at 64–66.

40. *See Universal Studios* v. *Reimerdes*, 111 F. Supp. 2d 294, 324 (S.D.N.Y. 2000); *Universal Studios* v. *Reimerdes*, 82 F. Supp. 2d 211 (S.D.N.Y. 2000).

41. *See, e.g.*, Julie E. Cohen, *Copyright and the Jurisprudence of Self-Help*, 13 Berkeley Technology Law Journal 1089 (1998).

42. *Baker* v. *Selden*, 101 U.S. 99 (1879); *Sony* v. *Connectix*, 203 F. 3d 596 (9th Cir. 2000); *Sega Enterprises, Ltd.* v. *Accolade, Inc.*, 977 F.2d 1510 (9th Cir. 1993); *Atari Games, Inc.* v. *Nintendo of America*, 975 F. 2d 832 (Fed. Cir. 1992).

43. Such noncommercial alteration would be actionable only if it worked a large-scale interference with the author's ability to exploit the work commercially. Authors of works are not intended for commercial distribution that are commercially distributed without authorization would, of course, be able to recover, but authors whose works are adapted, misattributed, or altered for personal, private, or limited noncommercial consumption would not.

44. "Integrity right" is a term of art for an author's right to object to or prevent mutilation or gross distortions of protected works. *See generally* Edward J. Damich, *The Right of Personality: A Common-Law Basis for the Protection of the Moral Rights of Authors*, 23 Georgia Law Review 1, 15–23 (1988). The Berne Convention, a treaty the United States ratified in 1989, requires its members to protect authors' moral rights, including integrity rights. The United States has relied chiefly on the Lanham Trademark Act, 15 U.S.C. §§ 1051–1127 (1994), to fulfill those obligations. The integrity right I propose is probably more consonant with the Lanham act's approach to trademark issues than the Copyright act's approach to authorship rights in any event. For a different spin on integrity rights and the Internet, see Mark A. Lemley, *Rights of Attribution and Integrity in Online Communications*, 1995 Journal of Online Law, art. 2.

45. See Visual Artists Rights Act, codified at 17 U.S.C. § 106A.

A S OF THIS WRITING, THE future is murky. A wholesale reconceptualiza-
tion of copyright law seems unlikely. Inertia may be the most powerful of all natural forces. Even if there were the energy and commitment to
reexamine what copyright means, and how it should be structured to "promote the progress of Science and the useful arts," adoption of a regime anything like the proposal I made in chapter 12 seems impossible. It isn't only
that it would take very public-spirited copyright lawyers to cooperate in a
scheme designed to write them out of a job. Years of thinking within the
peculiarly counterintuitive constraints of copyright law have a way of man-
gling one's mind and distorting one's imagination until more prosaic ways
of seeing the world simply seem *wrong*.

There are not many Don Quixotes in Washington. The conflict
over the scope of copyright in a digital age may have been fueled by differences in principle as much as narrow self-interest, but it is being fought in
the usual way: representatives of private interests are simultaneously jock-
eying for advantage while offering to sit down at the bargaining table and
negotiate a deal that they find satisfactory. Senators and representatives
make general pronouncements about the importance of the issues raised
and the need to find the right answer, while assuring the various interests
that their doors are open and that they would be delighted to broker a
negotiated solution.

I have gotten much more cynical than I used to be about this eagerness
to be the member of Congress who secures a negotiated solution. I used to
think that it derived primarily from a lack of congressional expertise or
interest in the nitty-gritty of copyright laws. More and more, though, it
seems likely that at least many of the legislators who seek to promote interindustry consensus are hoping to score a substantial portion of the money
being poured into copyright lobbying. A dozen years ago, when I attended
copyright hearings in the House and the Senate, they were perfunctory

things. The chair of the subcommittee would open the meeting attended by one or two staffers. A couple of senators and representatives would poke their heads in long enough to announce that while the press of urgent business prevented their attendance, they would be sure to read the transcripts of the testimony with utmost care. The witnesses would begin to speak, with no one but the chair, the couple of staffers, and the lawyers for the other witnesses to listen. (Rarely, there were also press in attendance. They came out in droves, for instance, whenever the recording industry flew in one of its artists to testify about the need for stronger copyright laws. Senators and representatives tended to attend those sessions, too, at least so long as the celebrity—who always got to speak first—was at the witness table.) At one point, the chair would ask a pro forma question or two; somewhat later, he might yield the gavel to a newly arrived colleague and leave the room.

These days, congressional hearings are a little different. Senators and representatives still don't appear to listen to the testimony. Indeed, it seems extraordinarily common for them to stay out of the hearing room until the witnesses have finished making their statements, and to slip in to their seats just in time to use their allotted five minutes to pose questions to the panel. I'm sure there are some legislators who think up their own questions, but there aren't very many of them. Most of the questions seem quite clearly to have been written by a lobbyist for one of the groups affected by the legislation, and parroted by our elected representatives in order to get some statement or question into a record that nobody but lobbyists (and academics like me) will ever read.

After reading the prefabricated questions into the record and receiving a rehearsed response, the legislator, often solemnly, offers his services as a deal-maker. Affected interests looking for a bargaining table where they can sit in favored chairs may take him up on it, or seek to negotiate under the auspices of one of his colleagues. Thus is U.S. information policy crafted.

The solutions Congress adopts to the problems posed by the digital revolution, then, will inevitably be negotiated solutions. Individuals must trust to the public-spiritedness of the manufacturers of hardware and software, the telephone companies, the libraries and schools, the professional associations, the writers and organized consumer groups, and the civil liberties clubs—the interests, in short, who employ paid Washington lobbyists to speak up for the needs of unrepresented citizens. No wonder the copyright laws we enact come out the way they do.

There are not many Don Quixotes in Washington. No Mr. Copyright

Smith to insist to his colleagues that the Congress needs to get it right because it's the right thing to do. No lobbyist worth her not inconsiderable pay is going to stand up in front of the people she is hired to manipulate—oh, excuse me, I meant to say "persuade"—and cry out "Shame on you!" So the best available solutions are difficult ones.

One could hope that enough of the businesses and institutions at the bargaining table have some constituency among their individual customers and clients, or are subject to enough of the same concerns, to attempt to address some of their needs as well, if only in a derivative way. As solutions go, that one isn't a very good one. It is hardly calculated to produce laws that are wise. The process is not, truth to tell, very attentive to promoting the "Progress of Science and the useful Arts," and it has historically tended to do so only by accident. So it behooves the rest of us to look at our copyright laws with a more jaundiced eye. The information that is available in our information society and the uses to which it can be put will inevitably be shaped by the structure of our copyright laws. They are no longer laws only for specialists. If we can't figure out a way to influence their form, they will shape what we are able to read, write, view, hear, and say in ways so insidious that we may not even notice what we've lost.

The failure of the Digital Future Coalition to achieve any concessions of substance in connection with the Digital Millennium Copyright Act should give us pause when we consider trying to participate in the copyright legislative process on its own terms. Copyright lobbying is not a sport for amateurs. Yet, the law is moving us closer to a day when reading, viewing, and listening may be subject to control by copyright police. Copyright owners have asserted rights to control unauthorized copies, to control unauthorized access, to control Internet hyperlinks to unauthorized copies; to control devices and methods that might help make unauthorized copies or gain unauthorized access, and to control links to sites offering devices and methods for making unauthorized copies or gaining unauthorized access. In early returns, courts have been receptive. While later court decisions may yet introduce some limitations into the law, the legislative machine is poised to close any significant loopholes.

As I have watched the copyright wars intensify, however, it has seemed to me that consumers' widespread noncompliance offers a very real ray of hope. I don't expect large crowds of Napster-deprived citizens to rise up in civil disobedience against a law they perceive as unjust—even in the post-Napster world, copyright will not be a hot issue. Instead, I expect that most people will continue to ignore a law written in barely comprehensible prose that makes no sense whatsoever from their point of view. Without copyright lawyers to tell them that reasonable-seeming behavior is nonetheless illegal, even the most cynical of them will continue to believe that Congress intended the law to make sense, and continue to go about their business.

Copyright owners' enforcement strategy so far has been limited to threats, litigation, and slick and unpersuasive campaigns to educate Americans to disapprove of unauthorized use. That strategy works well against commercial and institutional actors, and far less well in deterring individuals from engaging in undesired behavior. The music and motion picture industries have therefore concentrated on identifying and taking out intermediaries. What's so frightening about the Internet is that in many contexts, intermediaries are, while extremely useful, nonetheless optional. A variety of applications have appeared to permit individuals to engage in precisely the same behavior that has inspired litigation, without providing any intermediary to sue. The glut of digital copyright lawsuits has only encouraged this trend. Thus, in order to actually enforce the rights that content owners claim the statute gives them, it will be necessary to enforce it against individual consumers. And here, widespread noncompliance will matter a great deal.

The less workable a law is, the more problematic it is to enforce. The harder it is to explain the law to the people it is supposed to restrict, the harder it will be to explain it to the prosecutors, judges, and juries charged with applying it. The more burdensome the law makes it to obey its proscriptions, and the more draconian the penalties for failing, the more distasteful it will be to enforce. The more people the law seeks to constrain, the more futile it can be to enforce it only sporadically. Finally, the less the law's choices strike the people it affects as legitimate, the less they will feel as if breaking that law is doing anything wrong. In other words, if a law is bad enough, large numbers of people will fail to comply with it, whether they should or not.

People don't obey laws that they don't believe in. Governments find it difficult to enforce laws that only a handful of people obey. Laws that people don't obey and that governments don't enforce are not much use to the interests that persuaded Congress to enact them. If a law is bad enough, even its proponents might be willing to abandon it in favor of a different law that seems more legitimate to the people it is intended to command. Even if copyright stakeholders refuse to give the public a seat at the bargaining table, they may discover that they need to behave as if they had.

GLOSSARY

ADHESION CONTRACT. Standardized form contract offered to consumers on a take-it-or-leave it basis, without the opportunity to negotiate terms.

ANALOG. Conventional recording technology records sound and pictures by continuous measurement of its properties. Analog recordings of music, for example, translate the sound waves into electrical signals of the same frequency. Analog data cannot be processed by computers unless it is first translated into **digital** form. As analog data is transmitted over distances or rerecorded, it is subject to degradation in the quality of sound and picture.

ASSIGNMENT. In copyright law, an assignment is the transfer of one or more exclusive rights. Assignments must be accompanied by a signed, written document. All other transfers are considered to be **licenses**.

COMPULSORY LICENSE. A **license** prescribed by law. Compulsory licenses are an exception to the general rule requiring the copyright owner's permission in order to reproduce, adapt, distribute, publicly perform, or publicly display a protected work. The copyright statute includes several compulsory licenses, all of which require the payment of money to the copyright owner in return for automatic permission to engage in specific limited uses. The mechanical license allows recording artists to record previously released songs in return for a statutory fee paid directly to the copyright owner. The cable TV license permits cable systems to transmit broadcast signals to cable subscribers in return for a statutory royalty that is paid into a pool divided among copyright owners in an annual arbitration proceeding. The satellite TV license is narrower, but operates similarly. Some digital public performances of **sound recordings** are covered by a compulsory license (analog public performances of sound recordings are wholly exempt). The statute contains a backup compulsory license for the benefit of public broadcasting in the event that public broadcasters and copyright owners are unable to negotiate terms.

COPY. The statute defines "copies" as tangible things (such as books, CDs, floppy disks, or statues), in which a work is embodied (or "fixed") in permanent form. Copying a work, therefore, means making a copy: One copies a work when one reproduces it in fixed, tangible form. That can happen when one makes a verbatim copy, or when one creates a new work containing expression copied from the old work. Performing or displaying a work does not, without more, create a "copy" of it, although it may under some circumstances infringe the copyright owner's independent exclusive rights to publicly **perform** or **display** the work.

COPYRIGHT. Copyright is a bundle of exclusive rights to permit or forbid particular specific uses of a work. In the United States, copyright is defined by statute: Congress has granted copyright to authors of works. The copyright gives the author, the author's employer, or anyone to whom the author transfers her rights the legal ability to control who may **copy**, adapt ("create **derivative works**"), **distribute**, publicly **perform** or publicly **display** her work, subject to particular legal exceptions. Under the U.S. Constitution, copyrights may last only for limited times.

DECOMPILE. Decompilation involves the use of computer software tools to **reverse-engineer** a computer program by mechanically translating the machine-readable code into language that's comprehensible to people. Computer programs are initially written in "source code," which is a language intelligible to people, expressing the tasks and routines that make up the program. A "compiler" program is then used to translate the program into code that will run on a computer. Thus, *de*compilation is an attempt to reverse that translation process.

DECRYPTION. Decoding data that has been **encrypted**, i.e., translated into a secret code.

DERIVATIVE WORK. A derivative work is a new work that incorporates protectable expression from an underlying work. Films are often derivative works based on stories or books—they incorporate protected plot, character, and dialogue elements from the stories. **Sound recordings** are usually based on (and incorporate) musical works. Translating a book into a different language or writing a musical arrangement for a song is creating a derivative work. The U.S. copyright statute gives the copyright owner control over the creation of derivative works.

DIGITAL. Information recorded in the form of numbers, especially 0 and 1, so that it can be processed electronically.

DISPLAY. To "display" a work means to show a copy of it, either directly or by means of a film, slide, television image, or computer image. The U.S. copyright statute gives the copyright owner control over some but not all public displays. It does not give the copyright owner control over private displays.

DISTRIBUTE. To distribute copies of a work means to transfer tangible copies from one person to another. The statutory **publication** right is in fact a right to distribute copies to the public by sale, gift, rental, lease, or lending.

ENCRYPTION. Translating data into a secret code, so that it cannot be read without a password or key.

FAIR USE. Fair use is a long-standing legal privilege to make unauthorized use of a copyrighted work for a good reason. Claims of fair use are evaluated by courts on a case-by-case basis. There is no hard and fast rule setting forth how much of a work may be used—despite popular perceptions, there has never been any magic number of words one may quote or notes one may copy.

FILE-SHARING UTILITY. A computer program that facilitates the exchange of computer files among different computers. File-sharing utilities are key to the operation of computer networks, from LANs to the Internet.

FIXED. The copyright statute deems a work to be "fixed" when it is embodied in a material object with sufficient permanence that it can be perceived or communicated for a period of more than transitory duration.

FORMALITIES. Until 1989, the United States conditioned copyright on complying with a variety of formal requirements. One of the most familiar formalities was the requirement for copyright **notice**. From 1909 until 1978, publishing a work with the required copyright notice (the word "copyright" or the symbol ©, the name of the copyright owner, and the date of first publication) was in most cases necessary for federal copyright protection. Publishing a work without the required notice thrust it into the public domain. In 1976, Congress enacted a new copyright law that, effective 1978, made copyright protection automatic for all works, whether published or not. Even under the new law, however, distributing copies of the work without the prescribed copyright notice could dump the work into the public domain. Other formalities included requirements that copyrights be registered, that the person designated by the statute as the proper claimant for the copyright renewal term apply for renewal within a twelve-month window, and that certain texts be printed from type set in the United States. In 1989, the United States abandoned formal prerequisites to copyright protection when it ratified the Berne Convention.

HYPERLINK. A string of code in an electronic document that links to another electronic document or to another location in the same document. People using the World Wide Web commonly encounter hyperlinks embedded in Web pages; by clicking on the links, they can follow them to new Web pages or resources.

HYPERTEXT. A language permitting nonlinear association of data. Related pieces of information are connected by links that allow the author of a hypertext document to combine multiple sources of data in a single document, and to allow a user to follow associative trails to different documents and data. The linked data may be text, pictures, sound, or executable computer programs.

INFRINGEMENT. An invasion of legal rights. Copyright infringement consists of reproducing, adapting, distributing, publicly performing, or publicly displaying a work protected by copyright without either a legal privilege or the permission of the copyright owner.

LICENSE. Permission to reproduce, adapt, distribute, perform, or display a work. Licenses need not be in writing; they may be granted orally or inferred from circumstances. When someone sends a letter to the editor of a newspaper, for instance, that behavior supports an inference that the writer intended to grant the newspaper a license to print the letter in the "Letters to the editor" section of the paper, and to edit the letter for length. It does not, however, support a conclusion that the writer transferred the copyright to the newspaper, since the copyright law requires all **assignments** or transfers of ownership to be in writing.

LITERARY WORKS. The copyright statute defines literary works to include any works expressed in words, numbers, or other verbal or numerical symbols or indicia. Novels, essays, and grocery shopping lists are literary works under the statutory definition. So are databases and computer programs.

NOTICE. Copyright notice is now optional; until 1989, U.S. law required that any publicly distributed copy bear a notice consisting of the word "copyright" or the symbol ©, the name of the copyright owner, and the date of first publication. This book, for example, bears the copyright notice "© 2001 Jessica Litman." Commercially released recorded music often bears two copyright notices: a © notice covering the artwork and any lyrics and a ℗ notice covering the performance of the music and the dubbing and mixing of recorded sound. Through an accident of history, it has never been necessary to affix © notice to sound recordings to preserve the copyright in the songs on the recording.

PATENT. A patent is an exclusive right to make, use, or sell an invention for a period of twenty years.

PERFORM. The statutory definition of perform says: "To 'perform' a work means to recite, render, play, dance, or act it, either directly or by means of any device or process or, in the case of a motion picture or other audiovisual work, to show its images in any sequence or to make the sounds accompanying it audible." Singing a song is performing it; turning on the radio in your car is performing the music being played on the radio; playing a prerecorded tape or watching television are performances. The copyright statute gives copyright owners control over most public performances, but not over private performances.

PORTAL. A portal is a site on the Internet designed to lead to other sites.

PRIVITY. The relationship between two parties to a contract, or between two people whose interests are sufficiently congruent that the law will treat an agreement by one as binding the other.

PUBLIC DOMAIN. Material not subject to copyright protection, either because the material is not protectable by copyright (e.g., ideas, facts, processes, systems) or because copyright protection has expired (e.g., Mark Twain's *Tom Sawyer*) or been forfeited by failure to comply with a statutory condition for copyright. The public domain comprises material that the public is free to use in any way it pleases.

PUBLICATION. The distribution of copies of a work by sale, rental, loan, or gift. A public performance or display of a work does not constitute publication.

REGISTER OF COPYRIGHTS. The Register (not "Registrar") of Copyrights is the head of the Copyright Office, which is a department of the Library of Congress. The Copyright Office is responsible for registering claims to copyright (hence the title "Register"), promulgating copyright regulations, advising Congress and the executive branch on copyright law, and managing the statutory **compulsory licenses.**

REGISTRATION. A work attains copyright protection independently of any registration of the copyright. Until 1978, however, registration of copyright protection was mandatory, and failure to register could ultimately result in forfeiture of the copyright. In the 1976 Copyright Act, effective January 1, 1978, registration was made optional. U.S. citizens must register their copyrights before suing for copyright infringement, but registration may occur at any time during the copyright term.

REVERSE ENGINEERING. Analyzing a product by taking it apart in order to reconstruct its design.

ROYALTY. The term "royalty" is used generally to describe money paid in return for the use of property. In the copyright context, it means money paid in return for copying, adapting, distributing, performing, or displaying a copyrighted work.

SEARCH ENGINE. A computer program that searches documents for specified keywords or symbols and returns a list of documents where the keywords or symbols were found. Search engines combine search algorithms with a database of documents to be searched. Search engines that locate documents on the World Wide Web do not, typically, execute the computer program on the Web at the time that the user types in a query. Rather, the search is run on a database assembled by sending a computer program (called a spider) to follow links to Web pages and record the content and location of each Web page it finds, and then indexing the resulting records. The copies made in that process are **copies** within the scope of the copyright owner's reproduction right, and may infringe the copyright, except to the extent that they fall within a statutory privilege, such as **fair use**.

SOUND RECORDING. A sound recording is a copyrightable work of authorship comprising the performance, recording, dubbing, and mixing of sounds. The copyright in a sound recording is independent of the copyright in a musical work that might be recorded. Industry practice calls for sound-recording copyrights to be controlled by record companies. If Clara Composer writes a song and Sam Singer records it under a contract with Retro Records, whose technicians mix the vocal track with an instrumental accompaniment played by Big Band, then the copyright in the song is owned by Clara, while the copyright in the work created by combining Sam's performance, Big Band's performance, and Retro Records' mixing of the tracks is separate from Clara's copyright and owned by Retro Records.

STREAMING. Streaming is the continuous transmission of digital information. Streaming audio and video transmits content to consumers in a stream that permits them to watch or listen as the data is transferred. This has three principal advantages. First, streaming avoids overwhelming constrained resources (slow modems, congested networks, limited computer memory) by transferring data a little bit at a time. Second, consumers can view or listen to streamed material immediately, without waiting for the download of an entire file. Finally, because the entire file is not transferred as a unit, streamed content cannot easily be saved by the recipient. Copyright owners have therefore been more willing to make their content available over the Internet in streamed format than to release it in downloadable format.

TRADEMARK. A word or symbol used to distinguish one business's product from products of other businesses.

URL. "Uniform Resource Locator," the global address of documents and other material on the Internet.

USENET NEWS. A free-floating collection of more than twenty thousand subject-specific online discussion groups, offering virtual conversation on any imaginable topic. Usenet preceded the World Wide Web, and was one of the most popular recreational uses of the Internet in the late 1980s and early 1990s. It is entirely text-based. Although it has been eclipsed by the World Wide Web, it continues robust operation despite the fact that nobody "owns" it and it doesn't easily lend itself to moneymaking. To sample Usenet news, visit deja.com's Usenet archive at <http://www.deja.com/usenet>.

INDEX

access to copyrighted materials, 82–83, 175
  control over, 82–84, 131–32, 138–39, 144, 167, 170, 176, 184
  unauthorized, 82, 133, 138, 194. *See also* copyright infringement; piracy
access to information
  digital technology and, 12, 13
adaptations of copyrighted materials, 40–41, 176
Adler, Allen, 140
Aimster, 166
Alexander, Joshua, 41
American Society of Composers, Authors, and Publishers (ASCAP), 29, 42–44, 65n.12, 113, 117, 119n.8, 164n.6
Audio Home Recording Act (AHRA) (1992), 36, 59–60, 64n.4, 85, 124, 159, 177
authors, 13, 185

Barlow, John Perry, 119n.8, 151
Ben Hur, 40–41
Berne Convention (1989), 36, 76n.10, 184–85
Bliley, Tom, 137
Bloom, Sol, 43
book publishing industry, 126, 139, 140, 169
Boucher, Rick, 137
broadcasting industry, 18
Broadcast Music, Inc. (BMI), 66n.17, 113, 119n.8, 164n.6

cable television. *See* television broadcasting industry, cable television

campaign contributions, 62
Cary, George, 56
Church of Scientology, 128
churches, use of copyrighted materials, 18
civil rights groups, 123, 127
Coble, Howard, 137–38
competition, discouraging, 172
computer software industry, 93, 123, 126, 136, 137, 139, 140
computers, 26–28, 60–61, 82, 91. *See also* online service providers
Congress, U.S., 23, 26, 31–32, 35–63, 74, 134, 193–94
Consumer Project on Technology, 127
consumer protection organizations, 123, 127, 132, 134, 137, 138
consumers, 51, 70–74, 154, 167, 185, 195
  right to cite copyrighted materials, 183
  right to gain access to, extract, use, and reuse ideas and facts, 184
  right to give, loan, or sell copyrighted materials, 16, 71, 83, 161, 167. *See also* fair use doctrine
  right to make noncommercial copies of copyrighted materials, 167
  right to read, view, or use copyrighted materials, 115, 183, 194
content owners. *See* copyright owners
content scrambling system (CSS), 152, 153, 169
copies, definition of, 99n.15, 174, 180
copyright infringement, 19, 34, 131–33, 135, 136, 160, 163, 169, 171, 173, 178, 180
  detection of, 25

205